D1456871

Also by ROLAND FLAMINI:

Scarlett, Rhett, and a Cast of Thousands:
The Filming of Gone With the Wind

Pope, Premier, President

The Cold War Summit That Never Was

ROLAND FLAMINI

MACMILLAN PUBLISHING CO., INC.

New York

Macmillan Publishing Co., Inc.
866 Third Avenue, New York, N.Y. 10022
Collier Macmillan Canada, Ltd.

Library of Congress Cataloging in Publication Data

Flamini, Roland.
  Pope, Premier, President.

  Includes index.
  1. Catholic Church—Relations (diplomatic) with the
United States. 2. United States—Foreign relations—
Catholic Church. 3. Catholic Church—Relations
(diplomatic) with Communist countries. 4. Communist
countries—Foreign relations—Catholic Church.
5. Johannes XXIII, Pope, 1881–1963.   6. Paulus VI,
Pope, 1897–1978.   7. Popes—Biography.
I. Title.
BX1406.2.F52   327.45′634′073   80-17532
ISBN 0-02-538680-8

10   9   8   7   6   5   4   3   2   1

Printed in the United States of America

To my son Nicholas

Contents

I   *A Man from the East*   1

II   *Pope and Council*   17

III   *The Making of a Pontiff*   36

IV   *On Borrowed Time*   54

V   *At Arm's Length*   70

VI   *Treating with the Devil*   85

VII   *A Pope Dies*   105

VIII   *The Vacant Throne of Peter*   125

IX   *Princes of the Church*   141

X   *Conclave*   161

XI   *Pope and President*   175

XII   *The "Visitor" Departs*   199

XIII   *Agreement—of Sorts*   216

Index   223

Pope, Premier, President

CHAPTER I

A Man from the East

He stood on the balcony gripping the balustrade, arms outstretched before him. The imperial stance, forceful face, and resonant baritone bespoke a strong sense of authority. Below him thousands cheered, enclosed in the vast embrace of Bernini's circular colonnade, its ring of stone saints outlined against the soft white cathedrals of the clouds. Rome does not ordinarily convey a feeling of being a capital, but when a pope is elected it becomes again what it once was —the center of the world. There is an overwhelming sense of historic continuity extending beyond the papacy to the Roman emperors. Yet the papal election of October 1978 broke with tradition in the very act of perpetuating it. The formal Latin announcement was made as usual from the central balcony above the main portico of Saint Peter's Basilica by Cardinal Pericle Felici, as head of the Order of Deacons of the College of Cardinals: the new pope was Karol Wojtyla. He had chosen the name of John Paul II.

For an instant there was silence while the breathtaking significance of this news ricocheted around the crowded square like a bullet. The conclave in the Sistine Chapel had broken the Italian monopoly of the papacy. The 111 cardinal electors had audaciously chosen the first "foreign" pope since the Dutchman Hadrian VI in 1522. Their choice was, moreover, a *coup de theatre* on the international political stage because Wojtyla came from a communist country: he was the archbishop of Cracow, Poland's second largest city.

Soon the new pope himself was standing on the balcony, and the crowd liberated their excitement by shouting, cheering, and waving white handkerchiefs at the small figure, newly robed in his purple *mozzetta*, with the gold-embroidered papal stole hanging from his shoulders.

Few people in Saint Peter's Square, or for that matter in the world at large watching Pope John Paul II on their television screens for the first time, had much of an inkling what sort of a man had been elected. His ecclesiastical career, though evidently successful, had been spent in his native Poland, which testified to his courage and suggested a strict doctrinal traditionalism but gave little clue as to where he stood on the major problems awaiting his attention. Only in a peripheral way did his election signal the ascendancy of one approach to these problems over another, as the election of Paul VI fifteen years earlier had seemed to proclaim the triumph of progressives over conservatives. The excitement was rather for the sheer boldness of the act itself and in a larger sense reflected the particular drama created by the remarkable succession of papal events.

The death of Pope Paul VI, the one-day election of Albino Luciani as John Paul I by near acclamation, his unexpected popular impact, then his sudden death, plus the hypnotic ecclesiastical ceremonies at every turn witnessed worldwide with mass-communication immediacy never before tested on such a scale—all of it had generated a burst of interest and fervor that was difficult to define.

Luciani's achievement was to give the papacy a smiling face once again, chasing away the gloom left behind by the long-failing Paul VI and touching a religious and popular nerve that had not responded since John XXIII. The fact was that in Rome—not the most devout of cities despite its role as the home of the popes—priests noted an upsurge of attendance at mass and confession. Elsewhere, African prelates reported a wave of enthusiasm among their parishioners for a Church that Luciani suddenly seemed to render less grandiose and more comprehensible. United States bishops were struck by the way non-Catholics as well as Catholics appeared to look up and listen. The ecumenical movement suddenly acquired new hope of great progress. Somehow, Luciani's thirty-four-day reign seemed to make the notion of a non-Italian pope slightly more plausible than in the previous conclave. Even so, there had been other non-Italian cardinals with better electoral prospects than the fifty-seven-year-old Polish prelate who now intoned his first papal benediction: *"Urbi et orbi,"* "To the city and to the world."

One question, at least, was soon answered when the new pope addressed the crowd in fluent Italian. His brief speech, confessing his trepidation and apologizing for his faulty Italian (which it was not) immediately made him seem less "foreign." This time the roar was a collective expression of acceptance. The pope had been on the balcony for less than five minutes, but the plain man-to-man talk, brimming with good nature, had disarmed the crowd with a shining debut.

A non-Italian pope was clearly an idea whose time had come, even more than anyone realized. After the initial surprise, in fact, what was surprising was how easily the modern precedent of a "foreigner" was accepted in Rome at all levels. For the most part the Italian cardinals, who had in effect lost control of the papacy after nearly five centuries, swallowed hard and managed to look unbowed. This was possibly because Cardinal Wojtyla had in any case been a candidate of some influential Italian electors who felt that his noted anti-communist position would provide a counterweight to the looming prospect of the Communists gaining power in Italy.

Below them the Curia Congregations, the principal sectors

of the Vatican bureaucracy, appeared to offer accommodating ground. Curial offices had long been heavily populated
with non-Italians as a result of Pope Paul's concerted internationalization of the Church's central machinery. There in
the curial offices, in fact, differences—doctrinal, political, or
merely conversational—tended to be related to age rather
than nationality.

In the parishes of Rome, the reaction was virtually unani-
mously favorable. The simple, forthright style of his balcony
speech, using the first person instead of the pontifical plural,
was a reassurance that he had noted the impact of the short
papacy of cheerful Cardinal Luciani, and would not put the
clock back to the rigid formalities of the recent past.

Though Wojtyla's election clearly carried political implications, it was not deliberately designed as a political move,
except among his Italian backers in the conclave. But the de-
nouement did in fact take place within a particular climate of
thinking among a number of strategic-minded churchmen.
Like other geopolitical thinkers, some had been concerned
that detente may have been wobbling on its pedestal and that
the death, when it came, of the aging generation of communist
leaders in Eastern Europe, including Leonid Brezhnev in the
Soviet Union and Yugoslavia's Josip Broz Tito, could lead to a
new and prolonged East-West crisis.

In that event, it would make sense to have entrusted the
Church to a pope who was fully equipped by his personal
experience to deal with a possibly risky new era of changing
power politics. But that was a climatic factor, not a deliberate
purpose. What was deliberate was the pronounced impulse to
pay tribute to the Polish church with the award of a pontiff: an
act of homage to the Polish people, to their fidelity, to the
absolutely unswerving manner in which they have stood fast.
There could, after all, be no greater tribute.

Pope John Paul II's choice of name, on the other hand, was
more than a tribute to the thirty-four-day wonder who had
preceded him. It was a proclaimed intention of following in

the footsteps of Pope John XXIII and Pope Paul VI in their determined pursuit of a single objective: to bring the Church once again into the midst of the world—"Almost," as Pope Paul once said, "to run after it in its rapid and continuous change."

This determination explains why the world's Catholic bishops in the Second Vatican Council, the greatest religious event so far witnessed in this century, should have devoted so much of their energy and attention to contemporary social and political problems. After the council, this emphasis on the need of the Church to make itself relevant to local conditions often raised serious problems of excess in its application. For example, "liberation theology," the notion of transforming faith into revolutionary commitment—usually Marxist—pushed the Church into opposition in many Latin American countries, often jeopardizing its position. In the hinterlands of Argentina, young *banderillo* priests were flirting with condoned violence in revolutionary struggles of the past decade between peasants and landowners; in San Salvador in 1979, government troops attacked a Jesuit-run retreat house which, the regime claimed with some justification, had been used as a base by anti-Somosa guerrillas.

This determination also explains the rapid evolution of a less intransigent approach to communism which replaced a policy—so deep-set in the postwar years as to seem irreplaceable and even immortal—of anathemas against the communist East from a spiritual authority which could be relied upon to strike at the enemies of the West. The ideological war against communism which had been joined with such religious fervor was abandoned under John XXIII (except insofar as the official teachings of communism were concerned), and the change was made with striking forthrightness.

Wojtyla's election has to be seen in the context of these developments: Vatican relations with communist states were better than ever before. The Church was under greater pressure from some rightist military regimes in Latin America than it had experienced in Eastern Europe in nearly two decades. Wojtyla himself was an eloquent reflection of the Church's changed condition in communist countries. In a way, he was a product of it. At the 1963 conclave which elected Paul VI, only one cardinal was present from the Communist bloc; that was the Primate of Poland, Cardinal Stefan Wyszynski. The other hierarchies in Eastern Europe were then still in a state of disarray. The other surviving East European cardinal, Joszef Mindszenty, was a voluntary captive in the United States legation in Budapest where he had taken refuge after the 1956 Hungarian revolution collapsed. But even then the process of recovery and reconstruction through direct negotiation with the regimes involved had already started, and at John Paul II's election, there were six cardinals from communist countries, including the newly elected pope himself. The single Polish cardinal had become three, but one was too ill to attend. In addition, there was a resident cardinal-archbishop each from Hungary, Czechoslovakia, and Vietnam, and a curial cardinal residing in Rome who came from Yugoslavia.

The credit for pursuing what amounted to the Vatican's own policy of detente goes to Pope Paul. Throughout the fifteen years of his pontificate, Paul's commitment to improving the situation of Catholics living behind the iron curtain resulted in a careful cultivation of the Church's former enemies. The communist regimes, for their part, were not slow to respond. A papal audience became a fixed point on the schedule of communist heads of state visiting Italy. The Soviet foreign minister, Andrei Gromyko, had seven separate meetings with Paul VI over the years.

This policy, however, had its genesis in a series of remarkable events that were without precedent, and that had taken place in the latter half of Pope John's reign. Minor episodes at first, but each nudging the Church a little farther from a political course it had followed for nearly two decades, and from a historic tendency to align itself with one or more powers against others—with France in the fifteenth century, with Spain during the era of the Hispanic conquests.

The first indication came in January 1960. Cardinal Alfredo Ottaviani, secretary of the Holy Office, and, in his own mind at least, commanding general of the garrison of the City of God, publicly denounced Italian President Giovanni Gronchi's planned state visit to the Soviet Union. Addressing a gathering in the basilica of Santa Maria Maggiore, the cardinal thundered, "In the twentieth century, it is still necessary to condemn genocide, mass deportations, slaughters like Katyn Wood, and massacres such as Budapest. But some still shake the hand of the new Antichrist and exchange sweet smiles. Can a Christian, confronted with one who massacres Christians and insults God, smile and flatter? Can a Christian opt for an alliance with those who prepare for the coming of the Antichrist in countries still free? Can we consider any relaxation of East-West tensions when the face of Christ is once more spat upon, crowned with thorns, and slapped?"

In reporting Ottaviani's speech, the Vatican newspaper, *L'Osservatore Romano,* added a little brimstone of its own to the cardinal's fire by quoting Pope Pius XI's 1931 encyclical *Quadragesimo Anno:* "Socialism, considered either as a doctrine or as a historic fact, or as a plan for action, cannot be reconciled with the teaching of the Catholic church. No one can be at the same time a good Catholic and a good socialist." Gronchi's Moscow visit was postponed, ostensibly because the president was indisposed.

What was surprising was that a week later, under pressure from Pope John, Cardinal Ottaviani gave a rare interview to the Catholic newspaper *L'Avvenire d'Italia* in which he made an even rarer retraction. He had, the prelate said, been misquoted. "Cardinal Ottaviani was giving a doctrinal sermon on the Mystical Body," the paper reported. "The thought of Cardinal Ottaviani was simply and profoundly theological . . . and in omitting this presupposition, as many newspapers did, his words acquired a wrongly political significance." The following month, Gronchi recovered and left for Moscow.

By April 1961, Pope John's social encyclical *Mater et Magistra* had been drafted and awaited his approval. For a further three months, the pope honed and refined the document, removing all critical mention of communism, adding a section on the values of "socialization" (strongly opposed by his more cautious advisers), and finally releasing it in the summer. It is hard to suppose that the detailed advice it contained on how to administer farms will go on being read for generations to come; but the passages defining as "unjust" any economic system which "compromises the dignity of those who work in it, or removes from them a sense of responsibility, or hinders them from expressing their personal initiative," constitute a landmark in the Church's social thought, a great leap forward from the cautious language of Leo XIII's *Rerum Novarum*.

Meanwhile the pope had also turned his attention to the young countries of Africa which were then arriving swiftly, and not always fully prepared, to full autonomy. It was John who ordered the immediate consecration of thirteen native bishops, and who in his speeches and encyclicals criticized traditional colonialism and spoke as a champion of the under-privileged. It was also John who brought the first African-born bishop into the Sacred College of Cardinals. The appointment of Cardinal Laurean Rugambwa of Bukoba, Tanzania, was strongly opposed by curialists as too great an innovation. But a cardinal is the pope's personal creation, requiring neither prior consultation nor approval.

John, who liked to keep things simple, turned the whole episode into an anecdote: "You know, when he (Rugambwa) was made a cardinal not everybody was in agreement," Pope John once confided to the Italian sculptor Giacomo Manzù while the latter was modeling the pontiff's head·in clay. "But I thought, *beh*, let's do it! Let's make him a cardinal! A little bit of black among so much white will give us a nice *caffè-latte*."

On September 10 of the same year, Pope John addressed a message to a meeting of non-aligned nations in Belgrade, urging them to work for peace, and it produced a response from an unexpected quarter. Two days later *Pravda*, the Soviet Communist paper, published a comment by Premier Nikita Krushchev. As a communist and as an atheist, he said, he did not fear the judgment of God, but he did believe in the responsibility of the heads of governments. "We cannot fail to welcome an appeal to work in the interests of peace," Khrushchev stated. "I wonder if such fervent Catholics as John Kennedy, Konrad Adenauer, and so many others will know how to heed the words of the pope." *L'Osservatore Romano* described Khrushchev's comment as the first recognition by a Soviet leader of the Church's work on behalf of peace. It was, said the paper, "a new fact to be noted." After all, *L'Osservatore* went on, the Church was not directed against any particular objective, but was universal. This tentative exchange was as distant from Stalin's contemptuous question: How many divisions has the pope? as it was from Pius XII's clear, unmitigated condemnation of communism, and it indicated rethinking in both Rome and Moscow.

To Pope John, the "new fact" seemed providential. The Church was then preparing for the Vatican Council. In moments of crisis the Church has often resorted to councils— meetings of all its bishops to decide on its future course. The Counter-Reformation was a product of the Council of Trent. The renewal of the Church in the twentieth century—the search for ways of leading it into more direct relation with modern life—would be entrusted to the Second Vatican Council which was due to open in the following September. It was the thirty-second council of the Church, and only the second to be held in the Vatican itself, the first having taken place in 1870.

Pope John used to use another anecdote to describe how the idea came to him in an inspirational flash on January 20, 1959, during an audience with Cardinal Domenico Tardini, his secretary of state. They were discussing, he would say, the troubled state of the world, and the Church's need to set an example of peace and concord between men when suddenly, "without having given it any prior thought," as he put in his private diary, he blurted out, *"Un concilio!"* Tardini's response was immediate and enthusiastic: *"Sì, sì, un concilio!"*

In reality, Pope John's version telescoped into one epiphanic moment several months of careful thought and discussion. The idea of a council was first broached to him by two cardinals in the conclave at which he was elected. The notion took hold in his mind; shortly after his election it came up in conversation with Monsignor Loris Capovilla, his secretary, who was noncommittal but privately felt that it would be too tall an order for a pontiff so advanced in age. Pope John brought up this subject with other prelates, including Archbishop Dell'Acqua. But the moment of decision came during his meeting with Tardini, when, on an impulse, the pope decided that the time had come to test curia reaction. Then, encouraged by Tardini's response, he opened a drawer in his desk and produced for the astonished prelate, who thought this a new idea, twelve pages of notes for a speech announcing the Council, which the pope duly delivered five days later.

To demonstrate what he thought the council would accomplish, Pope John would go to his window overlooking Saint Peter's Square and open it to let in the fresh air. He spoke of it as a method of restoring "the simple and pure lines that the Church of Jesus had at its birth." It was *"un balzo in avanti"* —a leap forward.

Liturgical reform; the Church's approach to social problems; the growth of ecumenism; the need to overhaul the entrenched Curia in order to introduce more of a sense of the wider feeling of the community and less of a characterization of "them" and "us," the central bureaucracy and the Church at large—these were some of the dominant problems on which John expected the council to focus its attention. But his underlying concern was that religion was failing, and that to combat growing indifference not only the Catholic church but all Christian churches needed to seek ways to bring back freshness to Christianity. This conviction was at the heart of his invitation to other Christian churches to send observers to the Second Vatican Council.

As the opening of the council drew nearer, there was still no indication of how many Catholic bishops from Eastern Europe would attend. In the summer of 1959, to help draw up an agenda for the council, questionnaires had gone out to the world's 2,594 archbishops, bishops, and abbots, inviting their views on which topics they considered the most pressing. Though the response was generally overwhelming, only a handful of replies came from behind the iron curtain. The Vatican had addressed each questionnaire to the bishop's last known address, but the Vatican did not know how many Eastern European bishops still survived, much less their whereabouts. The single exception was Poland, where the Church had managed to survive intact and the lines of communications with Rome had remained open. But this still did not mean that the regime would permit Poland's bishops to travel to Rome for the council. With the publication of Khrushchev's statement, however, John perceived, or thought he perceived, a faint glimmer of light at the end of the tunnel, and his natural optimism propelled him toward it.

A vision of the Church's role in international events was taking shape in the pope's mind—a vision of daring scope and proportions which would place the Church in the midst of the complexities of cold war politics and which was to dominate his thinking until his death. It stemmed from his conviction that, while the superpowers might understand each other's positions, and, in their own ways, share a common anxiety for world stability, they were incapable of establishing a satisfactory basis for direct communication.

"It is not merely that arm matches arm, or that muscle matches muscle," John once explained. "It is that mouth does not match mouth. They speak no common language. And we? We Christians are doing nothing to break the fatal silence." By addressing itself to the good will that exists in all men, by demonstrating its political neutrality and at the same time its commitment to finding solutions to the world's problems, the papacy, John felt, could provide the bridge to break that silence.

But if the Soviet leader's statement was indeed a signal, then the next move was up to Rome. The question was what the move should be. Direct contact was clearly premature. Great caution was essential to avoid the risk to the Church of a potentially disastrous rebuff. But one of John's gifts was his ability to involve others in his undertakings. One of his friends, Don Giuseppe De Luca, a distinguished Italian priest, had communist contacts. Realizing this, the pope suggested that he sound out high party functionaries, and De Luca eventually found himself in direct contact with Palmiro Togliatti, the party secretary.

De Luca, a noted church historian whom many felt was destined to become a cardinal, had remained in touch with the *Communisti Cattolici,* the communist fringe group excommunicated by Pius XII, or more correctly, declared to be equivalent to "apostates." It was in Rome in the home of Franco Rodano, leader and chief theoretician of the *Communisti Cattolici,* that the pope's emissary had his first encounter with the leader of the largest Communist party in the West. They met late at night for added secrecy: Khrushchev's statement had struck a responsive chord in Rome, the priest said. The pope would now welcome a clearer indication of the Soviet premier's desire to initiate a dialogue. The form that this initiative would take was up to Khrushchev, but Pope John's eightieth birthday, on November 25, might provide a suitable occasion.

Togliatti replied that of course any improvement in relations between the Church and Moscow was an attractive prospect, and he undertook to act as intermediary. For the communists, and the Italian left in general, the timing was significant. Negotiations were in progress between the Christian Democrat Party, which needed outside support to have a stable parliamentary majority, and the non-communist left to form a center-left coalition. The powerful Italian Bishop's Conference had launched a full-scale offensive against this historic phase in Italy's postwar politics. The clergy had been instructed to denounce it from the pulpit. The Christian Democrats were threatened with withdrawal of support in the Catholic press and vital financing from Catholic backers unless the party abandoned *l'apertura a sinistra* (the opening to the left).

The Italian bishops' opposition grew out of their concern that the Socialist party, which was considered largely procommunist, would prove to be a Trojan horse for communist policies and intentions in the coalition. By giving the left greater legitimacy, the opening to the left could in the long run turn out to be an opening to direct communist participation in the government. As Patriarch of Venice, the pope himself had effectively scuttled an early center-left experiment at the local government level in his city by browbeating the Christian Democrats into quitting the coalition. But as pontiff, he saw Italian politics in the broader context of the Church's universal responsibilities. Publicly, he remained neutral and tried with limited success to persuade the Italian Bishops' Conference to do the same. Privately, he had come round to the view that a transfusion of left-wing ideals might hasten Italy's much-needed social reforms.

Togliatti transmitted to Moscow Pope John's interest in improving relations, together with his own assessment of the impact such a development would have on the Communist party in Italy. He saw it first as a neutralizing counterweight to the continued opposition of the Italian hierarchy. If a rapprochement did indeed blossom between Rome and Moscow, the advantages to the party could be enormous in terms of increased popular support and greater prestige. Moscow's reaction is not known but is easy to infer from the fact that over the next six weeks De Luca and Togliatti met more than once at Rodano's house until, on the eve of one of Togliatti's periodic visits to the Soviet Union, they sat down together at Rodano's desk and drafted a birthday message for submission to Khrushchev, and the pope's reply, both of which Togliatti took with him.

Pope John celebrated his eightieth birthday with a solemn high mass in Saint Peter's Basilica attended by Catholic reigning sovereigns and heads of state. The United States was represented by John McCone, Director of the Central Intelligence Agency and a practicing Catholic. The Soviet Union did not send a representative, but later in the day, while the pope was at lunch in his private apartment on the third floor of the Vatican Palace, Cardinal Amleto Cicognani, the secretary of state (Tardini having died meanwhile) was ushered in with the message from Khrushchev. The Soviet ambassador to Rome had delivered it to the papal nuncio to Italy, the Holy See's official representative to the Italian state. The astonished prelate, who had no inkling that all this was in the making, had rushed with it to the Vatican.

Typed on a single sheet of Soviet embassy paper, the note, addressed to the nuncio, stated: "I am instructed to ask you to convey in the name of Premier Khrushchev to His Holiness Pope John XXIII, on the occasion of his eightieth birthday, congratulations and sincere best wishes for his continued good health and for success in his noble aspiration to contribute toward strengthening and consolidating peace on earth and also toward the resolution of international problems by means of frank negotiations." The pope immediately ordered champagne from his well-stocked wine cellar. His secretary, Monsignor Loris Capovilla, protested that the pontiff was supposed to be on a diet—for he was vain about his appearance and fought a losing battle to reduce his ample waist—but John brushed his admonitions aside. When one of the prelates present asked for a soft drink instead, the pope exclaimed exuberantly, "What, you don't drink? You don't know what you're missing!" In the afternoon, Pope John went for his customary walk in the Vatican Gardens and knelt for a long time in prayer before the statue of Our Lady of Lourdes (a copy of the original in France). "Something is moving in the world," he told Capovilla. "The Lord is using my humble person to move history. Today, we have had a sign of Divine Providence." Two days later, a Jesuit ventured into the Soviet embassy in Rome like Daniel into the lion's den, to deliver the pope's reply, written in Russian in Cyrillic characters. "His Holiness Pope John XXIII sends thanks for your greetings," it said, "and for his part extends, also to the Russian people, cordial wishes for the spread and consolidation of universal peace through fraternal understanding and good will, and for this he offers fervent prayers."

The Church of Pius XII had been the Church of the cold war, aligned to the mystique of McCarthyism and John Foster Dulles. It was the Church that had condemned the trial of Cardinal Mindszenty in 1949. The movement of history for which Pope John was responsible dislodged the Church from its Western moorings and brought it into neutralist waters. Through a combination of flexible politics and personal warmth he succeeded in bringing about a thaw in the cold distrust between the Church and the Communist bloc.

The United States and other Western governments, concerned about its effect on their own dealings with Moscow, viewed this development with growing concern. Many Catholics were scandalized and dismissed the exercise as a betrayal in principle and a dangerous futility in practice. Pope John, who had no illusions about the nature of communism but possessed his own ideas about what ought to matter in mankind's various orders of priority, thought the game was worth the candle. The first gain was access to information about the state of the Church in Soviet countries. When the Secretariat of State established contact with the Hungarian regime a year later, the Vatican did not even know how many of its bishops had survived, still less where they were.

The second was freedom of Church leaders to travel to Rome where they could be consoled, encouraged, and brought up to date on theological developments. Thirdly, there was the chance to improve the extremely troublesome church-state relations in countries with large, devout Catholic populations and Communist governments, notably Poland, Czechoslovakia, and Hungary. Finally, it held the promise of an opportunity to extend Pope John's influence in the area which, in his closing years, he increasingly regarded as the most vital—world peace.

CHAPTER II

Pope and Council

THE SECRETARIAT OF STATE is responsible for the Vatican's relations with the outside world. During Pope John's reign it was divided into two sections: the Ecclesiastical, or Ordinary Affairs, Section dealt with the administrative problems of Catholic dioceses around the world (except in missionary countries which came under the jurisdiction of the Congregation for the Propagation of the Faith); the Extraordinary Affairs Section was responsible for implementing the foreign policy of the Holy See, and was thus the Church's principal channel of contact with the secular power. The head of the Ordinary Affairs Section was Archbishop Angelo Dell'Acqua, who had the title of substitute secretary of state, while his counterpart in the Extraordinary Affairs Section was Archbishop Antonio Samoré.

Both prelates were career diplomats, but their opposite views and contrasting personalities made them mortal enemies. Dell'Acqua was a genial, ruddy complexioned churchman whose practical good sense and open mind had made him one of Pope John's closest collaborators. Samoré, a pale, aquiline, Curia man, belonged to the Ottaviani camp.

Technically, the pope's contacts with Moscow ought to have been made through Samoré's section, which controlled the Holy See's diplomatic service. In the late nineteenth century, the Vatican lost its temporal power, but the international character of the Holy See was never doubted either in law or in practice. Papal sovereignty continued to be assured under international law, and a Vatican network of more than a hundred diplomatic missions (papal nunciatures and apostolic delegations) stretches across the globe with the avowed purpose of promoting the Church's pastoral mission and creating conditions of justice and peace in which the Church can operate. (Many countries, such as Egypt, have reciprocal representatives with Rome, even though they do not recognize the pope's authority as a spiritual leader.)

In fact Samoré wasn't even told of the pope's secret contacts with Togliatti. He almost certainly learned of them from his own sources, but this did not give him the authority to go to the pontiff and warn him of the consequences of his intentions. One reason why John had circumvented his own diplomatic network was his fear that if the proper officials were involved he would try to scuttle the whole endeavor. Samoré's inflexible anticommunism was based on domestic political concerns. Any relaxation in the Church's rigid stance towards the Communist bloc would benefit Togliatti's party in Italy and harm the Curia-backed Christian Democrats. Pope John, on the other hand, was more concerned with the broader scope of the negotiations.

But besides differences in style and essentials from the Roman Curia, the pope had another reason for preferring to work outside the limits of the Vatican bureaucracy, and that was to reduce the Church's direct involvement in, and implied responsibility for, his admittedly adventurous course of action. Thus, while Don Giuseppe De Luca's dealings with the Italian Communist party were *authorized,* they were not *official,* since De Luca occupied no position in the Roman Curia. As the scope of John's Eastern initiative grew, so did his parallel diplomacy, entrusted to a small group of faithful collaborators directly responsible to him.

The most influential of these was Capovilla. The young, soft-voiced priest had been a journalist and broadcaster in his native Veneto region before the newly appointed patriarch of Venice, Cardinal Angelo Roncalli, appointed him his secretary in 1953. The appointment raised ecclesiastical eyebrows because Capovilla, then only twenty-eight years old, shared many of the ideals of the Socialist party and appeared to have little in common with his apparently traditionalist archbishop, who was more than forty years his senior. But the choice had a certain logic and served Roncalli's purpose. Loris Capovilla knew the area well and had a wide network of contacts; he also shared the patriarch's fondness for being on the move. In a short time, Cardinal Roncalli was no longer a stranger in his new diocese. More than that, thanks to Capovilla's good public-relations sense, Cardinal Roncalli became one of the best known senior churchmen in Italy and gained a reputation for great personal warmth and open mindedness.

It was Capovilla, too, who exposed the cardinal to currents of progressive thought in the Italian church. For instance, through his secretary Roncalli came into contact with the Jesuits of the Instituto Sant' Ambrogio in Milan, a center for advanced social ideas. Roncalli became the Jesuits' unofficial protector, interceding on their behalf whenever they got into difficulty with the archbishop of Milan, Monsignor Giovanni Battista Montini, to whom Roncalli was linked by a growing friendship.

In 1958, Capovilla accompanied Cardinal Roncalli to Rome and served as his conclavist in the papal election from which the patriarch of Venice emerged as John XXIII. The new pope appointed Capovilla his cup bearer, an ancient post in the papal household, thus enabling him to keep the young priest by his side, for the position of secretary to the pope is not officially recognized in the Vatican.

The pope relied on him to do a great many things; for example, to coordinate the work of others on important projects such as his developing relations with Eastern Europe; to carry confidential messages (Pope John rarely used the telephone to talk to anyone outside the Vatican, fearing that the lines might be tapped); to read the newspapers every morning and mark with a red marker the items of interest for his attention; to make sure that the pope stuck to his diet in his constant struggle to lose weight. In politics especially, it was often difficult to determine where Capovilla's ideas ended and those of the pope himself began. It was true, however that the young priest was a seminal influence on his pontiff's thinking and decisions.

The pope still had daily audiences with his secretary of state, Cardinal Amleto Cicognani, whose office corresponds roughly to that of prime minister of the Holy See, but it was mainly because he enjoyed Cicognani's company, for at eighty-three the cardinal was beginning to show, and sometimes to act, his age. John's actual right-hand man in the Secretariat of State, and the second most important member of his inner circle, was archbishop Dell'Acqua, the substitute secretary.

Dell'Acqua's nominal chief mildly acquiesced to this situation. Other curialists, however, resented it. In 1960, Dell'Acqua survived an attempt by Curia cardinals to remove him by persuading Pope John to send him to Paris as papal nuncio so that Archbishop Samoré could step into his shoes. The move would have assured the Curia party of control over both sections of the Secretariat of State. The pope was tempted, since the post virtually guaranteed his trusted associate a cardinal's hat at the end of his stay in France. But in the end he refused to part with him, and Don Angelo (as the pope had called him since the time when they had served together in Istanbul twenty-five years earlier, the pope as apostolic delegate and Dell'Acqua as his secretary) stayed put.

Cardinal Augustin Bea, head of the Secretariat for Promoting Christian Unity, enjoyed the pope's complete trust and was consulted on many problems besides those relating to Christian unity. Igino Cardinale, the Vatican's chief of protocol, was the last member of the papal inner circle, although others were added as the occasion arose. A specialist in Vatican diplomatic practice who had written an authoritative book on the subject, the young monsignor had a well-stocked mind and was already a diplomat of ripe experience. His first language was English, having grown up in Brooklyn, to which his Italian parents had emigrated when he was a child, and he often acted as interpreter for Pope John during audiences with English-speaking visitors.

Pope John's attitude toward those around him was intensely familial. "It is difficult for you to comprehend how the Holy Father thinks of us and we of him," one of them told a visiting American. "None of us have wives, children, or social obligations. Nor do we live a prescribed communal life like monks. We who are here in Rome very often read, talk, and listen to music together.

"The Holy Father is our real father; to him, we are literally sons. Sometimes, we tell him new things which interest him and he is proud of us. Sometimes, he tells us to stop talking nonsense and to go away and learn wisdom. Ottaviani is not an enemy. To the Holy Father, he is an old uncle who is often difficult and must be circumvented but is still respected. Cicognani is an old friend of great experience who has become one of the family, like a trusted doctor. Wyszynski is a younger brother who lives far away and does great and difficult things with which we must help."

The visiting American was James W. Spain of the Central Intelligence Agency's Office of National Estimates, so called because the CIA's operational budget in a particular country was based on this department's projections of long range political developments. The Vatican prelate had no idea that he was talking to a CIA agent, for Spain had a cover. He posed as a scholar preparing a study on Italy on a Foreign Service grant.

The CIA's interest in the Catholic church went back to

1945, when the Vatican Curia and the Office of Strategic Services (OSS), its forerunner, found themselves working together to help the Christian Democrat Party come to power and to keep the communists out. At the same time that James Jesus Angleton, the brilliant head of the Rome station of the OSS, was busy building an intelligence network in Italy, Pope Pius XII was setting up his own information-gathering service to keep himself informed about political developments.

As described in an OSS report to Washington at the time, the pope's new service, which was largely dependent on the Jesuits, comprised several sections, each of which was ordered to report directly to the pontiff. Cardinal Enrico Gasparri, Prefect of the Roman Rota, was responsible for direct relations with the Christian Democrat Party. The General of the Jesuits, Father Norbert de Boynes, and the provincial of the Italian Jesuits, the report said, "have the task to organize and direct through the members of the Society of Jesus scattered in Italy a scrupulous service of secret information about the clandestine activities of the Italian communists and their relations with Moscow."

In addition, Cardinal Pietro Boetto, the archbishop of Genoa, also a Jesuit, "has organized in the diocese of Genoa an information service of Jesuits that operates separately in the north of Italy to collect secret information. He contacts the Pope separately from the (Jesuit) General House." The substitute secretary of state, Monsignor Giovanni Battista Montini, was "to maintain relations with the Italian Episcopate and to direct through it the activities of all the parish priests of Italy, and to be informed by them about the feelings of the population."

A lot of the information collected by the Vatican about the sentiments of the faithful and the activities of its enemies trickled to Washington through the CIA's network of contacts and friends in and around the Curia. It was thought to facilitate relations with Church sources if the Rome station chief of the CIA was a practicing Catholic, and this was almost invari-

ably the case. In the 1950s, when the Church's anticommunist
crusade was at its most militant, the Rome station chief was
William E. Colby. A decade later, he headed the CIA's vast
and generally notorious Vietnam operation. Intelligence officers who served under him in Saigon recall that Colby still
went to mass every morning before starting his day at the CIA
headquarters. He maintained good relations with the Vietnamese hierarchy, and several Catholic priests collaborated
with the agency.

Nor were these the only instances in which the CIA had
found the Catholic church cooperative in the common anticommunist cause. In Latin America, the agency could for
years count on the help of sympathetic churchmen at all levels. A decade later, the agency itself lifted a corner of the
curtain on this aspect of its activity when it was reluctantly
forced to admit at the congressional hearings on its activities
that it had recruited American missionaries in several Latin
American countries to act as informers and part-time agents.

In 1962, the CIA still considered the Church a vital prop to
the Italian Christian Democrats. This belief was reflected in
the year's allocation of "project money" for Italy, estimated at
$6 million, which included a number of contributions to the
charities, orphanages, schools, and other religious and welfare
projects supported by the agency's Vatican connections. But
in the Vatican itself, the crusading spirit was gradually giving
way to more flexible attitudes. Pope John's attempts to impose
political neutrality on Italian bishops had split their ranks
right down the middle, with half of them obeying the pope's
wishes and the other half persisting in their open support of
the Catholic party.

The exchange of messages with Khrushchev was confirmation to American intelligence circles that the Vatican could no
longer be taken for granted as an ally. The CIA station chief
in Rome, Thomas Hercules Kalamasinas, was instructed to
raise the priority of the station's spying on the Vatican. The
son of Greek immigrant parents, Kalamasinas was born in Sta-

ten Island and raised in the Greek Orthodox faith, converting to Catholicism after his marriage to a Roman Catholic girl. A New York racket-busting lawyer before the war, his espionage background was typical of many agents of his generation: he joined the army as a private at the outbreak of the war, was recruited into the OSS, served in various European countries; in 1945, he got his first exposure to militant communism in Greece, the land of his forebears, during the communist take-over attempt and instantly recognized the enemy. He was still in Greece when he transferred to the newly formed CIA, later serving in France and Italy. Pope John's embryonic *Ostpolitik* was hardly likely to appeal to a man of Kalamasinas's anticommunist convictions and, in fact, the Rome station's reporting did little to reverse the impression in Washington of a dangerous leftward drift.

In Washington, CIA studies with such titles as *The Catholic Church Reassesses Its Role in Latin America* attempted to articulate the impact of Pope John's policies on the Church in different regions. These reports projected a picture of increasing commitment to social change in the world and to some extent, to political change as well. For example, agency analysts predicted increased criticism of military regimes by Latin American hierarchies, and correspondingly more sympathy toward left-wing opposition groups such as Salvador Allende's party in Chile. They foresaw the emergence of militant social churchmen in the same mold as the Brazilian Bishop Helder Camara, who championed the cause of the slum dwellers in his diocese. In short, the Catholic church was becoming less dependable as a supporter of the established order.

The CIA's attitude toward developments in the Church was colored by the fact that Director McCone took a personal interest in the situation. Unfortunately for the agency's Italian station, it was required to keep a closer watch on the Vatican just at the time when some of its best sources found themselves shut out as a result of John's tendency to operate out-

side his own bureaucratic system, especially in his dealings
with the Communist bloc.

"Why didn't you tell me about De Luca?" a CIA operative
asked his Secretariat of State contact one day.

"Because we were in the dark ourselves," the contact lamented. "As we very often are these days."

It is ironic that while the CIA was striving to increase its
"intelligence capability" in the Vatican, the Kennedy Administration was trying equally hard to keep Rome at arm's length.
Pope John had hoped that the presence of a Catholic in the
White House would facilitate the improved relations he
sought with the United States to counterbalance his contacts
with Moscow.

His closest advisers argued the opposite. The first Catholic
president of the United States was going to lean over backward to avoid any whiff of Vatican influence on his policy
decisions. Throughout the 1960 presidential campaign, the
pontiff remained optimistic that a closer understanding was
inevitable. He even made light of their fears. Receiving Archbishop John Wright of Pittsburgh, he asked how Americans
rated Kennedy's chances of winning the election. Kennedy's
chances were considered very good, the bishop replied.
"Well, don't expect me to run a country with a language as
difficult as yours," John commented.

The pope's advisers were soon proved right. Of all the messages of congratulations from foreign heads of state received
by Kennedy on his election, only the one from Pope John
XXIII was kept secret by the White House, and the Vatican
was asked to do the same with Kennedy's own equally harm-
less reply.

Religion had been one of the toughest issues in the campaign. In the triangle of Bible states with Indiana at the apex
and Oklahoma and Mississippi at the base, the key factor was
not the racial factor, but the religious factor.

Despite Kennedy's insistent promise—at the famous Houston confrontation with southern Protestant and Baptist minis-

ters and at other times during the campaign—that his religious
beliefs were his personal affair and would in no way influence
his decisions as president, bigotry, political sniping, and also
genuine concern combined to keep the issue alive even after
his election.

To many Americans, the presence of a Catholic in the White
House spelled the end of the sacred principle of the separation of church and state. One theme persisted: that the pope
would soon be governing America. Determined to calm genuine concern, neutralize a powerful political weapon against
him, and at the same time isolate unrelenting bigotry before
the next election campaign, Kennedy adopted a strict policy
of total public detachment from his church, and especially
from its visible head in Rome.

Years later, Theodore Sorensen, one of Kennedy's special
assistants in the White House, was to explain it this way: "The
hardcore religious opposition . . . would remain and flourish
to be cited by future conventions against the practicability of
nominating a Catholic, if he (Kennedy) lowered the bars between church and state, yielded to the pressures of the hierarchy, or otherwise confirmed the religious opposition's
suspicions. But if his conduct of the office was in keeping with
his campaign pledge and constitutional oath, while unreason-
ing bigotry would always be raised, the unwritten law against
a Catholic president would not only be temporarily broken
but permanently repealed."

This approach was clearly understood at the White House
and rigidly followed. But the administration's hypersensitive-
ness about the Vatican did not interrupt the Central Intelligence Agency's spying activities in Rome, nor its use of
members of the Church in other countries. It was not an era in
which the activities of the CIA came under public scrutiny,
but if they had, the agency could have argued that the separation of church and state was less strictly observed in several
countries crucial to the security of the United States, for ex-

ample, Italy itself. Therefore, the agency was justified in monitoring the political activities of churchmen.

A discreet contact was also maintained on the diplomatic level in both Rome and Washington. Though not exactly secret, it was not an arrangement either side was keen to publicize. In Washington, senior State Department officers would, as the occasion arose, meet privately with the apostolic delegate, Archbishop Egidio Vagnozzi. The Italian churchman was not the Holy See's accredited representative to the United States government, but the Vatican's representative to the American hierarchy. However, he was an experienced diplomat, quite at home in such situations.

A couple of times a year, too, Vagnozzi and McGeorge Bundy, Kennedy's Special Assistant for National Security Affairs, arranged to meet by accident at a reception or dinner at the Georgetown home of the Italian ambassador. They would slip away unobtrusively to the ambassador's study, conduct their business, and then return to the party.

It cannot be said that Pope John's interests were well served by this arrangement. Vagnozzi was an Ottaviani man with a conservative's skepticism about the pontiff's reforms which he did not hide from his State Department contacts. Moreover, he had been counsellor in the nunciature in Paris when Pope John was papal nuncio, and had formed a low opinion of John's abilities, which he freely expressed in Washington.

In Rome, there were more frequent, but equally informal contacts between William Sherman, a political officer at the American embassy, and Monsignor Igino Cardinale. These meetings, which usually took place in Cardinale's cluttered office near Archbishop Dell'Acqua's on the third floor of the Vatican Palace, originated with one of those accidental circumstances that occasionally comes to the aid of diplomatic practice. Sherman's predecessor in Rome was a distant cousin of Monsignor Cardinale, and in the absence of any formal contact between the Holy See and the United States, the two had occasionally collaborated to resolve specific problems, such as, for example, arranging papal audiences for distinguished Americans, and looking after official delegations at important papal functions.

Before leaving Rome at the end of his tour early in 1962, Cardinale's cousin had introduced the prelate to his successor, William Sherman. The two diplomats had much in common. They were both young, capable, and inclined to be low key —ideally suited for this delicate diplomatic maneuver. With the encouragement of Pope John on Cardinale's side, and of the American ambassador, Frederick Reinhardt, on Sherman's, a regular channel of communication was established. Sherman was expected to maintain the relationship in addition to his regular duties as the embassy's contact with the ruling Christian Democrats. In fact, Sherman's dual function provided a plausible answer to awkward questions about his meetings with Cardinale. Since the Christian Democrat party was strongly influenced by the Italian hierarchy, some contact with senior Vatican prelates was not only reasonable, but useful.

In this manner, the embassy was able to pick up and transmit to Washington useful information about Pope John's aims and intentions in situations and spheres in which the United States had a direct interest, such as his recent contacts with Moscow. What had started out as a convenience rapidly acquired greater importance in the pope's politically eventful closing years. Reinhardt's view was that the Vatican's political activities during that period were becoming too important for this casual arrangement, and he said as much to Washington.

Reinhardt owed his post to Kennedy's policy of appointing career diplomats to former political plums. At fifty-one, he was a rising professional with the old-school knack of never seeming to be under any sort of pressure. Some of his subordinates in Rome mistook this for laziness, but his ability was recognized in Washington where it counted, and where he was generally considered destined for greater things. So the Department of State set about testing the water at the White House.

First, a senior officer from the department discreetly sounded out influential White House advisers, putting forward all the arguments for giving serious consideration to re-establishing regular diplomatic contacts with the Vatican. They pointed out the distinction between the Holy See as a sovereign state with the pope as its head and the Vatican as the central mechanism of the Catholic church. The political influence of the Church, especially in Catholic countries, was vast and significant, even though churchmen would argue that it was also incidental to the Church's main mission. In the Holy See, Rome had a structure with which a secularized power such as the United States could deal on a political and diplomatic level without breaking the fundamental principle of the separation of church and state.

Kennedy's closest advisers agreed that the question was worth looking into, but only the president could make the decision. Some days later, Dean Rusk, the secretary of state, brought up the subject at the close of a cabinet meeting, while the cabinet room was emptying out. Kennedy listened to Rusk's arguments staring out of the window at the White House lawn. Then he shook his head firmly. No, he said, that was going to have to wait. It was an issue for another president —or, at any rate, another term.

It did not matter to Kennedy that the United States had actually maintained relations with the Holy See for almost as many years as it had been without them. When Benjamin Franklin was living in Paris during the years of revolution, the Vatican consulted him on the appointment of new bishops in America. Consular relations were established with the Papal States in 1797, followed by full diplomatic relations from 1848 to 1868.

But in 1868, the United States mission in Rome came under attack in Congress on the basis of its political usefulness and the apparent religious intolerance of the Papal States. Mr. Wil-

liams, who first moved in the congressional debates to strike
Rome from the bill of diplomatic appropriations, said, "It was
on the score of political insignificance of the Papal Government that I moved the amendment." To this was added a
general desire for economy (Mr. Morrill: "It is a useless expenditure, merely to provide a place for someone who wants
a position").

Then came a specific objection to a report that the pope had
banned Scottish Presbyterian worship in Rome. The Scottish
Presbyterians, it was said, had been ordered to hold their services outside the city limits. The report later turned out to be
false, but by then Congress had voted to close down the U.S.
Embassy to the Papal States and funds had been cut off.

After that, it was not until 1939, when Franklin Roosevelt
appointed Myron C. Taylor as his personal representative,
with the *honorary* title of ambassador (thus bypassing the
problem of obtaining congressional approval), that a form of
regular contact was re-established between Washington and
the Holy See. Taylor left Rome in 1941 before the entry of the
United States into World War II, but his deputy, Harold Tittman, remained behind and spent the war years living in Rome
under the protection of the Holy See, a state of affairs which
the occupying Germans accepted without question.

Taylor's appointment was renewed in 1947, but when he
resigned because of ill health three years later, President Truman, strongly influenced by a Catholic lobby led by Cardinal
Spellman, decided that the time was ripe to put relations on a
more normal footing. Accordingly, in October 1951, Truman
nominated General Mark Clark, commander of the United
States Army Field Forces and incidentally an Episcopalian,
not as his personal envoy, as Taylor had been, but as full
ambassador. The nomination thus required the approval of the
Senate Foreign Relations Committee, whose chairman, Senator Tom Connally, a Texas Democrat, promptly announced
that he would oppose it. Connally's avowed hostility was not
conditioned solely by the anticipated opposition of Southern

Baptists. General Clark also had the misfortune of being personally unpopular among Texans, many of whom held him responsible for heavy losses suffered by a Texas National Guard regiment during the Italian campaign of World War II. Clark had ordered the Thirty-sixth Division to advance across the Rapido River in the face of great odds. The unit had suffered many casualties, and the Texans never forgot it.

The Senate Foreign Relations Committee's procrastination about holding nomination hearings allowed Protestant opposition to the appointment to mobilize. Church groups all over the country, but especially in the Bible Belt, staged protest meetings. In Washington itself, about five hundred Protestant clergymen demonstrated outside the White House against Truman's decision to establish diplomatic relations with the Holy See. Among the demonstrators was the president's own pastor. Truman refused to receive a delegation of the protesting clergymen: he sent word that a meeting would be of no avail because his mind was made up.

The enraged leader of the group, Reverend Carl McIntire, president of the International Council of Christian Churches, exclaimed, "[Truman] has driven a sword deep into the heart of Presbyterian America. Communism is an enemy. We are all against it. But we have another enemy too, older, shrewder. It is Roman Catholicism and its bid for world power. In the United States, it is called Spellmanism." When this was reported to Spellman, who was in Boston, his retort was, "It would be better if they donated a pint of blood for the boys in Korea. That would be much more useful."

In pressing Truman to make the controversial nomination, Cardinal Spellman was an instrument of Pope Pius XII's strong desire to cement the Catholic Church's relationship with its strongest political ally. There seemed to Pius to be a certain logic in the notion that the spiritual and temporal leaders of the Cold War should have diplomatic ties. It would serve as a confirmation of their unified stand against the common enemy.

Spellman also had a hand in selecting an active military man as the United States representative to the papacy. The Archbishop of New York was a very active Catholic Military Ordinary (Senior Chaplain) and an unabashed admirer of such soldierly virtues as devotion to duty, to God, and country. He probably felt more at home in the company of generals than he did among his own ecclesiastical peers. He knew the upper echelons of the armed forces well, and Clark was one of his favorite generals. The gossip in church circles at the time was that the nomination of a United States envoy to the Vatican was important to Spellman in a personal way in that the cardinal felt it would enhance his prestige in Rome and possibly his chances of filling the vacant post of Pope Pius XII's secretary of state, for which he was then mentioned to be the front-running candidate.

But on January 14, 1952, the White House announced General Clark's retreat. Clark asked to be withdrawn from the nomination, citing "the controversy that has developed." Truman, doubtless prodded from the wings by Cardinal Spellman, who had been summoned to Rome to report on Clark's withdrawal to Pope Pius, said that he would nominate another ambassador in Clark's place. Years later, Truman was to say that he underestimated the opposition of other churches. He believed that, without the exacerbating factor of Senator Connally's personal enmity toward Clark, the hue and cry would eventually peter out. But the protests continued and the matter threatened to become an issue in the 1952 presidential election.

Some weeks after Clark's withdrawal, a group of Presbyterian ministers passed a resolution "to work for the defeat at the polls of any man or party which is disposed to undermine our Constitution," in which, as the text stated, the First Amendment assures the separation of church and state. Church groups and individual churchmen continued to sound the same warning of the political consequences of establishing formal ties with the Vatican. On May 14, the president of the

Southern Baptist Convention warned that Baptists could not "in conscience sake countenance any candidate, even one of their own number, who does not make it crystal clear that he opposes any and all missions to the Vatican." Ten days later, the American Baptist Convention, meeting in Chicago, reaffirmed its opposition to "any kind of formal diplomatic relations on the part of our government with the Vatican." The Convention claimed to be voicing the objections of 3.6 million followers.

Truman did not drop the subject, despite the opposition, but neither did he nominate a new ambassador. While Truman waited for the fury to abate, Pius despatched Monsignor Giovanni Battista Montini, the undersecretary of state, to urge him to "formalize" relations between the two states. *L'Osservatore Romano* delivered a prod by publishing President Lincoln's letter of April 7, 1882, nominating an envoy. The Vatican paper added no comment, but none was needed. The inference was clear. There was historical precedent for what Truman was trying to achieve.

But an election year imposes its own political priorities. In August, shortly before the Democratic convention Truman announced that the question of the nomination of a United States ambassador to the pope had been shelved. And some weeks later, the Democratic presidential nominee, Governor Adlai Stevenson of Illinois, declared that, if he were elected, it would remain on the shelf. Such an appointment he said, "would be highly incompatible with the theory of the separation of church and state."

Pope Pius wrote to President Truman that he would not accept a return to the Roosevelt formula. Myron Taylor's nomination had been accepted by the Holy See as a "provisional" arrangement, but it was now time to put relations on a more regular footing. Henceforth, admonished *L'Osservatore Romano* on February 12, 1953, echoing the pontiff's letter to Truman, "there can be no question of anything but official and stable diplomatic representation."

The United States continued to send high-level representatives to attend important events in the Church, such as the funeral in 1958 of Pope Pius XII, and the coronation of Pope John XXIII. But even this limited contact seemed too much for the overcautious Kennedy administration.

In September 1962, the Holy See invited the United States Government, along with other governments, to send an official delegation to the opening of the Vatican Ecumenical Council. About eighty nations accepted, but not the United States. Washington's official refusal, transmitted through the Rome embassy, explained that the traditional separation of church and state precluded representation at a religious conference.

Cardinale immediately sought a meeting with Sherman at which the normally cheerful prelate gave vent to his dismay. It was not a matter of attending the Council *debates,* he argued—they were closed to everyone except the bishops anyway. The Council opening was an important ceremonial event in the life of the Holy See, the type of occasion to which the United States had not hesitated to send its representatives in the past.

If the United States chose to ignore the opening of the Council, it would be committing a serious blunder. Reaction in Catholic countries would be very critical, especially in Latin America, which looked to the United States for guidance and leadership. Other countries would be represented by royalty, heads of state, ministers, and senior statesmen. This was a measure of the importance attached to the Council throughout the world. Washington could play down American attendance by sending a low-level representation but could not ignore it. While American presence need not be conspicuous, American absence certainly would be.

"Why, if the Holy See as much as dropped a hint that Russian official attendance would be welcomed, Khrushchev himself would be on the next plane," Cardinale concluded.

Sherman had never before seen the Vatican prelate agitated.

With the opening of the Council ten days away, the American diplomat lost no time in transmitting the Vatican's deep vexation to Washington.

The reply was equally prompt. The White House, not the State Department, had decided, and (as the telegram stated) "at the highest level," that the answer was still no. Kennedy apparently felt that representation at coronations and funerals was generally understood by the public to be purely ceremonial, but the presence of an official delegation at the opening of a religious conference of such significance laid the administration open to criticism and misrepresentation.

That had a ring of finality. No diplomatic arguments about adverse Latin American reaction were going to compete with the danger (real or imagined) of critical sermons from scores of southern pulpits and the accumulation of fresh ammunition for use against Kennedy in future campaigns.

But the Vatican was not yet prepared to take no for an answer. On October 3, 1962, Vagnozzi sought a meeting with the State Department. He had, he said, a personal message to Kennedy from Pope John. The pope was sorry to hear that the United States may not be represented at the opening of the Council, and he hoped that the American ambassador would be able to attend.

In the face of a direct request from the pope for a token presence, Kennedy backed down. Reinhardt was told to attend the ceremony in Saint Peter's, taking William Sherman with him. His instructions were specific, and came straight from the Oval Office: "If queried, you should treat your presence as a completely natural thing to do under the circumstances."

And, instead of the white tie and tails normally worn by diplomats at papal functions, he was told that he should wear a dark suit.

CHAPTER III

The Making of a Pontiff

KENNEDY'S RETICENCE perplexed and disap-
pointed Pope John, but the memory of it was soon forced aside
by the breathtaking whirl of last-minute developments leading up to the historic opening of the Council itself.

On September 27, 1962, the pope presided over a gathering
of members of the *Famiglia Pontificia,* the papal household.
Cardinals, *monsignori,* priests, technicians, gardeners, and a
handful of nuns packed the Hall of Benedictions in the Vatican Palace. When the pontiff walked into the room, they broke
into cheers and applause. John smiled warmly, settled into
the large red throne, and began as usual to tap the ground with
his red slippered feet, while Monsignor Pietro Parente, asses-
sor of the Holy Office and an Ottaviani henchman if ever there
was one, conveyed dutiful greetings on behalf of all.

Then John launched into an intimate discourse, dispensing
with the pontifical "we" and speaking instead in the first person singular in order to emphasize the "familial" nature of the
occasion. He urged the gathering to "live the council," and
also to pray for an important special intention.

Hardly anyone present knew with any certainty what that

special intention could be. But as John was speaking, his thoughts were probably with Monsignor Jan Willebrands, secretary of the Christian Unity Secretariat, who was boarding Czechoslovak Airlines flight 502 bound for Moscow. His mission: to approach the ruling hierarchy of the Russian Orthodox church and persuade them, as representatives of some forty million Orthodox church members, to send observers to the council.

Over the next four days, the poker-faced Dutch theologian had a series of meetings with the Orthodox patriarchate to explain the purpose of the council, and the intended role of the observers from other Christian churches. These representatives, appointed by their hierarchies, were intended by Pope John to be more than window-dressing symbols of the church's new openness and its willingness to establish a dialogue with other Christian faiths. They would attend the closed sessions, receive all the literature, and thus be in a position to lobby and to be consulted on matters relating to ecumenism.

Equally important were Willebrands's assurances that the council would undertake no anticommunist polemics, that John's political approach was not that of Pius. Rome could be friends with Moscow.

Willebrands returned to Rome on October 3, with the official answer from Moscow: "The Moscow Patriarchate does not see its way clear to announce the sending of observers to attend the first session of the Second Vatican Council." Both he and Cardinal Bea, his superior, understood. The Russians were coming—but in their own good time. Places were reserved for them in Saint Peter's Basilica, where the council was to meet, among the other observers expected from the Protestant Churches of the West, and other Orthodox hierarchies from the East (but not from the ecumenical patriarch of Constantinople who decided, after much discussion, that the time was not yet ripe to accept the Roman olive branch).

To Pope John this was wonderful news. But one question still weighed heavily on his mind: what of the Catholic hierarchies in Eastern Europe? Would the glimmer of a thaw in relations between Moscow and Rome make it possible for bishops in Poland, Czechoslovakia, Hungary, and Yugoslavia to come to Rome to attend the council?

The Pope's associates, to pave the way, had spread the word to those Vatican diplomats abroad whom they knew to be sympathetic to the notion of a Vatican Council to make it their business to cultivate their Soviet counterparts with two objectives in mind. Firstly to try to discover Soviet intentions regarding the attendance at the Council by Eastern European bishops, and secondly, to reassure the Kremlin that the pope was determined not to let the historic gathering become a forum for anticommunist sentiment.

In due course, news was received of a conversation between the apostolic delegate in Turkey, Archbishop Francesco Lardone, and the Soviet ambassador. The ambassador had assured Lardone that Moscow was doing its utmost to induce Eastern European regimes to allow their bishops to go to Rome. There was no further word from the Russians on the subject, but three days before the opening of the council, the pope was told that Cardinal Wyszynsky had arrived from Warsaw at the head of the Polish hierarchy, consisting of twenty-three bishops. Two days later, John singled out from the twenty-five hundred bishops and heads of religious orders present the two bishops from Hungary and four from Yugoslavia for a private audience. That afternoon, he almost wept with joy when he learned that a lone Czech bishop had just flown in from Prague. Then, on October 10, the day of the opening itself, Cardinal Bea brought him a telegram from Moscow: the Russian Orthodox observers would be appearing on the scene the following day.

The opening ceremony of the council represented one of those moments when history changes gear. Pope John was carried in on his portable throne, the *sedia gestatoria,* which

he hated because the swaying movement upset his stomach.
He was an absolute monarch, the last of Europe's crowned
heads in *plenitudo potestatis*, presiding over an environment
within which thrived a social framework with some of the
creases of the wider society carefully ironed out and others
carefully pressed in.

It was a world of courtly bows, swishing silks, and whispered conversations in marble galleries where life moved
with the measured grace of a Haydn quartet; a world full of
color—scarlet-caped cardinals, bishops in violet, Swiss
Guards in slashed doublets and breeches of red, yellow, and
blue, Noble Guards in plumed helmets and bright red coats
—yet at the same time strangely somber, and so rigidly formal
that the pope's official photographer wore white tie and tails
at all papal functions, even in the morning; a world in which
the domestic vocabulary of everyday family life was a distant
echo from outside the walls, and where the human side revealed itself in the sight of a doddering old cardinal wiping
his sniffly nose, or perhaps a junior prelate paying court to a
senior one.

This domain is Vatican City State, a 108-acre sovereign territory within Rome's city limits and with a predominantly
male population of about 700, plus about 3,000 more who
come from Rome each day to work, with its own standing army
and police force, its own bank, post office, radio station, daily
newspaper, railroad station, and jail. The whole area is divided into three roughly equal parts: offices and residences;
gardens; and churches and museums, the latter housing one
of the world's outstanding collections of art treasures and
books.

After the pope, its most important citizens are the twenty or
so cardinals who reside in the Vatican and preside over the
various aspects of the Roman Curia. Strong umbilical cords of
geography and history tied the Vatican and Italy together;
popes had been Italian since the death of Hadrian VI in 1523.
Italian priests still filled most of the posts in the Vatican bu-

reaucracy. In the Church at large, the Curia had a well-deserved reputation for being lethargic, narrow, provincial, prim, bourgeois, and not a little hypocritical.

Both Pius XII and John XXIII had made serious attempts to reduce the length of religious ceremonies in Saint Peter's, but tiring hours officiating in long liturgies under the weight of richly embroidered vestments were still a burden on the pope's physical stamina. Pope John made it a point not to go through such occasions on an empty stomach: halfway through the opening ceremony of the Vatican Council he had a reviving cup of espresso and a sandwich while sitting on his throne in the basilica, concealed behind a wall of cardinals and prelates.

With the Council, the old Church began a process of self-renewal amounting to a revolution from within. In a few years the process of rapid change was to alter many things, not least the face of the papacy. The great irony was that the architect of this change should be John XXIII.

Pitchforked into the papacy after a long and difficult conclave as a result of a pragmatic alliance between several factions, each of which had failed to elect its own candidate, he was not chosen Bishop of Rome because of any program of *Aggiornamento*. Few cardinals, if any, dreamed that he would call an ecumenical council. He was supposed to fill a quite different bill.

In his last years, Pope Pius XII had become constitutionally reluctant to commit himself to a definite line of policy; he hated to cross or burn a bridge. When he died in 1958, an old, innocuous, accommodating prelate was sought to succeed him. Someone who would replenish the diminished ranks of the cardinals and make routine decisions, largely prepared by the Curia, but would do nothing strikingly new while the problems of Pope Pius's stifling personal rule were gradually ironed out behind the scenes and until things were ready to pass into the hands of a more modern pope with a distinct policy.

Cardinal Spellman, who sat opposite him in the Sistine Chapel during the voting, used to relate how, as the votes mounted in Roncalli's favor in successive ballots, he watched him closely and was surprised to see no change at all in his expression or demeanor. When, immediately on his election on the fourth day and eleventh ballot, he was asked the ritual question, "By what name do you wish to be known?", he calmly produced from his pocket a long speech in Latin, which he had prepared in advance, and in which he announced that he would take the name John. Among the reasons he gave for his choice was the observation that, "Nearly all popes named John had a brief pontificate," thereby making it clear that he realized he had been chosen as a transitional pope. He was then seventy-six years old.

It quickly became apparent, however, that in picking Cardinal Roncalli the advocates of a transitional pontificate had greatly miscalculated. Old he may have been, but the "interim" pope soon showed that he had no intention of being either innocuous or accommodating. To the confounding of the prophets and the discomfiture of the Curia, he turned out to be a great innovator.

"No one anticipated that Pope John was indeed destined to be a pope of transition in the very special sense now evident to us all," the Jesuit historian, Robert A. Graham has written. Thomas Carlyle, the great English nineteenth-century historian, says that the history of the world consists of the biographies of great men. In the same way, the history of the papacy has its roots in the lives of its popes. Certainly, the events that shaped the pontificate of John XXIII can be explained by one thing: his whole life.

The Catholic Church is democratic in advancing priests who show promise: it has offered splendid careers to many men of humble origin. Cardinal Ottaviani was the son of a Rome baker. Cardinal Bea's father was a village carpenter in the Black Forest in Germany. Cardinal Siri grew up in Genoa, subsequently his archdiocese, in an apartment block where

his father was the janitor. Pope John was of North Italian peasant stock.

The two hundred sixty-first successor to the throne of Saint
Peter was born Angelo Giuseppe Roncalli on November 25,
1881, in Sotto Il Monte, a small hillside village nine miles
from Bergamo where the Alps flatten out into the fertile plain
of the River Adda. His father was a tenant farmer eking out a
grim existence on means that were out of proportion to the
size of his family—Angelo was the third of thirteen children,
ten of whom survived childbirth, and the eldest son.

The Roncallis were a prolific clan typical of the Bergamo
region. A Vatican list of everyone who could legitimately lay
claim to kinship with the pope, published shortly after his
accession in order to make things more difficult for impostors,
contained over four hundred names. As the eldest son, Angelo
was steered toward the priesthood, a common practice in Italian peasant families partly through piety, and partly because
a priest in the family enhanced its prestige. A boy in the seminary also meant one child less to feed and clothe at home.

The decision was taken by his mother, a gentle, pious
woman, whom he revered all his life, and by the local parish
priest. When he was twelve, he entered the seminary at Bergamo and did well enough there to win a scholarship to finish
his ecclesiastical training in Rome. So, at nineteen, the Lombard farm boy found himself transplanted to the Accademia
dei Nobili, a seminary for the sons of Italian aristocratic families noted as a recruiting ground for the Roman Curia. Admission presupposed wealth and a good pedigree; Roncalli
possessed neither, but his openness and irrepressible good
nature helped him bridge the social gap, and he was popular
with both his colleagues and teachers.

When he was ordained in Rome in 1903 he was twenty-
three years old. He hoped for a parish assignment, preferably
close to Sotto Il Monte. But before this wish could be fulfilled
the Accademia had a visit from Monsignor Count Giacomo
Radini-Tedeschi, the Bishop of Bergamo, who was looking for

a young *bergamasco* priest to become his secretary. The choice rapidly narrowed down to two candidates, one with a good academic record, the other with a cheerful disposition. The bishop recruited the latter, who was Don Angelo Roncalli.

Bishop Radini was a strong influence in the life of the young priest. An aristocrat and social reformer, this distinguished churchman was well known in Italy as the founder of the Catholic Workers' Movement, but it was said in Vatican circles that his activism had marred a promising Curia career and caused his removal to Bergamo. Being out of the mainstream of ecclesiastical life failed to dim his reformist spirit; through him, Roncalli was brought into contact with currents of social thought and the alarming facts of economic life in Europe in the years leading to World War I. From him, the young priest not only learned the social reformist theory of the time, but drew the inspiration to apply it in practice.

In 1909, Radini openly supported a textile workers' strike in Bergamo with money from his own pocket (the first known instance of a local bishop backing a strike), and his secretary mobilized Catholic youths to feed and help the strikers, in defiance of the Vatican's well-known suspicion of such radical action. Radini saw the Church as a shield for the elemental human liberties of the poor and the weak, and Roncalli learned to see things from the same reformist perspective.

In most other respects, Bishop Radini-Tedeschi was a traditionalist cleric. Life in his household was sober, dignified, and orderly. This too made a lasting impression on Roncalli, who always acknowledged Radini as his model of priestly behavior. An entry in his diary when he was papal nuncio in Paris deplores his staff's tendency to gossip, especially about Church personalities.

In Radini's household, he recalls, "There was never a single reference to a Vatican official that lacked reverence, affection, or respect." About women there was "never a word, never."

In World War I, Roncalli enlisted as an army chaplain; then

came a stint as a seminary professor and university counsellor in Bergamo, during which time he established a national network of Catholic student hostels; but the pastoral work that he felt was his true calling continued to elude him.

Roncalli's association with Radini-Tedeschi again influenced the course of his career in 1921. The bishop had died seven years earlier, in his secretary's arms. Among his bequests to Roncalli were his love of travel and the goodwill of his many friends, who had included two prelates who later became popes. One was Pope Benedict XV, to whom Roncalli now sent a copy of his just completed biography of Radini. This evidently jogged the pontiff's memory about Roncalli, who was immediately summoned to Rome and appointed president of the Italian branch of the Society for the Propagation of the Faith.

This organization was entrusted with raising money for missionary work, mainly through Sunday church collections (Roncalli's counterpart in the United States was Monsignor Richard Cushing of Boston). Although he came on the Roman scene as a new man at the age of forty, he was given sufficient authority by Pope Benedict to transfer the Society's center of operations from Lyons to Rome and to modernize its financial structure.

It was a peripheral curial post, but it gave Roncalli a chance to display his considerable gifts as an organizer and to indulge his love of travel. Besides visiting every diocese in Italy, he inspected the society's more effective centers in France, Germany, Poland, and the former Austro-Hungarian Empire. He left the society, three years later, in considerably better shape than he found it, and it proved substantially effective in supporting the Italian foreign missions.

Following a brief stint as lecturer in Patristics at the Lateran University in Rome, he was made an archbishop and dispatched to Bulgaria as apostolic visitor. His mission was twofold: first, to establish contact with the scattered and disorganized Catholic and Uniate (Orthodox in communion with Rome) minorities which had a hard existence in a region dominated by an unfriendly Orthodox Church; second, although as Apostolic Visitor he was the pope's temporary representative to the clergy and faithful in Bulgaria and had no diplomatic status, he was instructed to try to establish a permanent Vatican presence in Sofia.

Roncalli had no formal training as a diplomat. He was not a product of the Pontifical Ecclesiastical Academy, the Vatican's prestigious school for prelates destined for the foreign service. He left for Sofia in 1925 believing his excursion into diplomacy to be a temporary one, but at forty-six he was embarking on a new phase in his life that was to last three decades.

He had barely set foot in Bulgaria when he got into hot water with Rome. Hearing that the synod of the Bulgarian Orthodox Church was meeting in Sofia, the new Apostolic Visitor sent a message of greeting. The bishop's reply was to invite him to address the synod, something no papal representative had done for at least three centuries.

This seemed to Roncalli a providential opportunity to establish contact with the Bulgarian Church, and he cheerfully appeared before the synod where he made a short, safe speech recalling the Christian heritage of their two churches. The Vatican took a dim view of this unauthorized encounter, and he received his first reprimand.

Shortly afterward, Archbishop Roncalli visited Rome where he had an audience with Pope Pius XI, who had by that time succeeded Pope Benedict. Pius brought up the incident, and lectured his visitor on the risks to the Church, as well as to his own soul, of such unauthorized contacts with alienated—and often alien—churches.

"I did what I thought best," stammered Roncalli.

"Well," replied the pope consolingly, "perhaps you sowed that others may reap."

His Bulgarian assignment lasted ten long years. For, having succeeded in persuading the Bulgarians to accept a permanent Vatican representative to the local Catholic hierarchy, he was himself appointed the first apostolic delegate. From Sofia, he was then shifted to Istanbul in the same capacity at a time when an anti-religious and secularist government was proving hostile to the Catholic community.

On April 25, 1935, shortly after Roncalli's arrival in Turkey, the United States ambassador in Istanbul, Robert P. Skinner, reported to Washington that the new apostolic delegate had called to introduce himself. "He dwelt pointedly upon the fact that the Church in its history had known how to bend without breaking, and that as far as he was concerned he intended to bend in Turkey wherever it might be necessary and thus maintain as long as possible, intact, the Church organizations, religious, educational, and philantropic."

His first task was to persuade members of the clergy and religious orders to comply with the new Turkish law that prohibited the wearing of ecclesiastical dress in public. He later told his diplomatic colleagues that, while the Catholic priests and monks in Turkey complied without protest, the nuns put up a strong resistance, and it required all his powers of persuasion to win them over to his point of view.

From the earliest phases of World War II, Roncalli was extremely active in keeping the Turkish pipeline open for escaping Jews. According to testimony in his canonization proceedings, he was personally responsible for helping over twenty-four thousand Jews to escape from Nazi-occupied countries in Central Europe. This he did by issuing safe-conduct passes (often certifying the bearer to be a Catholic) so that they could obtain permission from the authorities to remain in Turkey and thence arrange for passage to Palestine. At the time, the Turkish government was reluctant to admit large numbers of Jewish refugees, fearing a retaliatory German invasion.

Beginning in September 1940 with a full account of the first of many encounters with groups of fleeing refugees, Roncalli was meticulous in keeping the Holy See informed of all that he saw and heard regarding the plight of East European Jews.

He did it with a growing sense of shock, and Rome's failure to speak out against such acts was at first puzzling and then painful to him. (Archbishop Tardini, the substitute secretary of state, once remarked with a sigh, "Monsignor Roncalli's reports are always such—eye-openers!")

Pius XII's wartime conduct raises and leaves unanswered crucial, nagging questions. The pope himself never gave a full explanation of it. The publication of many of the acts and documents of the Holy See relating to World War II sheds only partial light. Pius has been accused of relinquishing the moral leadership inherent in his great office by failing to make even one specific condemnation of the crimes and cruelties of war. It has been said that he had at his disposal against Hitler the two greatest weapons in the world—excommunication and martyrdom—and that he used neither one.

The pope himself felt that he had sufficiently condemned Nazi misdeeds himself, and that he was exerting all the pressures that he could through his personal representatives and other church leaders in various cities. He was firmly convinced that an open denunciation of the Nazi regime not only would not deter Hitler from his course, but would have the opposite effect of exposing Catholics in German-occupied lands to savage reprisals and Catholic institutions to suppression.

In the eyes of the pope, and of many others of his Curia, compared with the calamity of communism, fascism was merely an inconvenience. They appeared to have a generous sympathy for the Nazi regime's self-characterization as the scourge of communism. If Germany was totally defeated, Pope Pius foresaw—prophetically, as it turned out—an Eastern Europe dominated by Moscow and for all practical purposes lost to Rome. This fortified his resolve to preserve a meticulous neutrality, hoping to shorten the war by offering himself as a mediator acceptable to all the belligerents.

In 1942, he explained to Harold Tittman, the American chargé d'affaires, that he could not be specific about Nazi atrocities without also specifying the atrocities committed by the Bolsheviks, and this the other Western Allies presumably would not like. For all the pope's rationalization, it is difficult not to conclude that he ended up sinning by omission where a violation of simple human rights cried out for condemnation.

Roncalli went as far as he dared in urging the pope to speak out—too far, in the view of his superiors. Cardinal Maglione, the secretary of state, used to complain, "I have received from Monsignor Roncalli yet another attempt to persuade the Holy See that now is the time to intervene." Typical of this divergence of approach between the Vatican and Roncalli was the Franz von Papen case. The German ambassador to Istanbul had assiduously cultivated Roncalli's friendship. Once a week, he served mass for the apostolic delegate in the latter's private chapel. Afterward, while the ambassador's wife and daughter cleaned the chapel, the two of them discussed the progress of the war.

One day, von Papen confided to the delegate that he was in touch with the anti-Hitler group in the German High Command, whose objective was the overthrow of the Führer and his replacement with a leadership that would negotiate peace with the Allies. These high-ranking conspirators, he said, had accepted the reality which Hitler refused to accept: the Germans would lose the war. To accomplish their mission they needed the help of the pope. For if he issued a strong public condemnation of Hitler it would enhance the moral aspect of their endeavor, and inspire Catholics to rally to their cause. Once Hitler had been overthrown, they looked to the pope to persuade the Allies to agree to a negotiated peace settlement with Germany's new leaders.

Roncalli reported von Papen's request to Rome, leaving no doubt of his own total belief in the ambassador's personal honesty and deep concern for his country. Pius XII, on the other hand, found many reasons to be skeptical. He distrusted von Papen, whom he had once refused to accept as German envoy to the Holy See. There was little evidence to support von Papen's story. If his claim of a highly placed opposition to Hitler in the German military was true, why had the Holy See not heard it from other papal representatives—from the nuncio in Berne, for example, or Lisbon?

This was one question raised by the Vatican in its reply to Roncalli. The pope needed more proof. Otherwise, was it not possible that von Papen was setting a trap to provide Hitler with a pretext to move against the Church? Or perhaps he wanted to establish with the Vatican a secret reputation as an anti-nazi, as insurance against the possibility that Germany might lose the war.

Roncalli could only repeat his complete faith in von Papen, whom he described as a devout Catholic deeply concerned for his country. But Pope Pius refused to act. It is true that he was convinced that the Allies would settle for nothing less than their stated objective of unconditional surrender, so that negotiation seemed out of the question. But in the end, the pope's decision reflected his lack of confidence in Roncalli's professional judgment.

This is not surprising, for Roncalli's superiors tended to regard him as something of an amateur with poor judgment, and his word carried little weight in the Secretariat of State. When Roncalli was elected pope, the first concern of Archbishop Tardini was to remove from the new pontiff's personal file all the derogatory comments that he had written about him. Pope John evidently bore him no ill will, for Tardini was made a cardinal and appointed secretary of state.

The truth was that diplomacy made faults out of some of Roncalli's best qualities. He had a tendency to see only the best in people, a commendable quality which often led to faulty judgments about personalities and situations. His faith in von Papen remained unshaken, leading him to the extraordinary view, which he expressed to fellow diplomats, that von Papen would make an ideal leader for postwar Germany. Even assuming that von Papen had the necessary qualities of leadership, which was questionable, his Nazi past would have ruled him out. He relied heavily on his instinct and on the work of Divine Providence, whereas the bureaucrats in the Vatican would have preferred a more critical approach.

Yet he had a rare gift for establishing close personal relationships with people without conceding matters of principle —the essence of the diplomatic method. Many diplomats who knew him thought him agreeable and capable of great patience, another essential quality in diplomacy.

During the war, he once recorded in his diary with evident satisfaction, "My relations with the Turkish authorities, and the Italian representatives, the French, English, German, and the others are excellent." In fact, he managed to stay on good terms with both the official Vichy representatives in Istanbul and the Gaullist faction, for whom he sometimes relayed messages to and from the French Resistance movement in France through the Vatican diplomat bag.

When he finally left Turkey in 1945, the large group of Turkish government officials and diplomats that saw him off testified to his popularity, for as apostolic delegate he had no official standing. Duff Cooper, the British ambassador in Paris, once summed him up to the foreign office as, "A pleasant type of Italian priest, urbane, well informed and not averse to the pleasures of the table. He has a fund of historical anecdotes." Paris was Roncalli's next assignment on leaving the Balkans after more than twenty years.

And from Turkey to Paris was a spectacular leap up the ranks of the diplomatic ladder. It virtually assured him of a cardinal's hat at the end of his career. Somewhat dazed by the appointment, he thanked Monsignor Tardini. "Don't thank me, for no one in the Secretariat of State had anything to do with it," Tardini replied with characteristic bluntness. "You owe your post to no one but the Holy Father."

This was the mystery in his sudden elevation: why had Pope Pius raised him to a position of such prominence? The contemporary version—and still the most plausible—was that Roncalli's appointment was intended as a sign of papal displeasure with General Charles de Gaulle. The president of the newly created Fourth Republic had insisted on the removal of the nuncio, Valerio Valeri, because he had remained at his post under the Vichy regime. Pius took Valeri's expulsion badly, made the retiring nuncio a cardinal, and peevishly retaliated by not appointing one of his senior diplomats to fill the post, thus by implication reducing its importance.

Whatever the reasons for the choice of Archbishop Roncalli, he arrived on the scene during a particularly delicate phase in relations between the Holy See and France. The French hierarchy was in disarray because the government was pressing for the removal of thirty allegedly collaborationist bishops, including the archbishop of Paris, Cardinal Suhard. On August 25, 1944, the cardinal had been barred from attending the victory service in his own cathedral of Notre Dame.

By a combination of persuasion and prevarication—requests for more specific evidence, delays in replying to correspondence, and other ruses—Roncalli managed to hold the government at bay until public anger against the bishops had subsided, and in this way succeeded in reducing the number of proscriptions to three. The years in Paris brought Roncalli into contact with the problems of the Church in a new world striving to rebuild its social and political foundations. The French worker-priest movement, a bold attempt to combat growing indifference to the Church, was just starting. The idea of priests living in lay surroundings and working in regular jobs in factories and on farms was not compatible with Roncalli's personal view of the priesthood ("Christ engaged neither in politics nor sport, but His word touched every man's heart," was his standard reply to people who argued that priests should be politically and socially in the thick of things). Yet in an atmosphere made heavy by Rome's concern to maintain control, he followed a policy of noninterference that helped the movement grow and test its mettle.

His relations with de Gaulle remained formal, perhaps because the French president could not forget the rebuff inher-

ent in Roncalli's appointment, but the nuncio was highly
regarded in France in political as well as ecclesiastical circles
(the collective backing of the French cardinals was to be an
important factor in his election as pope). When Piux XII made
him a cardinal in February 1952 and transferred him to the
patriarchate of Venice, apparently feeling that the French situation needed to be placed in firmer hands, the friends he left
behind came from a wide area of French political life:
Georges Bidault, Georges Schumann, Leon Blum, and Michel
Herriot, the colorful socialist president of the National Assembly. Roncalli's successor was Giacomo Marella. He arrived in
Paris on March 5, 1953, with instructions to bring the worker-
priest experiment to a close.

The years in Venice were the happiest of Angelo Roncalli's
life. Here at last was the pastoral work that had eluded him for
so long, and on a scale beyond anything he had dreamed. He
was seventy-two years old when he moved to Venice, and he
fully expected to end his days there: his precedessor had been
seven years younger at his death. But he ran his sprawling
diocese, which included a large chunk of the industrial main-
land, as well as the historic city on the canals, with a deft, light
touch. He made it a point to be highly visible, attending all
official functions. Every year, he gave a reception for the participants in the Venice Film Festival (which his predecessor
had ignored altogether). He toured the Venice Art Biennale
without batting an eyelid at its more outrageous entries.

At the same time, he was known to be strict with his priests,
expecting them to dress neatly and live by example, instruct-
ing them to keep off the streets of Venice in summer to avoid
having to look at the scantily dressed women tourists who
invaded the city, discouraging them from owning a television
set because television interfered with the priest's spiritual
role and was an assault on the intelligence. He was also
against any relaxation of the rule of celibacy, which he regarded as a voluntary sacrifice of great value.

When he left for Rome on October 18, 1958, to attend the

conclave following Pope Pius XII's death, he was aware that his name was being mentioned as a possible candidate, but he told a group of well-wishers who saw him off that he expected to return to his archdiocese shortly.

In the days leading up to the election, he was visited by a stream of other cardinals, which was taken as an indication that he was in the running. His young secretary, seeing the interest in his archbishop and the extreme respect with which Roncalli was treated by the electors, became convinced that Roncalli would be the next pope.

On the morning of the conclave, Capovilla was sitting outside the cell his cardinal had drawn by ballot. He was questioned on Cardinal Roncalli's chances. Capovilla said nothing but pointed to the large notice over the door of the cell. The notice said, *Il Commandante* ("The Commander"). Roncalli was lodged in the quarters of the Commander of the Noble Guard. Four days later, Roncalli was pope.

CHAPTER IV

On Borrowed Time

A LOVER OF TRAVEL all his life and a naturally gregarious man, Pope John felt hemmed in by the combined restraints of Vatican pontifical protocol and the inherited and acquired responsibilities of his great office. He would have liked to get about more, and he chafed at being bottled up in the frescoed, marble confines of the Vatican Palace.

But though his movements were limited, and he could not get about to see people as much as he would have liked, he encouraged them to come and see him. He did not live in seclusion, which was a major and bitter grievance against his predecessor. He reinstated the papal audience *a tabella* thereby making himself regularly accessible to dozens of senior Curia prelates and officials on fixed days of the month. A whole gallimaufry of prelates and dignitaries of the Papal Court also had the right to be received at regular intervals. They included the heads of the religious orders in Rome, the commanders of the Swiss Guard, the Noble Guard (open only to members of the papal aristocracy, all of whom had the rank of lieutenant colonel, except for the prince commander, who was a general), the Palatine Guard, the Papal Gendarmerie, the heads of the tribunals of the Sacred Roman Rota, and the envoys of foreign countries accredited to the Holy See.

The world's bishops, on their *ad limina* visit to Rome every five years, also hoped for an audience with the pope, and usually got it. And, unlike Pius XII, who had always taken his meals alone, he loved company at lunch or dinner: diplomats, visiting prelates, members of his staff, would sit down with him to simple, well-cooked meals and good wines from his well-stocked cellar.

But though he listened attentively to the flow of visitors and was open to outside arguments, he never lost sight of his own aims and intentions. He was shocked when the Curia's financial department told him the projected cost of the ecumenical council. He was even more shocked when he was told that, in spite of a generous subsidy from the United States hierarchy, the Vatican was still going to have to dig deeply into its capital to cover the cost, something that Pope Pius XII, with his firm grasp of money matters, had always refused to authorize. But ultimately financial considerations carried little weight with Pope John, and he ordered the capital expenditure.

To further reduce his sense of isolation, Pope John instituted his regular Sunday appearances at the window of his third floor study overlooking Saint Peter's Square to recite the noon Angelus, and deliver a short, impromptu discourse. His "window on the world," he called it, and the occasion provided him with a rare moment of pastoral contact with his universal flock. He was the local parish priest in his pulpit, variously urging his parishioners to love one another, drive carefully, dress warmly, and even on one occasion to pray for a Soviet cosmonaut in orbit.

On Sunday October 27, 1962, the feast of Christ the King, the pope appeared as usual to recite the noon devotion. He crossed himself, and then began the Angelus, enunciating the Latin with great care as if to ensure that his words were understood: *Angelus Domini nuntiavit Marie* ("The Angel of the Lord announced unto Mary.") The crowd below replied: And she conceived of the Holy Ghost. . . . When it was over, he stood for an instant, taking quick and satisfied note of the many mothers with their children, the priests, and the groups of young seminarians from all over the world wearing around their waists the distinguishing colored sashes of their Roman colleges. Then he began to speak, recalling that three days ago war had seemed imminent, but today there was peace in Christ's kingdom. "The word of the Gospel is heard from one end of the world to the other, and finds a way into men's hearts," he said.

In the opaque language of public papal pronouncements there was no place for any direct mention of the Cuban Missile Crisis. But on October 25, at the height of the confrontation, Pope John had appealed publicly for peace. The tension had eased the following day when the Soviet Union began dismantling its missiles in Cuba, and rightly or wrongly the pope clearly felt that his words had contributed to the outcome.

The pope's involvement in the Cuban crisis was the result of a request from an unexpected quarter. On October 24, Archbishop Dell'Acqua received a telephone call from Andover, Massachusetts, where a meeting of the Dartmouth Conference, a joint Soviet-American peace conference attended by scientists and writers from both countries, was in progress. The call was from two of the conference members. One was Felix Morlion, a brilliant, Belgian-born Dominican friar whose colorful past included a stint as an OSS agent during the war (although, as he often assured people, not on the killing side). His wartime American contacts, including fellow agent Clare Boothe Luce, helped finance a private university, Pro Deo, which he had founded and ran in Rome. Morlion was also a figure on the fringes of Vatican ecclesiastical circles, and Dell'Acqua was one of his patrons. The other caller was Norman Cousins, wealthy publisher of the *Saturday Review*, philanthropist, peace activist, and one of the founders of the Dartmouth Conference. And Jewish.

Many of the conference participants, including several Russians, were gravely concerned about the worsening crisis and the possible catastrophic consequences of the confrontation, they said, and were anxious to find a voice that could bring some sanity to the situation. Pope John's moral authority was recognized and respected by both sides. Would not the pope agree to make an immediate appeal for peace?

To Pope John, only one reply was possible: an appeal, yes, for it would help dramatize the widespread public alarm at the deteriorating situation. But only with the prior agreement of both sides. For if one government rejected it, the pope's intervention would immediately acquire partisan overtones and would thus have failed in its purpose.

When this stipulation was transmitted to Father Morlion and to Cousins, they quickly set about trying to contact the Soviet and American authorities. Through the leader of the Soviet delegation at the peace conference they were able to reach the Soviet ambassador in Washington. Without hesitation, he undertook to relay the proposal to Moscow. Two hours later, he communicated Moscow's reply: Premier Khrushchev had agreed to an appeal from the pope.

The White House was relatively easy to contact, for Cousins knew some of the members of Kennedy's staff personally, but it was harder to persuade. When Cousins outlined the pope's offer the reaction was unpromising. Later, Ted Sorensen telephoned Cousins from a Washington pay phone in order to make it more difficult to trace the initiative to Kennedy. The president was not opposed, Sorensen told Cousins. He would welcome a message from the pope, as long as the pope agreed to certain conditions.

It should be a general appeal, avoiding any reference to the Soviet ships carrying missiles then approaching Cuban ports, or for that matter, to any specific aspect of the situation. Kennedy feared that a detailed statement might compromise the American negotiating position. Besides, Sorensen went on to warn Cousins, Kennedy "would be very distressed indeed if the public was led to believe that the president of the United States had been forced to change his course because of anything that the pope had said." Further, no hint should be allowed to leak out that the White House's prior consent had been sought and given. As the afternoon of October 24 wore on in Washington and the city glowed in a long autumnal sunset, Sorensen called once again from his pay phone to stress the importance of following Kennedy's stipulations.

It was already nighttime in Rome when Pope John began to compose his appeal. Pacing the marble floor of his study, he dictated a first draft to Monsignor Cardinale, who took it down on the pope's portable Olivetti, while from time to time Archbishops Dell'Acqua and Capovilla and Cardinal Bea weighed in with suggestions. Then he told them, "While you continue to work on the final text, I'm going to be doing something equally important to this undertaking." And he went to his private chapel to pray.

The pope's text was then delivered to the United States and Soviet embassies in Rome for immediate transmission to Washington and Moscow, but neither side offered any objections. Then, on the evening of October 25, the pope broadcast his message over the Vatican Radio. In his appeal, which took four minutes to read, he called on the leaders of the United States and the Soviet Union to forsake brinkmanship and resolve the crisis through negotiation: "Let them continue to negotiate because this loyal and open attitude has great value as witness for the conscience of all of us, as well as before history. To promote, favor and accept negotiation at every level and at all times is a prudent and wise principle that attracts the blessings of heaven and earth."

On October 26, the Soviet premier backed down, and war was averted. *Pravda* reported Pope John's appeal on its front page, noting his reference to the wisdom of negotiation. When he heard this, John remarked, "It is now said that when the pope speaks of peace, men listen."

It is at least arguable that the pope's appeal fortified Khrushchev's hand against the hawks in the Soviet Politburo who were pushing him toward a confrontation because it enhanced his moral stature as a world leader. The pope certainly thought so, and the episode left him more convinced than ever that the papacy could no longer remain aloof from world events if it was to be effective as an instrument of peace.

He was equally convinced of the need to establish regular channels of communication with Washington. Kennedy's deliberate aloofness disappointed him. He felt that, in the contrasting light of the Kremlin's friendly approaches, the White House was pursuing a narrow and short-sighted policy. Knowing little about America, which he had never visited, and having no trusted American prelate to offer advice as Cardinal Spellman had done for Pius XII, John failed to grasp the full significance of the domestic political considerations behind Kennedy's attitude toward Rome.

In his characteristically optimistic way, he diagnosed the problem as a lack of communication. If he could reach the right people in the Kennedy administration, they could not fail to respond to the changes that were taking place in the Church and particularly to the possibilities opened up by the pope's own willingness to play an active role in finding peaceful solutions to world problems.

In November 1962, Arthur Schlesinger, Jr., the White House's resident intellectual, received a visit from Ettore Bernabei. As Director General of RAI, the government-run broadcasting and television organization in Italy, Bernabei was a key political figure in his own right, and doubly so because of his close association with the then Premier Amintore Fanfani, and his friendship with Archbishop Dell'Acqua.

Ostensibly, he told Schlesinger, who had never heard of him in his life, he was in Washington to attend an international broadcasting conference, but in reality he had been sent by Pope John and Fanfani to discuss with Schlesinger the question of Vatican relations with the Kennedy administration, or rather the lack of them.

Bernabei's essential point was, "Pope John is presiding over a profound change in the Vatican, and the Catholic Church is now systematically enlarging its contact with—and hence influence on—the vital tendencies of the modern world."

Granted, the Vatican Council offered both opportunities and risks. For example, it was true that, in permitting Russian Orthodox observers to attend, Moscow was using the council to try to give the impression that freedom of worship existed in the Soviet Union. This would not get very far, Bernabei added confidently. But the interest shown in the council by the Soviet Union made American nonparticipation, "all the more disappointing, and even alarming," he said, evidently discounting the presence of the American ambassador at the opening ceremony. But that was all in the past. Looking ahead, he realized, he said, that official American representation to the Holy See was out of the question, but would it not be possible to do more in the way of informal private contact?

For example? Schlesinger asked.

Well, a senior White House official—such as Schlesinger himself—could come to Rome under the guise of giving a lecture or attending a conference and meet secretly with the pope. "In this way, it might be possible to begin continuous contact."

But the United States could maintain such contact through the embassy in Rome, Schlesinger pointed out.

Bernabei lifted his shoulders in an expressive shrug and made a wry face. He did not like to criticize able officials, Bernabei said and proceeded to do so: American diplomats in Rome were not sufficiently sympathetic toward the new directions of Vatican policy to maintain truly effective contact. No, what was needed was closer contact at a higher level. The inference was clear: the pope wanted to open a personal channel of communication to the White House.

All of which Schlesinger reported to Kennedy in a lengthy

memorandum classified "Secret," adding his own recommendation that "such relations should be established and that consideration should be given on a high level as to how this can best be brought about." But Bernabei's mission foundered on the rocky shores of Kennedy's determination to keep state scrupulously separate from church, and especially his church. The president read the document, said, "No, dammit," and shelved the whole idea. The pope waited in vain for an answer, for the Americans never again referred to Bernabei's visit.

John was disappointed. He felt ties of origin (both being of peasant stock), understanding, and even purpose with Khrushchev, the Marxist leader, but Kennedy the Catholic remained an unknown quantity to him. Meanwhile, however, preparations had begun for Kennedy's projected European tour in the summer of 1963. Since Italy was one of the countries on the presidential itinerary, the question of an audience with Pope John arose. At first Kennedy ruled it out. But when the State Department pointed out that in seeing the pope he would simply be doing what President Eisenhower had done on his official visit to Rome, he relented.

So careful was he not to go beyond established precedents in his dealings with the Vatican that he would probably never even have considered an audience with the pope if Eisenhower had not already been to the Vatican before him. He wasn't going to get himself into trouble on that score for such limited returns. But apart from his fear of appearing susceptible to Vatican pressure, Kennedy also had difficulty accepting the notion of the Church playing a substantive role in world politics.

He was a practicing Catholic in the old-fashioned Irish sense that he still found occasional solace in the mass. But his intelligence was fundamentally secular; he had no close friends among members of the American hierarchy or among the priests, whether liberal or conservative (though he greatly admired the Jesuit sociologist John Courtney Murray). Cardinal Cushing was a family friend, but he was closer to Robert Kennedy than to the president.

Bobby's religious outlook was more progressive, with a broader vision of the Church's role in modern society. The president was too traditionalist a Catholic to attach much weight to the Vatican Council view that the Church needed to demonstrate its relevance to the modern world. Kennedy had a strong admiration for Pope John. He was, in fact, fascinated by him. But it was a fascination based on the pontiff's character and engaging personality. He had probably categorized the pope's peace initiative as the work of a committed enthusiast.

It had at any rate become questionable whether John was the pontiff whom Kennedy would meet in Rome. For on November 4, 1962, the Rome station of the Central Intelligence Agency reported in a telegram to Washington that

POPE JOHN IS A VERY SICK MAN. HE HAS STOMACH CANCER WHICH IS SPREADING TO OTHER PARTS OF HIS BODY. HIS DOCTORS GIVE HIM ONLY A FEW MORE MONTHS . . .

John had wrestled with the disease since he went to Venice as patriarch, but now his doctors had come to him with the news that there was little time left—based on recent tests, perhaps six months. When Professor Antonio Gasbarrini, his personal physician, had raised the possibility of surgery, the pope had refused. He was not going to risk becoming the first pontiff to die on the operating table.

On the advice of his doctors, his public appearances and all except his most essential private audiences were canceled, and he was immediately confined to his bed. The official explanation was that he had been ordered to rest as a result of overwork in preparing for the council. Only a handful of senior prelates knew the truth.

On November 26, the pope suffered his first serious hemorrhage. The Vatican panicked and imposed a news blackout. Deluged with inquiries from all over the world, its press office barricaded itself behind a refusal to comment, and for over twenty-four hours it was virtually impossible to determine the real state of affairs in the Vatican Palace. A rumor started that John was dying—and even one that he was already dead. Indeed, only after large plasma transfusions had stopped the bleeding were the doctors able to say that he was out of danger. Finally on November 28, *L'Osservatore Romano* reported briefly that Pope John was suffering from "acute symptoms of gastrophy" due to "a recurrence of an old stomach ailment," which was rather like describing a brain tumor as a severe headache.

As the pope's condition improved, the Vatican became even more implacably opposed to telling the press and the public the truth about the situation. Spokesmen admitted that he was a sick man, but persisted in attributing his illness to overwork. But the apostolic delegate in Washington, meeting senior State Department officials, told another story. The pontiff was suffering from incurable cancer, he said. There was a more than even chance that he would not be the pope who received President Kennedy in the summer.

By December 2, John had made sufficient progress to be able to recite the Angelus from his window, afterward telling the crowd that he was on the road to recovery. Two days later, he presided at the closing ceremony of the first session of the Vatican Council. Instead of being carried in on the *sedia gestatoria*, he entered on foot—followed closely by his doctor. In his weakened condition he considered walking safer. The white-mitered bishops attending the council looked like a field of waving corn in their raised rows of seats stretching the length of the nave. When the pope passed, many noted that his face was ashen and his movements slow and deliberate; and the voice that intoned the invocation to the Holy Ghost was weak and rasping.

Then he sat down, fished out his glasses and began to read his speech. As he warmed to his theme, a review of the work of the council's first session, thanking the bishops, some of the

old vigor returned. He began to stress points with quick ges-
tures of his right hand, every so often glancing significantly
around him over his glasses as if to say, "Pay attention, this is
important." But as he wished them Godspeed and a safe journey home until the opening of the second session the following May, shadows of pain and fatigue darkened his kindly
face, the hollow rasp returned to his voice, and more than one
bishop closed his eyes in a silent prayer for the ailing pontiff.

Watching the pope from a balcony high above the nave of
the basilica was Norman Cousins, who had reappeared in Vatican circles. Using the contact established with the Soviet ambassador in Washington on the Vatican's behalf, the American
publisher asked for an interview with Nikita Khrushchev to
discuss problems of peace and disarmament. As the leading
light of the Dartmouth peace conference and an outspoken
advocate of disarmament, Cousins had the right credentials
for such a meeting, and the request was granted.

Cousins thereupon approached President Kennedy and volunteered his services as an intermediary. Kennedy received
him at the White House and asked him to try to glean something of Khrushchev's intentions in the Geneva Disarmament
Talks, then hopelessly deadlocked over the eternal question
of surveillance.

Having thus further strengthened his credentials, Cousins
next approached the Vatican and made the same offer, taking
care to mention the Kennedy assignment. The Vatican also
accepted, and Cousins was now in Rome to be briefed on
that aspect of his mission before continuing his journey
to Moscow.

Cousins did not see John himself, for the pope was rushed
to bed after his strenuous morning in Saint Peter's Basilica to
prevent a relapse in his condition. Instead, he was briefed by
Cardinal Bea, Archbishop Dell'Acqua, and Cardinal Gustavo
Testa, a close friend of Pope John's who was head of the Congregation for Oriental Churches.

The pope's assignment was vague, leaving plenty of scope

for initiative and personal judgment. Cousins was to convey the pope's profound concern about the danger of nuclear war and its consequences to the human race and his willingness to make himself and the Holy See available to help avert serious crises from developing, and to keep them from getting out of control if they did develop. The pope had no specific proposals for Khrushchev, no detailed diplomatic initiative to advance, but the implied scope was wide, ranging from helping to create an atmosphere of moral responsibility to direct mediation.

But all this was to be transmitted by implication. Cousins received nothing in writing from the pope for Khrushchev. In addition, Cousins was to try to raise the subject of enlarged religious freedom and its prospects in the Soviet Union, for example in such areas as the publication and distribution of religious literature. The only specific request came from Bea who asked Cousins to enquire about the whereabouts and condition of the Ukrainian metropolitan of Lwow, Josef Slipyi, who had been in Siberian exile for eighteen years, and if possible to broach the subject of his release.

Cousins's meeting with Pope John's closest associates left him with two distinct impressions. The first was the absence of an articulated policy. The group of prelates seemed linked by what Cousins thought of as "concerted inspiration." They all spoke and thought between the lines. It was all, "What if —but of course, it couldn't happen . . . but perhaps . . ." The second impression was the extent to which these prelates, all of whom held official posts, were functioning outside their own system.

Cousins did not see Cardinal Cicognani, the secretary of state, and he had the distinct feeling that Cicognani knew nothing of his projected trip and furthermore was not supposed to know. In fact, no one in the Curia outside the pope's circle had any inkling that a Jewish publisher from New York was being sent as the pope's personal emissary to the leader of Communist Russia on an historic mission with far-reaching implications. This was John's parallel diplomacy in action. Cousins suited John's purpose precisely because he had no official status. That way, if contacts with the Kremlin backfired, there could be no official repercussions, since the Holy See would not have been involved. The Vatican even asked Cousins not to write about the Moscow trip in his magazine, a self-denying ordinance which he accepted, presumably as the price for his involvement in the history-making process.

Cousins had a three-hour meeting with Premier Khrushchev in the Kremlin, during which he relayed John's offer to play a role in preserving world peace, and was struck by the Soviet leader's personal admiration for the pontiff. When he brought up the subject of Archbishop Slipyi, Cousins was surprised that Khrushchev recognized the name at once. Yet Khrushchev's familiarity with Slipyi's name was easy to understand: the Soviet leader was a Ukrainian and had, moreover, spent part of his youth in an Orthodox seminary. Slipyi, Khrushchev recalled, had been jailed for collaboration with the Germans. He had, however, paid for his crime and the Soviet premier promised to try to discover what had become of him and also to give some thought to the request for his release.

When Cousins returned to Rome a week later, the pope had recovered sufficiently to receive him in his study. Cousins had typed him a memorandum based on his notes from the meeting with Khrushchev and covering the main points on which Khrushchev and he had reached agreement. He now handed this remarkable document to Pope John. It read as follows:

1) Russia desires the pope's mediation, and Khrushchev agrees that it should not be limited to mediation in moments of crisis, but should be a continuous action by the pope in the cause of peace;

2) Khrushchev affirms that he wants to open lines of communication with the Vatican through private contacts;

3) Khrushchev acknowledges that the Church respects the principle of the division of church and state in many countries;

4) Khrushchev acknowledges that the Church serves all human beings for the sacred values of life and is not only concerned with Catholics;

5) Khrushchev acknowledges that the pope has acted with great courage, considering the internal problems that he faces, just as Khrushchev has internal problems in the Soviet Union.

Told of Khrushchev's personal admiration, the pope nodded and replied that he felt an instinctive understanding between himself and the Soviet premier based on their common peasant origins. "The Russian people are a wonderful people," he told Cousins. "We must not give them up because we do not like their political system. They have a deep spiritual heritage. This they have not lost. We can talk to them. Right now, we *have* to talk to them. We must always try to speak to the good in people. Nothing can be lost by trying, everything can be lost if men do not find a way to work together to save peace. I am not afraid to talk to anyone about peace on earth."

A few days later, the pope began to teach himself Russian from a grammar given him by Cardinal Gregory Peter Agagianian, the Armenian patriarch, who was a Curia cardinal. When word of this got around the Vatican, prelates speculated that the pontiff had begun to hope that he could himself meet Premier Khrushchev.

Six weeks later, came another indication of Khrushchev's desire to keep the Vatican-Kremlin exchange alive. Norman Cousins, by now back in the United States, received a call from the Soviet embassy in Washington: Archbishop Slipyi was free to leave the Soviet Union. Cousins immediately telephoned Monsignor Cardinale, who relayed the news to the pope, and John in turn entrusted Cardinal Bea with bringing the Ukrainian metropolitan to Rome, for the pope understood the message from Moscow: Archbishop Slipyi was not free to remain in the Soviet Union.

Bea dispatched Willebrands to Moscow for his second visit in six months. On arrival, he found Slipyi waiting for him in a room at the Metropol Hotel. The hardship of jail and the march of time had left their mark on Slipyi. His imposing frame was stooped, and the face drawn and lined, making him look twenty years older than his sixty-one years. His civilian clothes hung from his shoulders like becalmed sails, but he seemed alert, viewing his unexpected release with disbelief and suspicion, which did not diminish when Willebrands arrived without credentials officially identifying him as a Vatican representative. Could this be a KGB trick?

The Ukrainian prelate had had no no direct contact with Rome for nearly twenty years. Even the news of Pope John's accession had taken two years to filter through to the Siberian village where he had most recently been living under virtual house arrest. The name of Willebrands, one of the rising stars in the ecclesiastical hierarchy, meant nothing to him. Yet all Willebrands had to show him as proof of his identity was an autographed photograph of Pope John bearing a quotation from Tobias, and the pope's verbal message of Godspeed.

Slipyi led Willebrands out of the hotel room, which he assumed to be bugged, and took him to a nearby wood where for added security they talked in Latin. Having first established reasonably satisfactorily that Willebrands was who he claimed to be, Slipyi announced that he would not leave the Soviet Union. In his view, his departure would amount to desertion of the Ukrainian Catholic community of which, in spite of his long isolation from it, he still considered himself the spiritual leader. More than that, he saw himself as a symbol of the oppressed Church which the Kremlin wanted to remove, and he did not want to play into the regime's hands.

Willebrands used every argument he could think of in his efforts to persuade him to come to Rome, but when they parted for the night, Slipyi still seemed as immovable as a rock, even if remaining in Russia meant returning to house arrest. But the following morning, Slipyi came to Willebrands's room, knelt at Willebrands's feet, bowed his head, and said, "So be it, I shall do as the pope wishes."

Slipyi and Willebrands left Moscow by rail for Rome, the

former traveling with a Soviet diplomatic passport supplied by the Kremlin. In Vienna, they spent the night as guests of the archbishop, Cardinal Franziskus König. Meantime, the news of Slipyi's release had leaked out in Rome, and on the evening of February 17, the press massed at Termini Station to await his arrival. But no white-bearded metropolitan got off the train. To spare him the ordeal of such an encounter, it was explained, Slipyi had been taken off the train at Orte, thirty miles north of the city, where Capovilla was waiting to whisk him to the pope. It is also true that the pope wanted first to warn him not to make any statements against the Soviet regime.

CHAPTER V

At Arm's Length

JOHN WAS ELATED with the outcome of Cousins's Moscow trip. The pontiff saw Slipyi's release as further confirmation that he had been right to break the forty years of hostile silence between Rome and the Kremlin. The success fueled his resolve to press on along the same road. If he had a definite plan, he kept it locked in his own thoughts, but when Cousins saw him, the American publisher was given an exquisite sixteenth-century Russian icon from the Vatican's vast treasury of religious art objects to take to President Kennedy. The implication was clear. For the pope, Cousins's mission was not quite over. He was being asked to complete the circle by transmitting to the White House the same message of John's eagerness to play a role in the politics of peace.

John's men said nothing to Cousins about the discouraging antecedents of his Washington assignment. In fact throughout, very little was revealed to him of their aims and intentions or even of their assessment of the information which he provided. What little Cousins learned came mostly from that curious figure on the fringes of official Vatican life, Father Morlion. Still, having already experienced White House caution in connection with the pope's Cuban crisis message, Cousins contacted Ralph Dungan, the Irish special assistant responsible for religious affairs, with minimal expectations of a strong American response. Dungan, who not only was a veteran of the Kennedy presidential campaign but who had also helped write the Houston confrontation speech in which Kennedy solemnly vowed total and unwavering commitment to the principle of the separation of church and state, needed no prompting to know what to do, which was nothing at all.

But as the days dragged into weeks, Cousins received first one phone call, and then a second from Monsignor Cardinale, politely inquiring on Pope John's behalf about White House reaction. On January 16, 1963, almost five weeks after his interview with Khrushchev and exactly four weeks since his audience with John, Cousins fired off a telegram to Dungan. It said:

PLEASE FORGIVE ME FOR SEEMING TO IMPORTUNE BUT I HAVE RECEIVED TWO INQUIRIES FROM ROME ABOUT THE REACTIONS IN OUR HEADQUARTERS [i.e. the White House] TO SPECIFIC POINTS IN THE EXCHANGE. HENCE A MOST AWKWARD SITUATION NOW EXISTS THAT I HOPE CAN BE HANDLED REASONABLY SOON.

The telegram had the desired effect. Three days later over lunch in Washington, Cousins gave Dungan a full account of his conversations with John and with Khrushchev. The Cuban missile crisis, Cousins said, had left a deep impression on Pope John. It brought home to him how close to the surface was the danger of a sudden and devastating nuclear conflict in the prevailing atmosphere of tension between the two blocs.

The pope was ready to do everything in his power to help avert such crises in the future, and indeed to prevent them from aggravating beyond the point of no return if they did develop. Khrushchev had recognized and endorsed Pope John's desire to involve himself and the good offices of the Holy See in the search for peaceful solutions to world problems. The pope, for his part, had no desire to undertake any initiatives that did not have the blessing of both Washington and Moscow. In a written resume of his trip which Dungan was to deliver to Kennedy, Cousins argued that "it becomes necessary, with full respect for the difficulties, to communicate certain facts and obtain certain responses."

Dungan's reaction was reflexive—and totally negative. Kennedy simply could not afford to be linked with any action, either at home or on the international plane, that could expose him to the charge of allowing the pope to interfere in the policy-making process of the United States government. In reporting his meeting with Cousins to Kennedy Dungan wrote, "My own feeling is, after having talked to him (Cousins) at length, that it would not be a very useful conversation but I thought you might want to consider it."

Kennedy merely scrawled across Dungan's note, "Thanks for picture from pope," meaning the icon. The doors of the White House remained closed to Norman Cousins, at any rate on this occasion, but at the same time, cracks began to appear in the White House's studied aloofness from Rome: a file marked "Vatican" was started, with Dungan's memorandum as its first item. "Holy See" would have carried with it a certain diplomatic logic, but whatever the term, Washington's non-relations with the Roman pontiff simply refused to live up to their description.

On January 28, Cousins came up with a proposal designed to save his face and also that of the Kennedy administration, which he thought needed saving although the administration did not share this view.

"I agree completely with you and the president that he must in no way be connected to, or identified with, the communications between the Holy See and Moscow," Cousins wrote to Dungan. "There is, however, a genuine problem. I am sure you agree that we don't want to create the opposite impression; namely, that the president finds these developments distasteful or even that he had repudiated them. It is not unreasonable to suppose that the pope and the men around him would arrive at such an interpretation because of the lack of an appointment [i.e., for Cousins to see the president] even though more than a month has elapsed since my return.... Perhaps the problem can be met in another way. It may be that a letter from the president will serve the purpose; I can send a copy to the Holy See."

Early in February, Cousins was able to send to Pope John a letter received from Kennedy and dealing with the pope's peace initiative. It amounted to a very noncommittal communication taking note of the publisher's trip to Rome and Moscow, but making no mention of Pope John, and in particular, it was careful to commit the Kennedy administration to nothing. The most daring passage read, "Any betterment of the human situation in this world—whatever the country involved—is of importance to the United States. The national interest and the human interest come together in our fundamental objectives as a nation."

The letter was a disappointment to the pope, who had been hoping for something more substantive from the White House. Ever the optimist, he took comfort in the fact that a three-way dialogue, however tenuous, had been established. He would have been even more disappointed had he known—as he certainly never did—that even this innocuous document was not, strictly speaking, a White House initiative. The Kennedy letter had been drafted by Cousins himself. Sent to the White House, it was copied on official stationery, signed by Kennedy, and solemnly delivered to Cousins.

Useless in the broader sense of Pope John's global intentions, this deception served to preserve Cousins's credibility in Rome, and therefore his continued usefulness as an unofficial Vatican emissary. Cousins would later publish a full account of his experience as John's go-between. Full, but not quite complete. Kennedy's total rejection of the pope in this connection and Cousins's ploy to avoid having to reveal the truth about the situation were not mentioned.

Aside from rigid policy considerations, however, there were other reasons behind Kennedy's negative response. There was the problem of John's intensely personal style which was so strongly Italian in flavor. John's use of trusted individuals instead of qualified professionals to carry out extremely delicate missions, his tendency to improvise, his liking for secrecy —all of these things would have made him an unpredictable ally.

John's choice of Cousins as his emissary did not help the pope's cause in the White House. It was not merely that Kennedy found it hard to accept the presence of a Jewish publisher so close to the core of the Catholic church's decision-making apparatus. Kennedy was simply not very impressed with Cousins's ability and judgment, and, moreover, along with a lot of other people, considered him something of a self-publicist.

But what probably tipped the scales against a positive American response to the pope was the skepticism of the Central Intelligence Agency. Early in 1963, Kennedy received a secret fifteen-page memorandum written by James Spain casting serious doubts on the soundness of the pontiff's East European policy and strongly suggesting that this policy was based on unreliable information.

Pope John, the memorandum said, had developed "a surprisingly specific theory that fundamental change is taking place in the Soviet Union with Khrushchev representing a force for moderation, which must be supported."

According to the CIA, similar versions of this theory were sufficiently widespread in Rome to suggest that it had been discussed and authoritatively formulated at the highest level in the Vatican, that is, by Pope John. "This view holds that Marxism is losing its force within the USSR and is increasingly having to give way on specific points of human affairs to an underlying concept of man's rights and privileges as a human being (in Western terms, the natural law). Religious feeling is also said to persist very strongly among most

Russians, and the Vatican feels it must do what it can
to help strengthen the position of the Orthodox church."
The reason for this was that the Orthodox church was, for
the moment, in a better position to serve the religious
feeling.

"In addition, the current theory holds that Khrushchev is
clearly a force for liberalization in the USSR," the memorandum continued. "A detailed account is circulating among cler-
ical circles in Rome of how Khrushchev first defied the
hardline elements in the Soviet leadership by insisting on
publication of *One Day in the Life of Ivan Denisovich*, and
then a few days later defied them again by insisting on the
release of Monsignor Slipyi.

"Much is made of the alleged fact that Khrushchev in de-
fending Slipyi's release insisted that this must be done, not
because of its propaganda or political value, but because the
Soviet state is a civilized and moral one. Khrushchev is said to
have taken the position that Slipyi was a criminal but the
USSR did not simply kill him as Hitler would have. It made
him work out his debt to the state in labor camps. The debt is
now paid, Khrushchev insisted, and Slipyi has a right to go.
The Pope was said to have privately described Khrushchev's
act as one of 'the greatest political heroism.' "

Spain went on to complain that it was "extremely difficult
to reach any firm conclusion on the extent and reliability of
the Vatican's knowledge of communist affairs, the validity of
its analysis, and the effectiveness of its tactics. Many Vatican
priests talk of 'our dealings' and 'our negotiations' with the
communists but they supply little specific information on the
manner and mechanics of their approaches. They also talk of
'our sources' within the USSR and suggest that there are still
priests active underground there, but again details are not
forthcoming. While they have evolved a fairly precise analysis
of the fundamental factors in their own relations with the
USSR and of what they think is happening within the Soviet
Union, they do not seem to have tried to relate this image of

the Soviets to Soviet action and policies in other fields, such as Cuba and disarmament."

Still, Spain concluded, the "open door" approach to the communist world was likely to continue. "In this framework, the establishment of official relations with the USSR, Khrushchev's reception by the pope, and even a new series of concordats with the communist states are possibilities." But another concern was that "these beliefs resulted in a new approach toward Italian politics which is permissive rather than positive. Political matters, including the 'opening to the left,' in Italy are seen as the responsibility of voters and lay leaders rather than of the Church." At the same time, he lamented, there was a growing inclination to encourage the hierarchies in Spain, Portugal, and Latin America to disassociate from political regimes not compatible with the principles of social justice.

The document was the first detailed American appraisal of Pope John's policies, and it was widely read in the administration. Aside from a few elementary howlers—Willebrands, for example, was identified as Cardinal Bea's Jesuit secretary, whereas he was neither—it gave a reasonably accurate picture of the Church on the move, and not in a general direction which was useful to the CIA.

Spain admitted that he was unable to assess the pope's information on Eastern Europe and the Soviet Union because Vatican prelates had refused to reveal their secret sources to him (he sounded oddly indignant about this), and he had failed to discover them for himself. All the same, a skeptical tone occasionally crept into Spain's reporting, as if he found the whole notion of papal involvement in world politics incongruous.

The pope's men may not have known the truth about Spain's report, or about Norman Cousins's contrived letter to Rome, but they were fully aware of the prevailing skepticism in Washington. This may account for the reappearance at this time in *L'Osservatore Romano* of a famous defense of the

Catholic church's involvement in formal diplomacy—an address delivered by Archbishop Giovanni Battista Montini in 1951, when he was the pro-secretary of state, at the Pontificia Accademia Ecclesiastica, the Vatican's school for diplomats in the Piazza della Minerva, to mark its two hundred fiftieth anniversary.

People questioned the diplomatic activity of the Holy See, Montini said. Some asked why the Church had not brought this activity to a close when its temporal power ended in 1870. Others wondered if the profession of Machiavelli was a suitable field of endeavor for clerics. Still others felt that the Church should rely more on its own inner strength rather than on such worldly pursuits as diplomacy.

It all depended on what was meant by diplomacy, Montini continued. As practiced by the Holy See, he said, it was "The art of creating and maintaining international order, that is to say, peace." It was the business of establishing humane, rational, and juridical relations among people without resort to force or balancing material interests. If this was true, it was something the Church should definitely be engaged in, for the Church seeks world peace.

"If civil diplomacy tends to the unification of the world by making reason prevail over force, and to the growth of individual states in the harmonious concert of an everlasting international organization, it finds in ecclesiastical diplomacy almost a model toward which it can look with assurance . . . because of the ideal from which (ecclesiastical diplomacy) starts, and toward which it tends—the universal brotherhood of men."

When Napoleon I sent Francois Cacault to Rome, he instructed his personal representative to "deal with the pope as if he had two hundred thousand men at his command." In time, Cacault was recounting the story using the figure of five hundred thousand. Confronted with this discrepancy, Cacault shrugged and countered that the pope's position in Europe had in the interim improved by the equivalent of about three hundred thousand men. But a century later, the papacy did not hold Joseph Stalin in thrall. Advised by French Foreign Minister Pierre Laval in 1935 that Pope Pius XI had complained widely about religious persecution in the Soviet Union, Stalin replied with the famous question about the number of divisions commanded by the pope. Wiser statesmen knew better. "Laval's answer was not reported to me," wrote Winston Churchill later, "but he might have mentioned a number of legions not always on parade."

Premier Khrushchev seemed to have grasped that what the Holy See had was not power as it was usually perceived in the political context, but enormous influence. The pope influenced the world Catholic community and the societies contiguous to it. In the Soviet leader's attempts to repair the damage caused by the Cuban fiasco to his policy of peaceful coexistence and to his country's prestige, the pope could prove a useful ally. Though he still believed Khrushchev to be fundamentally a man of goodwill, Pope John did not fail to recognize his usefulness to the Soviet premier, but he considered the price worth paying to achieve his own objectives.

So Rome and Moscow continued to exchange signs of goodwill. Pope John was awarded the Balzan Peace Prize principally because the four Russians on the international jury had been instructed by Khrushchev to vote for the pontiff. Then early in March, the new detente faced its biggest test. Alexei Adjubei, Khrushchev's son-in-law and the chief editor of *Izvestia*, who had been traveling in Italy ostensibly on vacation, requested an audience with Pope John.

Caught off balance, the Vatican hedged. The pope, Adjubei was told, had his hands full with the preparations for the second session of the Vatican Council and was probably too busy to receive him, but how about an interview with Cardinal Bea? Adjubei agreed to see Bea, but continued to press for an audience with John as well, saying he had a personal message for the pontiff from his father-in-law.

On the day of the Bea interview, the pope still had not

decided whether to grant Adjubei his audience. He had consulted the Holy Office, and Cardinal Ottaviani had replied
with a memorandum strongly advising him against it. The audience would inevitably provide political capital for Communist parties in Western Europe, starting with Italy which was
on the eve of crucial national elections following the collapse
of Premier Fanfani's center-left government. Secondly, communist regimes would have a powerful card to play against
local hierarchies who resisted them, for they could portray the
audience as a significant sign of growing rapproachement between the Vatican and the Kremlin. Finally, Ottaviani also
raised a human point: the encounter, he warned, "would
wound in a certain sense those souls who suffer and are deprived of liberty (under communism), not to mention the thousands and millions of people in jail."

Weighed against the opposition of the Curia was the advice
of Monsignor Capovilla and other members of the pontiff's
inner circle who argued that if John failed to recognize Adjubei's presence he risked undoing the progress thus far
achieved with Moscow—and at a moment when its advantages to the Church were still more a promise than a reality.

With Adjubei almost at his door, Cardinal Bea telephoned
Archbishop Dell'Acqua. If asked, was he to say that the interview that was about to take place was intended as a substitute
for a papal audience, or had the pope also decided to receive
Adjubei after all? Dell'Acqua consulted Cardinal Cicognani,
and the aged Secretary of State produced a classic Curia reply:
"Tell Cardinal Bea not to say that there will not be an audience, nor that there will be one."

But Pope John had considered the arguments and decided
to grant Adjubei his audience. "I will see him," he said simply
to Capovilla. "This will be my act of heroism" (as the release
of Slipyi had been Khrushchev's). A formula was also found to
reduce the glare of publicity surrounding the audience. A
group of about fifty Italian and foreign journalists were invited
to the Vatican to watch John receive formal notification that

he had been awarded the Balzan Peace Prize. Alexei Adjubei was one of them.

On the morning of March 7, flashbulbs popped and Swiss Guards saluted as the Soviet communist functionary and his wife drove through Saint Anne's Gate into Vatican City. In the Papal Throne Room, Alexei and Rada Adjubei sat together in the third row. Behind them sat Father Alexander Koulic, a priest from the Russicum, the Russian Seminary in Rome, who was acting as interpreter. When the pope walked in, the Russian couple together with everyone else rose to their feet. As the pontiff received the official notification of the Balzan prize they joined in the warm, general applause.

In his speech of thanks the pope drew attention to the "perfect supranational neutrality of the Church and her visible chief. This neutrality must not be understood in the passive sense, as if the pope's role was limited to observing events and maintaining silence about them. On the contrary, it is a neutrality that is full of vigor. . . . We have said on many occasions: the action of the Church is not purely negative and does not consist only in urging governments to avoid recourse to the force of arms. It is an action that wants to contribute toward forming men of peace."

The pope, of course, made no reference to Adjubei, nor did he pay the slightest attention to him. Yet his point rang out like a trumpet call. Following the formal ceremony, the pope lingered in the hall for several minutes. He had a few words for everybody—everybody, that is, except the couple from Moscow. His composure was complete. Vatican officials, who appeared to be extremely nervous, then ushered everyone out except the Adjubeis. Trailed by Father Koulic, who was to be the only other person present, the couple followed the pope into his private study adjoining the Throne Room.

Adjubei began by telling the pope that he brought a very cordial personal greeting from his father-in-law Nikita Khrushchev. The audience was an historic occasion, he said. Just as Khrushchev was considered a reformer in the communist world, so the pope was an innovator in the Catholic world. Did the pope not feel that the time was ripe to establish diplomatic relations between the Vatican and the Soviet Union?

To this Pope John replied, "You are a journalist, and you surely know the Bible. The Bible states that God, in his omnipotence, took seven days to create the world: we, who are so much less powerful, must not rush things. We must go slowly in such matters, step by step, preparing the way. At the moment, such a step would be misunderstood." Adjubei assured Pope John that he would tell no one except Khrushchev what had been said on the matter.

Then the pope talked about Khrushchev who, he said, "seemed chosen by Providence to do great things, and in this way might find himself in the light of Christ, who desires peace for all men of goodwill. For the head of the Church, there are only brothers among men, without distinction of nationality or race." Then the pope turned to Rada and asked her (in French) the names of her three children.

Rada replied, "Nikita, Alexei, and Ivan."

"Ah, Ivan. Ivan is John, and John is myself. And John is the name I chose for my pontificate: it was my father's name, and it was my grandfather's name. It is the name of the hill overlooking the house where I was born. It is the basilica of which I am bishop, Saint John Lateran. When you return home, give your children a warm greeting from me, but especially Ivan. I'm sure the others won't resent it."

By the end of this speech the poor woman was in tears. In a report of the audience to the Secretariat of State, Father Koulic stated that even Adjubei's eyes were misty when the couple took their leave of the pope carrying a letter addressed on the envelope simply "To K" and a box full of papal medals designed by the communist sculptor Giacomo Manzu.

As he was on the point of leaving, Adjubei asked Pope John if he could write a few lines about the audience, but the pope demurred—when the press gets involved, things get complicated, he blithely told the editor of the biggest newspaper in

the Soviet Union. (The Russian acquiesced to this, and nothing appeared in the Soviet press except for Pope John's message to Khrushchev—a few simple lines of greeting.) The
news that Pope John had received Adjubei flew around the
world while the audience was still going on. Yet it was two
days before the Curia could bring itself to confirm officially
that it had actually taken place.

The eighteen-minute meeting sent shock waves through the
press in the West, where it provoked dismay, satisfaction, or
uncertainty, depending on the individual political point of
view, or lack of it. The main criticism was that, by receiving a
prominent party man from Moscow in a private audience, the
pope had immeasurably enhanced communism's respectabil-
ity in the eyes of Catholics, and this was certain to have its
effect at the polls. *LA CROCIATA NON SI FA PIU* ("the Crusade is over") trumpeted a Rome communist weekly, while
the opposite view was expressed by the right-wing satirical
weekly *Il Borghese:* Pope John's new Eastern policy "means
the end of *La Chiesa Cattolica Romana.*"

In an attempt to calm the storm of controversy that was
scudding down on him, Pope John ordered the publication of
Father Koulic's report, but the bureaucratic department involved, the Extraordinary Affairs Section of the Secretariat of
State, headed by Monsignor Samoré, ignored his instructions.

"When it is heard what I said, and what he (Adjubei) said to
me, I believe the name of Pope John will be blessed," the
pope wrote in his private diary. "The [Secretariat of State]
doesn't heed our instructions, and I am sorry it is so. A request
from the pope . . . When I was nuncio, or patriarch . . . I de-
plore and regret what a lot of unmentionable games are played
these days. But I forgive and forget."

Moscow was eager to press its advantage. Having seen the
pope, Adjubei had a meeting with Premier Amintore Fanfani
at which he raised the question of a Khrushchev visit to Italy.

"Aren't you informed?" Fanfani replied. "I discussed that

with your father-in-law in Moscow and we agreed that there should be no visit in the forseeable future."

"You can't go on like this indefinitely," Adjubei argued. "High Italian officials have been in Moscow."

But Fanfani was able to cut off further discussion by saying that he could hardly make any commitments since his government was in its final weeks.

The Adjubei audience jolted Washington. Ambassador Reinhardt sought the advice of Premier Amintore Fanfani, with whom he had good relations (some of Reinhardt's embassy subordinates thought them too good for American interests in Italy because Fanfani had convinced the ambassador to support the opening to the left). Fanfani said he did not believe that anything of substance had taken place in the audience. However, he suggested to Archbishop Dell'Acqua that the Vatican ought to do something to soothe American nerves. Dell'Acqua called in the American political counsellor and justified the pope's decision to him on the grounds that the pontiff had had little alternative. The Church had to consider the consequences to Catholic interests in many areas, especially Eastern Europe, if the pope had turned down Adjubei's request.

Besides, the release of Slipyi had raised hopes of similar concessions in the future—"The Church cannot afford to have martyrs every day," Dell'Acqua said. At the same time, the Slipyi affair had left the Vatican in Moscow's debt, whereas it was important to put one's adversaries in one's own debt. It was true that Adjubei's purpose in seeking an audience—or at least one of them—was part of a Soviet attempt to improve its international image in the area of peace propaganda, which had been undermined by the Cuban missile crisis. The audience also served to emphasize the Vatican's own desire to play a role in preserving peace.

But, protested the American, what about its impact on the forthcoming Italian elections?

"Those who had not intended to vote Communist will not now do so because of Adjubei's audience with the pope," was Dell'Acqua's reply. As for the talk of a Khrushchev visit to the Vatican: "Premature." The American noted that the prelate did not rule it out altogether.

"In any case, the Soviet Government would have to make substantial concessions before such a step could seriously be entertained," Dell'Acqua added. No, the real significance of the visit had been to underline the fact that the Church did not belong to any political bloc. To illustrate the point, Dell'Acqua asked the diplomat to take note as he left of who was waiting to follow him into the prelate's office. It was the Cuban ambassador.

If the meeting was intended to reassure the Americans, it was not particularly successful. At a reception, Reinhardt buttonholed Cardinal Bea, took him aside, and confided that the Adjubei audience had worried Washington. The cardinal looked at him speculatively and smiled. If the United States was worried about recent Vatican political initiatives, it would be even more so as a result of something else that the pope was planning in the near future. That "something" was the publication of Pope John's encyclical, *Pacem in Terris.*

CHAPTER VI

Treating with the Devil

Pope John began working on *Pacem in Terris* in January 1963, when the dark shadows were already steadily lengthening, and periodic relapses in his condition fired their warning shots. The drafting was entrusted to Father Pietro Pavan, a noted Catholic sociologist, and to the Pope's trio of close collaborators, Capovilla, Dell'Acqua and Cardinale. In the preliminary discussions Pope John told Pavan, "I want this to be a document which both Kennedy and Krushchev will want to read." The final version was written by John himself, picking at the keyboard of his portable typewriter with two fingers in the small hours of the morning, with occasional visits to his private chapel to pray for inspiration.

Traditionally known by the opening words of the "official" Latin version, an encyclical is a letter from the pope to his bishops on an important contemporary problem. John addressed *Pacem in Terris* to "all men of good will," in order to emphasize that its theme of world peace and social progress were not the concerns of the Catholic hierarchy alone, or even of Catholics alone. The encyclical incarnated the justification and aims of his political philosophy. He dwelt pointedly on the terrible consequences of a nuclear war. He stressed the importance of a strong United Nations Organization for the preservation of peace—a departure from the hostile attitude of past popes toward international organizations, which had its origins in the secularist overtones of the League of Nations. But what was to capture the world's attention when the encyclical was made public was a guarded passage which in effect enshrined the reversal he had set in motion of the Church's hard line toward the communist world.

In it, the pope distinguished between false and dangerous philosophical doctrines and the actual movements themselves in the context of the constantly evolving historical situation. "A false philosophy of the nature, origin, and purpose of men and the world," should not be identified with an economic, social, cultural, and political program, "even when such a program draws its origin and inspiration from that philosophy." Thus while rejecting atheism, he went on to suggest that cooperation in the quest for peace and social progress was possible even with people holding incompatible views of the ultimate meaning of life.

"It can happen then," John continued, "that meetings for the attainment of some practical end, which formerly were deemed inopportune and unproductive, might now, or in the future be considered opportune and useful." The pope made no direct reference to communism, but his meaning was clear: Marxist ideology was undergoing such a radical transformation—at least in reality, whatever its formal doctrine—that it was possible for Catholics to cooperate with communists in resolving international disputes that threaten peace, while at the same time continuing to disagree with their beliefs.

It was inevitable that Pope John would sooner or later have issued a justification of his continued contacts with the communists. Theoretically, he was acting in violation of Pius XII's ban, which was still in force. In *Pacem in Terris,* or at least that section of the encyclical dealing with communism and the communists, John did not repeal Pius XII's ban—popes rarely repeal each other's edicts—but John plainly indicated that, in taking a more flexible line, the Church was adapting to changes in world conditions and even in the attitudes of the communists themselves.

When the draft encyclical was circulated among the curia cardinals for their comments prior to its publication, this *de facto* rejection of the Church's traditional hard line drew strong opposition from the conservatives, led by Cardinal Ottaviani. As secretary of the Supreme Congregation of the Holy Office—the prefect was the pontiff himself—Ottaviani, who was then seventy-two, was responsible for the maintenance of orthodoxy, but he was conservative not only *ex officio* but also through deep personal conviction, fearful of the future and opposed to change.

The head of the most prestigious and influential of all the sacred congregations, which had appropriated for itself the title of "Supreme" with little apparent justification in canon law, was, of course, a force to be reckoned with in the Vatican. However, forty years of unbroken curial service had put this brilliant canon lawyer at the center of an interlocking network of personal contacts which in many areas made him as powerful as the pope himself.

Few people who saw him intoning from the missal during papal ceremonies in Saint Peter's realized that because of his appalling eyesight he had committed everything to memory. As his sight worsened, his memory became correspondingly more formidable. On a visit to Germany to attend a religious festival he wrote a speech, had it translated into German—a language he did not speak—and memorized it. On the night before he was to deliver it, however, he decided to rewrite a key paragraph about the importance of real faith. The new section was again translated; he learned it anew, and his delivery was word perfect.

His large round bulk, encased in his red silk robes trailing a three-yard train, stood out at religious functions. Born in Trastevere, one of thirteen children, he had a native Roman wit that charmed even his adversaries. There was a gentle side to him in his personal dealings. For years, he ran a school and a summer camp for poor children from the *borgate* near Vatican City, but in his attitude toward progressive trends in theological thought or scriptural studies his mind could be as hard as metal and as narrow as a chisel. The cardinal had once attacked Yves Congar and Teilhard de Chardin, and the other theologians of the French school, as "certain pygmies who seem to think that a theology can be pieced together like a crossword puzzle, and who therefore invent a new theology. They do not stand at the feet of Jesus, like Mary, but face to face with the serpent, like Eve, allowing themselves to be bewitched in order to be more easily snared and devoured."

Convinced that Pope John's decision to hold an ecumenical council had been dangerously misguided, he masterminded the curia's attempt to scuttle it and when that failed, led the fight to control it. He was one of the promoters of a letter to the Pope signed by thirteen cardinals expressing concern at the dangerous doctrinal views being aired in the council debates.

Toward the end of his life, Pope John would receive a confidential critique of the council's first session which described in detail how the Council Theological Commission, of which Ottaviani was president, had successfully dominated the work of the preparatory phase and the first session. As an example, it cited the fact that when the Theological Commission revised the schema, or draft document, *De Ecclesia* ("On the Nature of the Church"), following the close of the council, the amendments submitted to it by several bishops at Pope John's urging were simply ignored. The meetings of the commission itself were conducted in a manner that discouraged dissenting voices among its members and *periti.* Anyone who questioned the conservative cardinal's will was apt to receive a broadside of florid rhetoric.

Sitting day after day in his place in Saint Peter's and listening to the council debates on reforming the Liturgy he had grown increasingly alarmed at the flood of proposed changes —communion in both kinds, concelebration, the use of the vernacular. On October 30, 1962, he could stand it no longer. Mounting the speaker's rostrum, he asked, "Are these fathers plotting revolution?" Such changes as they were contemplating would scandalize the faithful. They had the support of only a small minority. Concelebration would turn the sacrifice of the Mass into pure, or rather impure, theater. The Liturgy was sacred ground: had not God asked Moses to remove his sandals when approaching the burning bush?

The presiding cardinal, who happened to be Alfrink of Utrecht, a noted progressive, warned him that his speech had gone over the ten-minute limit. When Ottaviani ignored him and thundered on in the same vein, Alfrink turned off the speaker's microphone. Ottaviani continued to speak for some minutes, then realized what had happened. The Cardinal secretary of the Holy Office sailed indignantly out of the basilica amid laughter and applause from the assembled bishops and boycotted the debates for two weeks.

Ottaviani's commitment to Italian political affairs ran second in importance only to his commitment to theological orthodoxy and stemmed from the same conservative convictions. As a young prelate in the Secretariat of State, he had been principally responsible for negotiating the 1929 Concordat between the Holy See and the Italian government of Mussolini, and, in defiance of John's insistence on a policy of *disimpegno* or noninvolvement, refused to distance himself from the affairs of his home country.

Every year, he delivered a series of strongly anticommunist political lectures to senior officers of the Italian armed forces, including the defense minister. Right-wing politicians, as well as Curia prelates, regarded him as one of their major spokesmen. So did the papal aristocracy, which had lost many of its ancient privileges under Pope John. Unlike Pius XII—himself a member by birth of the "black" nobility—Pope John had little time for titles and nobles, regarding them as an anachronism in the modern church. He tolerated them around him during papal ceremonies and received them en masse in audience once a year, but otherwise he virtually ignored them. There was only one occasion when he exercised his authority as head of this ancient nobility, and that was when he suspended Prince Raimondo Orsini from his hereditary post of assistant to the throne because he was publicly living with an English movie actress, Belinda Lee. This left only one prince assistant to stand beside the papal throne on public occasions—Don Aspreno Colonna, head of another historic Roman house.

At his *a tabella* audience, which was at three o'clock in the afternoon the third Friday of each month, Ottaviani launched into a long critique of *Pacem in Terris*. To support his arguments he produced the written comments of Father Lorenzo Ciappi, the Master of the Sacred Palace. The holder of this medieval title, always a member of the Dominican order, was in effect the confidential theologian of the Holy See. Father Ciappi had succeeded Cardinal Michael Browne when the latter received his red cardinal's hat. The Irish cardinal, one of the few non-Italian senior prelates in the curia, was a noted conservative who supplied the traditionalists at the Vatican Council with appropriate references from the schoolmen for their speeches. Ciappi came from the same conservative mold, and he found much to criticize in the new encyclical.

What it had to say about communism, and about international organizations, he wrote, undermined the continuity of papal teaching, since it ran counter to the pronouncements of previous pontiffs. Moreover, the danger of "contamination" was still very real. He therefore proposed that the passage which encouraged—or at the very least condoned—collaboration with communists be toned down by the addition of the cautionary phrase, "But in accordance with the social teaching of the Church and with the disposition of the ecclesiastical authorities." John was undeterred. He incorporated some of

Ciappi's suggestions, including the cautionary phrase, and made a few other token changes based on Ottaviani's objections. Then he ordered the immediate publication of *Pacem in Terris*. To Father Ciappi he wrote, "As long as the whole is theologically sound, *ubi plura nitent ego paucis non offendar maculis*." ("Where most things shine, a few blemishes don't offend me.")

Ottaviani had a personal motive for opposing *Pacem in Terris* and especially for wishing to postpone its publication until after the Italian general elections. The Curia had helped form, and was supporting, a new Catholic right-wing party which hoped to attract Christian Democrat voters disenchanted with the ruling party's electoral commitment to a center-left coalition. Among the leaders of this newly formed *Movimento Politico Cattòlico Italiano* were two right-wing politicians with Curia connections: Ottaviani's nephew, and the nephew of Monsignor Mario Nasalli Rocca, Baron Corneliano, major domo of the pope's own household. But John was a man in a hurry. As he continued to force the pace, he suffered intermittent reminders that death was not far away. His relapses would force him to bed for a few days, but he would spring back amid his doctors' protests as soon as the danger seemed to have passed. A leading Turin specialist, consulted early in 1963, ruled out radiation treatment on account of the advanced condition of the pontiff's illness, and John himself continued to refuse to consider the by now dangerous alternative of surgery.

Giacomo Manzù, the Italian sculptor, who was a communist, had been commissioned to make several busts of the pontiff, and the two had become friends, each impressed with the other's humanity. Manzù visited the pope after a long interval and was shocked by the signs of physical wasting away. The large face sagged like a partially deflated balloon, leaving the large nose and the large ears in even greater prominence than before, and black hollows underlined his eyes. He seemed to avoid the sculptor's gaze, as though he knew that nothing could hide what showed in his face and so caused discomfort to others.

Late in March, Norman Cousins, through Father Morlion, volunteered to undertake a second mission to Moscow on behalf of Pope John. When Monsignor Dell'Acqua acquiesced, Cousins approached the Soviet ambassador in Washington and asked for an interview with Khrushchev. As the pope's emissary, it was not difficult for him to obtain an assurance that Khrushchev would receive him, and Cousins once again set out for Rome and the Soviet Union. In the course of a brief audience, Pope John, who was in high spirits, presented him with two of Manzù's medals. One was for the publisher himself, said John, in recognition for his help. Then, with a perfectly straight face, he added, "As for the other one, I'm sure that you can think of someone appropriate to give it to." By now Cousins was sufficiently well-versed in the Vatican style to understand that the other medal was intended for Khrushchev, whom the pope, in fact, rarely mentioned by name.

More important than the medals, however, was the Russian language version of *Pacem in Terris* Cousins was given to put in Khrushchev's hands prior to its official publication (the White House, by contrast, did not receive an advance copy of the new encyclical). Cousins was also given an English translation for himself, which he read on the plane to Moscow. The American publisher and the Soviet leader thus became the first two individuals outside Vatican circles to learn the contents of the papal document. Cousins also had a meeting with Cardinal Bea, who asked him to broach with Khrushchev the subject of the release of Archbishop Josef Beran of Prague. The Vatican believed that Beran was being kept under house arrest by the Czechoslovak regime.

On April 12, 1963, Norman Cousins once more found himself face to face with Khrushchev in his improbable role of occasional papal envoy. The meeting took place at Khrushchev's retreat on the Baltic Coast. Cousins gave him the pope's encyclical, drawing his attention to the passages on disarmament, peace, and communism. He also passed on Bea's request for Beran's release. Khrushchev replied that he would do his best, but, of course, there was a limit to the amount of "persuasion" that he could exert on the Czechoslovak government.

Cousins was already in Moscow when it came out in the Vatican that he was once again traveling on papal business. Curia prelates were appalled. Conspiracy-minded, like Italians generally, some senior curialists had formed the theory that Cousins was not what he made himself out to be, that the whole undertaking smacked of the Central Intelligence Agency, and that Cousins was using the pope's name to provide himself with a cover. There was nothing substantive on which to base this belief, except perhaps Father Morlion's past association with the OSS, but word of it seems to have reached Pope John, and this may account for the fact that Cousins was not received on his return from Moscow.

Inevitably, the publication of *Pacem in Terris* three weeks before the Italian general elections was a gift to the Communist party. Henceforth, individual Italian bishops who defied the pope's insistence on remaining aloof from the campaign could rail against the Communists, but the papal document had cut the ground from under them. After *Pacem in Terris* a Catholic could vote Communist without placing his soul in jeopardy. But before the party could exploit this remarkable switch in papal teaching, it had to perform a dogmatic somersault of its own. Had not Marx said that "the criticism of religion is the beginning of all criticism" and freely predicted that the force of economic history would grind religion into oblivion? Clearly, some explanation was needed to account for the increased readiness of the Marxist leader of the Soviet Union to deal with the spiritual leader of the Catholic church and for the Italian Communist Party (PCI) to accept the support of the unconverted.

For a while the PCI hesitated, caught between dogma and the prospect of political games. Then Palmiro Togliatti faced the issue head-on at a rally in Bergamo. "Not only can a religious man aspire toward a socialist society," he pronounced, "but such aspirations can actually find a stimulus in the religious conscience itself. This is why we appeal for reciprocal understanding and agreement."

Pope John was aware that his actions had worked to the political advantage of the Italian Communists, but he was more concerned about the broader context of the Church's relations with Marxism. Only rarely was he influenced by arguments of the papacy's impact on the situation in his own country. Toward the end of his life, he wanted to keep a long-standing commitment to visit the rebuilt Abbey of Montecassino. His doctors would not hear of it, and, as usual, it fell to Monsignor Capovilla to deflect him from his course. In the first place, Capovilla argued, the monks at Montecassino had themselves postponed the original date of the visit because they were not ready to receive him. Therefore he need not feel bound by his commitment.

"The pope doesn't bargain with monks; it's not in good taste," the pope replied.

"Besides, the doctors say it's dangerous," Capovilla continued. "You could have a hemorrhage."

"I would go to bed. The monks would give me a cell in the monastery. Think of it. To die at Montecassino, the great abbey, the cradle of monasticism."

"Holy Father, don't say such things," Capovilla protested. But what persuaded the pontiff in the end was his secretary's argument that if John left Rome so close to the elections, the press might read some political significance into the trip.

"It's something to consider," the pope conceded. "Some newspaper might say that the pope was making the trip to help this or that political party." So the visit to Montecassino was called off.

The Communists gained a million new votes in the election at the expense of the Christian Democrats and the center-left parties, the Socialists, the Republicans, and the Social Democrats. The result dashed any hope of a strong anticommunist government in Italy. The center-left coalition was formed— no other alternative was politically or numerically possible— but the moderate faction of the Christian Democrat Party, which had proposed the center-left in the first place, was hard-hit by electoral losses. Control of the coalition passed into the unsympathetic hands of the party's right wing and lost its reformist character. During the eleven years that followed, the center-left would drag on as the Italian governing formula, weakened by infighting in the ruling party and differences with its partners. The Communists, meanwhile, would consolidate their 1963 gains in every election for nearly two decades.

The right-wing press stopped just short of calling Pope John a crypto-Communist. Other papers were more restrained, but few questioned that the Adjubei audience and the publication of *Pacem in Terris* had provided the springboard for the Communist party's spectacular leap forward. Moreover, it was noted that this was the first election in which the Christian Democrats did not have the public support of the Italian Bishops' Conference, and that, too, was in accordance with John's wishes. The pope was stung by the personal attacks but shrugged off the Communist vote. "The doctrine expressed in the encyclical is without doubt perfectly derived from the Lord's teaching, and in harmony with papal teaching over the past sixty years," was his reply to the charge that he was "soft on communism." He conveniently forgot Pius XII's document *Non Expedit,* which banned contact with the communists. When Spain, the CIA man, expressed his concern at the election results to a member of John's circle, the prelate replied, "Even if the (Communist increase) has been twice as great, we would not worry. We are on the offensive now. In a decade, if we give men true Christian teaching and social justice, there will be no Communist vote in Italy."

A less idealistic, but more immediate factor in Pope John's apparent lack of concern about the Italian situation was probably that his Eastern policy was beginning to bear promising fruit. There was now no longer any need for intermediaries such as Palmiro Togliatti and Father De Luca. The pope's secretary, Monsignor Capovilla, and the Soviet Ambassador to Rome discussed matters directly at occasional secret meetings. Through this channel, Pope John learned that Moscow's signal to its satellites was to cooperate with the Holy See. The pope received confirmation of this from the Primate of Poland, Cardinal Wyszynsky, who had been assured by the regime of Wladislaw Gomulka that it had received clearance from Moscow for a rapprochement with the Vatican. At the same time, Monsignor Agostino Casaroli, a senior prelate of the Secretariat of State, was on the point of leaving for Hungary and Czechoslovakia for talks with government officials in both countries about the situation of the Church, the first such contacts since the war.

To the pope, the Communist gains in Italy inevitably slipped back into second position in relation to the Church's improved prospects elsewhere. But the CIA was less sanguine. All indications pointed to a growing understanding between the Vatican and Moscow which could have disastrous consequences for the balance of political forces in Italy. In its evaluation of the election results, the Rome station reported to Langley: "One thing is certain. The (Adjubei) visit is a precursor to the establishment of diplomatic relations between the USSR and the Vatican. This appears to be an irreversible course, and the establishment of diplomatic relations is only a matter of time, quite possibly a relatively short time."

One of its informers, a prelate working in the Vatican Congregation of the Council, told the Agency that the papacy had become very sensitive about allowing any action that might seem anti-Soviet. For example, he said, the Catholic Action had asked permission of the Vicariate of Rome to affix commemorative posters on Rome churches honoring the "Church of Silence" during Lent. The poster made no mention of communism, but asked for prayer for those who suffered in the name of the Church. Permission was first granted without any questions being asked. Within forty-eight hours, however, it was withdrawn on instructions from one of the pope's close collaborators.

Another indication of what was going on in the Vatican, according to the prelate, was Cardinal Bea's secret meeting with the Soviet ambassador to Washington in Maryland, during the cardinal's United States trip in the winter of 1962. It was on this occasion that Bea secured Soviet acceptance in principle to the visit by Monsignor Casaroli to Eastern Europe.

There was much more, and the CIA pieced together a picture of disquieting changes in Vatican policy. The CIA's director, John McCone, had a meeting with President Kennedy and then flew to Rome for an audience with Pope John. Tall, silver-haired, austere, McCone marched purposefully into the pope's study and spoke his mind.

McCone began by telling the pope that he was speaking on behalf of the president of the United States. He then, in effect, asked him to stop the Church's drift toward the left. American Catholics were extremely disturbed by the conciliatory tone of *Pacem in Terris* toward the communists, he said. It was dangerous for the Church to deal with the communists because they could not be trusted. Besides, left-wing gains in the recent Italian elections amply demonstrated how damaging such a policy was to Catholic parties. Catholics were confused: Pope Pius XII had excommunicated Catholic members of the Communist party, yet now Pope John himself was being criticized in some quarters as a communist sympathizer.

Pope John listened in silence to McCone's arguments. Then he replied gently that his perception of world affairs was not necessarily the same as that of the United States government. He mentioned the Church's intensified interest in cultivating the underdeveloped countries; in maintaining contact with Catholics behind the iron curtain and in promoting social reform and justice in Europe and Latin America. All this, he said, represented the Church's considered view of the best

way to fight communism. At the same time, Catholics should
not turn their backs on anyone who wanted to talk about
peace, regardless of ideological differences: "I bless all people, and I withhold my trust from no one."

McCone returned to the attack. While Moscow was cooper-
ating in Eastern Europe, the CIA had reliable information that
the communists were persecuting Catholic priests in other
parts of the world, for example, in South America. Pope John
said he was grieved to hear it, but it only reinforced his
argument of the need for a better understanding with the
communists.

The audience ended in a stalemate, and McCone next tried
to lobby the pope's advisers. "These friendly overtures toward
communism are very disturbing to American Catholics," he
told one of John's associates. "Catholic political parties will
be harmed. Besides, a lot of people are getting the impression
that the pope has communist sympathies."

"Does the United States government have communist sympathies?" asked the prelate.

"Of course not," McCone replied sharply.

"Yet the United States maintains relations with the Soviet
Union."

"But that's different. There are many practical reasons for
regular contact—trade, for example."

"But the pope has to consider his trade too," the prelate
pointed out, "the trade of the soul, the good of mankind. He
has to think of the well-being of East European Catholics. He
has to work for world peace. These are his motives for keeping
the lines of communication open with the communist world."

Back in Washington, McCone reported to Kennedy that
the Church's leftward drift under Pope John was likely to
continue.

The audience caused McCone, and therefore the agency, to
revise his thinking on the usefulness of regular contacts with
the Vatican. Khrushchev had found a way to exercise a personal influence on Pope John XXIII, but the present situation

made it difficult for Washington to counter that influence. The Vatican was constantly in the process of making political decisions. It made good sense to be in a position to ensure that these decisions supported rather than obstructed American interests.

But aside from the importance of bringing United States influence to bear on such radical endeavors as *Pacem in Terris*, there was a second consideration. The Vatican's new relationships were opening up new channels of information—for example, with East European countries—and a diplomatic mission could prove to be a useful listening post and a useful addition to the CIA's information-gathering capability. McCone wrote the inevitable memo to President Kennedy, with the same predictable results . . .

McCone was the highest-ranking American official to visit Pope John. Perhaps this was why the pontiff felt—incredibly—that if his visitor represented him correctly to the White House, Kennedy would certainly come round to supporting his actions. His cherished hope of bringing the Soviet and American leaders together, possibly under his chairmanship, seemed closer than ever. Though this hope was expressed only to his closest collaborators, and then only by innuendo, a rumor started of an impending Pope John–Khrushchev–Kennedy summit. Venice would be the rendezvous. Inspired by John they would surely reach agreement. Everybody wanted to do what John wanted—or almost everybody; his own high-ranking bureaucrats were among the exceptions. When he was questioned about it, John smiled: he was, he said, always ready to do God's work. The dream of such an encounter faltered in Washington, where the President's policy of giving John the peacemaker a wide berth had not changed.

But even before McCone returned to Washington, Monsignor Casaroli, small, owlish, unobtrusive, had left Rome to embark on a new career as the pope's special negotiator with the regimes of Eastern Europe. Though he was Monsignor

Samoré's immediate subordinate in the Secretariat of State, Casaroli's instructions were to report directly to the pope. He had been recruited for John's "parallel diplomacy" by Cardinale and Capovilla because of his reputation as a diplomat and his extreme discretion. His first stop was to be Budapest, where he would have talks with representatives of the Hungarian regime and visit Cardinal Mindszenty. In John's eyes, the Church in Hungary had only two assets left: the faith of the masses, and the presence of Cardinal Mindszenty in the American legation. Only the latter asset was negotiable, and Casaroli's instructions were not to surrender it too lightly.

Casaroli's objective was to try to improve the state of the organizationally and financially crippled Church, excessively dependent on the regime's whim for its ability to function effectively. Of the eleven dioceses in Hungary, six were without a head, four were headed by men in their seventies and eighties, and one was headed by a sick man of sixty-one. Of the fifteen Hungarian bishops, at least five were in jail, and only seven were permitted to exercise their functions. The church had almost no property, no tradition of sizable contributions from the faithful, and depended totally on the regime for its financial support. Salaries paid to priests were manipulated to favor clergy willing to collaborate with the regime. In all, over one hundred priests had been suspended on regime wishes, or prevented from working in their parishes.

Preliminary contacts through Moscow, and through members of the Hungarian clergy had established the Kadar regime's apparent willingness to allow some improvement in the position of the Catholic church, partly as part of Hungarian leader Janos Kadar's drive for national reconciliation, and also because Moscow wanted it. But there was also the additional reason that the Hungarian government saw improved relations with the Vatican as a way of resolving the "Mindszenty problem." The presence of Cardinal Joszef Minsdzenty in the American legation as a fugitive from "justice" was a major embarrassment which prevented normal relations with the

United States and constituted a constant reminder to the world of the 1956 revolution.

It was after the suppression of the Hungarian uprising that Mindszenty took refuge in the Budapest legation. Being technically on American soil, he was immune from arrest, but two cars belonging to the Hungarian secret police had immediately taken up positions outside the legation waiting to pounce on him the minute he stepped through the door into the street. Seven years later, the police were still waiting, with their car engines running day and night, presumably to be quicker off the mark should the cardinal try to make a dash for it.

But the cardinal remained doggedly inside, at first out of fear of recapture (he had, after all, spent seven years in Nazi and communist jails), then out of a firmly rooted vision of himself as a symbol of the "Church of Silence," and an inspiration to Hungarian refugees the world over.

He lived a semi-reclusive life, rarely appearing uninvited outside the ambassador's two-room office suite which had been turned over to him as his living quarters, unless it was to hurry to the legation's tiny walled garden for his daily constitutional. He had slowly taught himself English and practiced it with growing confidence and skill on Catholic members of the legation staff and their families, for whom he said Mass and delivered a sermon every Sunday morning. The cardinal and his hosts treated each other with unfailing courtesy, the latter insisting only that he should receive no visitors, especially not Hungarian visitors, and give no interviews to the press. To avoid possible complaints that he was a burden on the taxpayer, the cardinal's upkeep was paid by contributions from American Catholics.

When Pope Pius XII died in 1958, Mindszenty received a telegram from the Dean of the Sacred College of Cardinals requesting his presence at the conclave. At the same time, the Vatican asked the United States government to try to obtain from the Hungarian regime his safe conduct to Rome. The prospect terrified Mindszenty, who was convinced that, were he to leave the embassy, he would suffer the same fate as Imre Nagy. The leader of the 1956 uprising was assassinated by the Hungarians after being granted safe conduct from the Yugoslav embassy, where he had taken refuge, to Yugoslavia itself.

But Mindszenty's dilemma was that he felt he had no alternative but to obey the summons to Rome, illness and old age being the only two reasons for not attending a conclave admitted in canon law. The United States, however, had never officially notified the Hungarian government of Mindszenty's presence in the legation. So when the American envoy, Garrett Ackersley, approached the foreign ministry in Budapest, the Hungarians feigned surprise. "You have a guest in your Legation?" he was asked. To Mindszenty's intense relief, the American request for safe conduct was turned down—a decision the Hungarians would have reason to regret in later years.

The Vatican had had no direct contact with Mindszenty since he had sought refuge in the legation. Occasionally, the American embassy in Rome relayed messages of greeting to or from the pontiff and sketchy reports on the cardinal's condition. Then, one day, shortly before Casaroli's departure, Pope John was discussing the situation of the Church in Eastern Europe with Cardinal König when he said something like this, "One of these days, why don't you make a trip to Budapest and drop in on Cardinal Mindszenty to see how he is?" Konig understood what was being asked of him. The pontiff wanted him to go to Cardinal Mindszenty first to determine his state of mind and general physical condition, and then to test his reaction to the idea of leaving Hungary and coming to Rome.

Accordingly, on April 18 König arrived in Budapest accompanied by a doctor from the United States Embassy in Belgrade. They found Mindszenty in good health, but intransigent in his determination not to leave, except on his own terms. Welcoming his Austrian "brother," his thin face was hard and his eyes, dark cold tunnels.

"What does the pope want of me?" he asked in Latin, even though his German was good, and König was at first taken aback by the harshness of his voice.

König replied that he had come at Pope John's behest to explain the Church's new approach to the problem of relations with the communists. Mindszenty dominated the conversation, leaving the prelate from Vienna in no doubt how he felt about the Church's new approach, but König departed with the Hungarian primate's conditions for his departure. If and when he decided to leave Hungary—and that was for the future because, as he told König, "I feel that my immediate departure would not be the best solution"—he insisted on (1) agreement between Mindszenty, the Vatican, and Hungary on the nomination of Mindszenty's successor, (2) Mindszenty's complete rehabilitation by the Hungarian regime, which meant abolition of the 1949 sentence of life imprisonment on charges of spying for the Germans during the occupation of Hungary, and (3) his freedom for a brief time before leaving his country to say mass and to consult with the Hungarian clergy.

König returned to Vienna deeply impressed by Mindszenty's bitter sense of betrayal. The Hungarian primate viewed the Church's new policy in Eastern Europe as a rejection of all that he felt he had stood for—and that the same Church had on so many occasions told him that he stood for —in the past twenty struggling years. But the Hungarian regime quickly made it clear that the ultimate price for any important concessions to the Church was his removal from the legation and from the country.

On his first visit to Budapest, Casaroli was able to secure the return from their places of exile of five banned bishops, but only one was immediately permitted to resume his ecclesiastical duties. It was a conciliatory gesture by the regime: now it was the Vatican's turn. Casaroli went to see Mindszenty, who was as immovable as he had been with König. To support his stand he produced a thick folder of "evidence"—

mostly newspaper clippings describing him as a symbol of the oppressed Church, and an inspiration to anticommunist resistance.

Typically, Pope John never *ordered* the cardinal to leave Hungary, for this would have forced the cardinal into open disobedience of his pontiff. Cardinal König put the case in very general terms. Casaroli spoke on behalf of the Holy See, not the pope himself. The decision was left to the cardinal's judgment—for the moment, at any rate.

CHAPTER VII

A Pope Dies

ON THE MORNING of May 21, 1963, Cardinal Wyszynski had a long audience with Pope John. Its main purpose: a thorough review of Polish church-state relations in the light of the regime's attempts to establish a rapprochement with Rome. This development, too, had its origins in Moscow. On November 4 of the previous year, Wladislaw Gomulka had paid a quick visit to Moscow where a principal topic of Polish-Soviet conversations was undoubtedly Poland's part in reviving Khrushchev's peaceful coexistence line following the Cuban fiasco (the Poles liked to be in the role of the foremost exponents of peaceful coexistence, and generally stood to gain from it). When Gomulka returned to Warsaw, the regime let the Polish primate know that it had received clearance from Moscow for a rapprochement with the Vatican.

West Germany and the Vatican would have been regarded by both Khrushchev and Gomulka as the natural targets for Poland. Formal Western recognition of its disputed Oder-Neisse frontier was one of the principal objectives of Polish diplomacy. Since, in Polish eyes, relations with the Vatican would constitute a form of recognition of the former German territories annexed after World War II, almost as much as would the establishment of diplomatic relations with West Germany itself, Poland immediately began to work for a rapprochement with both. The regime's West German overtures were left in the hands of foreign affairs specialists, but contacts with Rome were evidently too sensitive to be left to to professional diplomats. They became the exclusive concern of the party first secretary himself, and the Polish Politbureau's authority on church-state relations, Zenon Kliszko.

Gomulka assumed personal charge in order to act as a counterweight to the formidable primate, his nemesis. If the Polish Church belonged to the "Church of Silence" by geography, it certainly did not by temperament. Under Wyszynski's leadership, the Polish Church had not only survived the restraints of communism, it had grown steadily stronger, with Wyszynski himself constituting a challenge to the party leader's authority. Ironically, the Soviet Union had contributed to making Poland more solidly Catholic (with ninety-seven per cent of all Poles baptized in the faith) by annexing the eastern portion of the country, thereby siphoning off the Orthodox section of the prewar population.

Wyszynski was not popular with Pius XII, who preferred martyrs to survivors, but his policy of bending with the wind whenever possible came into its own under John XXIII when it served as a model for Vatican dealings with the governments of Eastern Europe. The prescription was simple: always be ready to negotiate but never waste an advantage; compromise if you must but demand written guarantees; don't compromise if the immediate gain will not be worth the eventual price; and—most difficult—try to put the regime in debt to the Church, and don't allow the Church to become dependent on the regime.

At first the Polish primate was central to the regime's approaches to the Vatican. He arranged with Rome for a papal audience on November 20 for one of Poland's leading lay

Catholics, Jerzy Zawieyski, in his capacity as a member of the Polish collective presidency, the Council of State. On the eve of his departure for Rome, Zawieyski apparently had a talk with Gomulka. Returning to Poland, Zawieyski gave an account of the audience with the pope, indicating that while the possibility of eventual diplomatic relations between Poland and the Vatican was discussed, it was made contingent upon "an atmosphere of mutual understanding and regard between the parties concerned."

But once it had established a foothold, the regime altered its strategy and attempted to go over the cardinal's head. On December 10, Kliszko delivered a lecture in Rome in which he was critical of the Polish episcopate and warmly appreciative of Pope John, whose speeches, he claimed, "render the attaining of a concordat not unlikely." Kliszko's remarks offended the pope and the Polish bishops, and they received a sharp rebuff in a *L'Osservatore Romano* editorial five days later, but the notion of bypassing the primate was not abandoned. Early in 1963, instead of facing up to the fact that in order to reach an accord with the Vatican it must first reach an accommodation with Cardinal Wyszynski and all the Polish bishops, the regime provoked another crisis in church-state relations by resuming attempts to restrict and control Catholic education.

It also launched a whispering campaign against the person of Cardinal Wyszynski, alleging disagreements between the pontiff and the cardinal. The campaign eventually found its way into the Polish press, provoking the cardinal to some unprecedented replies in his sermons, including a rather apt statement that "those who use lies become the first victims of lies." In April Gomulka told a Swedish editor that the Polish episcopate had not quite kept pace with political developments and that Pope John XXIII was a much more modern Catholic than the Polish primate. There was a lot of truth in Gomulka's statement. The Polish Church was strongly traditionalist and the primate a doctrinal conservative. But the implied distinction between a modern papacy prepared to deal with the communist leadership and an old-fashioned Church standing in the way of progress in their contacts was not well received in Rome. In attempting to deal directly with the pope, the Polish regime was following Moscow's lead, and possibly also its instructions. But during his visit to Warsaw in May, Monsignor Casaroli made it clear that no regime could expect an improvement of its relations with the Vatican without prior or concomitant accords with its national Catholic church.

The necessity of dealing with and through the Polish primate seemed to have been accepted at that point, but only with the added pressure of a wave of popular unrest at home which made an understanding with the Church advisable, if not imperative, for purely internal reasons. At the end of March, the Polish government had announced a steep price increase, doubling the retail price of coal, gas, and electricity, effective April 1. It became immediately apparent that this drastic and poorly justified measure evoked strong popular resentment and became a symbol of the constantly rising cost of living. Reports of slowdowns, factory demonstrations, and protests began to come in from all over the country. Gomulka was recalled from vacation to lend his personal prestige to salvaging the rapidly deteriorating situation. His address to Warsaw party activists, carried live on television on April 17, not only did not remedy the situation, but was believed to have seriously damaged the regime's principal asset—Gomulka's own image in the party and in the country.

Cardinal Wyszynski chose this moment to press the regime for a new church-state agreement. Jerzy Zawieyski opened the offensive with a speech in the Polish Sejm. Although Zawieyski could not always be regarded as a spokesman for the cardinal, in this case his speech most likely had Wyszynski's prior approval, since it spelled out the conditions for improved Polish-Vatican relations and the specific guarantees demanded by the Church in Poland.

After a brief summary of the Vatican's changed attitude and visible interest in Poland, Zawieyski characterized church-state relations in Poland as being "frequently downright bad." Then he proposed church-state negotiations with the aim of signing a new agreement which would supersede the 1950 Church-State Agreement and would "once again spell out mutual obligations and benefits."

"For the Church," said Zawieyski, "the most important problem is the possibility to teach religion freely and to develop Catholic culture through the press, publications, and education at the lower and at the higher level. For the government it is important that the Church should exert its moral influence on people's attitudes toward their duties to the state, teaching them respect for authority . . ." Then on April 21, the cardinal followed this up with a well-timed pastoral letter, read in all the churches, attacking the regime for interfering with religious education in violation of the constitution as well as the church-state agreement of 1950.

The cardinal's pressure had its effect, and six days later, the primate and Gomulka met for an entire day of talks, an unprecedented occurrence. The discussion centered on conditions for a concordat with the Vatican. When Wyszynski left for Rome shortly thereafter, he was carrying concrete Polish proposals for an accord. Over the next five days, he had a number of meetings with Pope John and his collaborators: the time had now come to draw conclusions and take his leave of the pope. As they stood together on the threshold of the pope's study Wyszynski smiled and said, "*Arrivederci* in September."

The pope lifted his shoulders in an expressive shrug. "In September you shall find either myself or another pope. As you well know, in a month it's possible to do it all—the funeral of one and the election of another." Then he added wistfully, "Were it not for this blessed protocol I would dearly like to accompany you at least as far as the gates."

The Polish prelate walked thoughtfully back to the elevator

through the glass-enclosed loggia with the Raphael frescoes showing scenes from the life of the Virgin and the marble galleries which increased in size and grandeur as he moved farther away from the pope's library. Beside him trotted Nasalli Rocca, the pope's fussy little Major Domo, who would accompany him to the main entrance of the papal apartments. At almost every doorway, Swiss Guards banged their halberds on the ground and sprang to attention in salute. Two Gentlemen of the Sword and Cape in black seventeenth century Spanish court dress bowed respectfully. A visiting bishop sailed past on his way to his audience with the pope, his purple *ferriolo* (cape) billowing behind him, and a young secretary, clearly on his first visit to the Vatican, trailing wide-eyed in his wake. The papal court bustled mechanically through another wind-up day of elaborate ceremonial, impervious in its own indestructibility to the approaching end of another supreme pontiff.

Little information leaked out on Wyszynski's conversations with the pope, but the CIA's Rome station pieced together a fairly detailed report of the Church's position and cabled it to Washington. The pope, said the report,

HAS LEFT THE QUESTION OF ESTABLISHING DIPLOMATIC RELATIONS WITH POLAND TO CARDINAL WYSZYNSKI. THE POLISH EPISCOPATE WANTS EITHER FULL DIPLOMATIC RELATIONS BETWEEN POLAND AND THE VATICAN OR NO OFFICIAL LEVEL RELATIONSHIP AT ALL. THE POLISH GOVERNMENT ON THE OTHER HAND WANTS TO ESTABLISH SO-CALLED CONSULAR RELATIONS PRIMARILY FOR PROPAGANDA PURPOSES SO THE POLISH STATE CAN SAY IT IS DEALING WITH THE VATICAN, BUT AT THE SAME TIME NOT PERMIT CLOSER RELATIONS. IF THE POLISH GOVERNMENT DOES NOT AGREE TO FULL RELATIONS THERE WILL BE NONE . . .

According to the agency's informers in Rome,

ALTHOUGH THE MAJORITY OF THE POLISH EPISCOPATE WOULD PREFER TO HAVE FULL DIPLOMATIC RELATIONS BETWEEN THE VATICAN AND POLAND, SOME BISHOPS BELIEVE THAT CONSULAR RELATIONS WOULD BE SATISFACTORY AND OTHERS WANT NO RELATIONS AT ALL. REGARDLESS OF THE NATURE OF THE RELATIONS, THE CHURCH REALIZES THE POLISH GOVERNMENT WILL USE THEM FOR PROPAGANDA PURPOSES AND THAT THE CHURCH WILL BE AT A DISADVANTAGE. WHILE THE CHURCH REALIZES THIS, IT IS WILLING TO ESTABLISH SOME FORM OF RELATIONS IN THE BELIEF THAT IN THE LONG RUN SOME BENEFITS WILL ACCRUE TO THE CHURCH. FOR EXAMPLE, THE PAPAL NUNCIO WOULD BE DEAN OF THE DIPLOMATIC CORPS IF FULL DIPLOMATIC RELATIONS WERE ESTABLISHED. THE POLISH DESIRE TO ESTABLISH ONLY CONSULAR RELATIONS IS AIMED AT AVOIDING THIS WHILE AT THE SAME TIME PERMITTING THE POLISH GOVERNMENT TO POINT TO ITS "LIBERAL" ATTITUDE TOWARD THE CHURCH.

WHILE THE POPE HAS LEFT TO CARDINAL WYSZYNSKI THE DECISION AS TO WHAT RELATIONS, IF ANY, ARE TO BE ESTABLISHED, THE POLISH GOVERNMENT DOES NOT WANT TO DEAL THROUGH THE CARDINAL, PREFERRING TO TALK DIRECTLY WITH THE VATICAN. THE POLISH GOVERNMENT HAS MADE SOME ATTEMPTS TO TALK DIRECTLY TO THE POLISH BISHOPS AND TO THE VATICAN BUT THESE ATTEMPTS HAVE NOT MET WITH SUCCESS.

The report accurately reflected what had transpired, and was obviously based on good information. Wyszynski was returning home with his hand considerably strengthened. But before a new round of negotiations could get under way, the process of rapprochement was interrupted by the pope's deteriorating condition.

On the morning of May 24, the pope woke in very weak condition and had to remain in bed. By evening, he was hemorrhaging and needed more transfusions. A noted Rome surgeon was called in; once again, the question of whether or not to operate was raised, and once again ruled out. True to form, the Vatican kept quiet about the pope's relapse. It simply announced that his Wednesday general audience in Saint Peter's and all his other public engagements had been canceled because he was going into spiritual retreat in preparation for the feasts of Pentecost and the Ascension.

On May 26, he again took a turn for the worse. Professor Gasbarrini was quickly summoned from Bologna, his home. Arriving in Saint Peter's Square as noon approached and finding it full of people, he feared the worst, but it was the usual Sunday crowd, still unaware of the situation, and waiting to see the pontiff at his window.

When the loudspeakers crackled into life, however, there was still no sign of the round, fatherly figure. Instead came an announcement that said: "The stomach ailment from which the Holy Father has suffered since last autumn and which had caused acute anemia in November has again caused anemia in the last few days, after a period of medical treatment and relative quiescence. It is at present being kept under control by suitable medical treatment." Then followed the recorded voice of Pope John himself reciting the Angelus. It did not take the crowd long to grasp the essential point: *Il papa sta male.* ("The pope is ill.") Too ill to appear at his window.

Yet many hesitated to leave the square, as if they hoped that the announcement would be given the lie by the appearance of the pope himself as usual. They remained there until it was dark, at intervals asking the Swiss Guards at the gates for further news and looking up to the pope's quarters, where lights could be seen behind closed shutters.

Though his hold on life was slight, the ailing pontiff insisted on conducting church business. He worked propped up on four pillows in the plain mahogany four-poster bed in which four other popes had slept before him, and in which three of

them had also died. The room had been Pope Pius X's cell
during the conclave at which he was elected, and he had decided to remain there in preference to moving into more elaborate quarters occupied by his predecessors on the floor
below. Since that time no pontiff had done much by way of
interior decoration, and the room still retained a cell-like quality with its few pieces of massive Victorian furniture and its
large collection of religious statuary and images.

Pope John's photographs on the walls provided the only
personal touch—his mother and father and other members of
the Roncalli family, and the pontiff himself at various stages
of his career: the newly ordained priest, sporting a crew cut,
with other members of his graduating class at the Accadèmia
dei Nobili; the medical corps sergeant, almost unrecognizable
behind a luxurious black mustache; posing with Bishop Radini Tedeschi; the apostolic nuncio in Paris standing in an
unblinking line with his four brothers.

The room hummed with subdued activity, unobtrusively
but firmly orchestrated by Monsignor Capovilla, who was
rarely out of John's sight. The pope was weak and in considerable pain. Documents had to be read to him; his signature
was a laborious scrawl. But when doctors protested that he
ought to rest, he cheerfully replied that they were right, and
went on working.

On the night of May 30, the CIA cabled headquarters in
Langley, Virginia:

THE POPE'S CONDITION HAS SHOWN A MARKED IMPROVE-
MENT IN THE LAST 24 HOURS. HE IS ENTIRELY LUCID, IS
FULLY AWARE OF THE SERIOUSNESS OF HIS CONDITION
AND, ALTHOUGH VERY WEAK, MAY, IF THE TREND CON-
TINUES, BE ALLOWED TO GET OUT OF BED FOR SHORT
PERIODS WITHIN A FEW DAYS. HEMORRHAGES HAVE NOW
CEASED COMPLETELY. STILL, THE NATURE OF THE ILL-
NESS DESPITE THE PRESENT IMPROVEMENT DOES NOT
GIVE MUCH HOPE.

VATICAN OFFICIALS ARE DISTURBED BY WHAT THEY
DESCRIBE AS THE HOLY FATHER'S INSISTENCE ON PLAN-
NING HIS FUTURE ACTIVITIES. THEY ARE AWARE THAT
TOO MUCH ACTIVITY COULD BRING BACK THE HEMOR-
RHAGES AND RESULT IN DEATH. EVEN UNDER THE BEST
CONDITIONS THERE IS NO REASON TO HOPE THAT THE
POPE WILL RECOVER ENOUGH TO RESUME HIS FULL DU-
TIES. THE LONGER TERM PROGNOSIS IS STILL THEREFORE
QUITE GLOOMY.

But hardly had the CIA Information Report arrived and
been circulated to the offices on the short circulation list—the
Director of the National Security Agency, the White House
Situation Room, the State Department's Bureau of Intelligence and Research, the Defense Intelligence Agency, and
the Chief of Naval Operations—when in came an urgent
chaser from Rome. It said, more succinctly:

POPE JOHN XXIII WENT INTO A COMA ON MORNING OF 31
MAY. HIS CONDITION HAS WORSENED AND IS EXTREMELY
SERIOUS. ITALIAN STATE RADIO BULLETIN OF 12:45
STATED THE POPE'S CONDITION TOOK A TURN FOR THE
WORSE IN THE LATE MORNING OF 31 MAY AND THAT EX-
TREME UNCTION HAD BEEN ADMINISTERED.

The fact that the CIA had learned of John's sudden relapse
from the radio was an indication of how very limited the news
was on the pope's condition. Access to his bedroom was carefully controlled by Capovilla, and limited to a small group of
prelates and doctors. Information could be released only by
Capovilla himself or by Dell'Acqua.

The procedure was as follows: the head of the press office,
Luciano Casimirri, stood by in a room close to the papal apart-
ments, together with the director of the Vatican Radio, Father
Paolo Pappalardo, and a member of the editorial staff of
L'Osservatore Romano. They were not allowed to enter the

pope's bedroom. Nor were they permitted to question, on their own initiative, anyone who had. From time to time Dell'Acqua or Capovilla (or occasionally someone deputizing for them) would emerge to brief them on the latest developments in the pope's condition, and supply them with a few details on what was going on inside. On the basis of this information Casimirri and the others would write a press statement which, however, required Dell'Acqua's approval prior to its release. It was not an arrangement calculated to keep the news flowing, or even trickling, because Dell'Acqua's many responsibilities often made him hard to track down, and Capovilla— who had his hands full with the pope—even more so.

It was actually in the small hours of Friday, May 31, that John suddenly woke out of his sleep and cried out for help. Capovilla, dozing in a chair by his bedside, sprang to his aid. An abcess had burst in Pope John's stomach and the pain shot through his body. Dr. Mazzoni fought feverishly to relieve the writhing man of his agony.

The hermorrhage was complicated by peritonitis, and the pope was worsening rapidly. His breathing was difficult and he was put in an oxygen mask. His arms hung limp by his side, and he recognized no one, not even his secretary. Some hours later, the pope's eyes snapped open and he regained consciousness. Capovilla approached the bed. "How do you feel?" he asked the pope.

"I feel all right now. But I'm also worried."

"Holy Father," said Capovilla gently, "as we agreed, I will do for you what you did for Monsignor Radini. Therefore I must tell you, that the final hour has come. This is the day you are called to paradise."

"Perhaps we ought to wait until we have heard what the doctors have to say," Pope John replied.

"Alas, the doctors have already had their say. The tumor has done its damage." And Capovilla burst into tears.

The pope consoled him. "Well, then, make all the arrangements to ensure that I die as befits a bishop and a pope. We have discussed the procedure, and anyway it is included in the ceremonies for bishops. We have worked hard. We have served the Church. We have not paused to pick up the stones that were thrown at us from one side or another, and we have not thrown any back."

Then he instructed Capovilla to hand over to the Secretariat of State what money he had locked in his desk. "I want the Lord to find me poor and owning nothing. We shall meet in paradise. You my son, must be courageous for you have to arrange everything, so start getting the people together."

The bedroom was cleared so that the pope's confessor, Monsignor Alfredo Cavagna, could hear his confession, as he had done every Saturday afternoon since the pope's election. Presently everyone filed back to the pope's bedside—the doctors; Capovilla; Cicognani; Dell'Acqua; Samoré; the pope's nephew, Monsignor Giambattista Roncalli, a parish priest in Bergamo; and Cardinal Cento, the cardinal-major penitentiary, whose duties included leading the prayers for the dying pope. The papal sacristan, Archbishop Canisius van Lierde, gave him the *Viaticum*, the Communion for the dying, and the last rites (Extreme Unction) anointing with holy oil the pope's eyes, ears, mouth, nose, hands, and feet—parts of the body that might have led him to sin. Van Lierde began reciting the *Proficiscor*, the prayer commending his departing soul to God, but Pope John was not quite ready to depart. Hauling himself into a sitting position, he whispered, "That's enough for now. I want to talk to everyone."

The kneeling group listened in surprise as the pope, often half-delirious, gasping, and twitching like some great white fish, beached and gaffed, offered his life for the glory of the Church and for the success of the Vatican Council. Then he began to recite, in chronological order, the names of the cities around the world where his ecclesiastical career had taken him, starting with Bergamo, where he was ordained, and ending with his pontificate in the Vatican, and to recall many of those who had worked with him. He asked forgiveness of all whom he might have offended or hurt since his youth and assured men everywhere that he loved them as brothers and wished them all to love him.

Searching out Cicognani, he told him, "Take my words to all the cardinals, and to the missions and dioceses of the world. First of all, about the council—what a heavenly inspiration. It will be a great event in the Church. Tell them that, and may all my cardinals be united with the bishops in the three aims of the council: to renew us from within, to bring our separate brethren into one Church, and to show the whole world, all mankind, that we are one family." To Dell'Acqua, his faithful collaborator, he said, "Never forget it—*Ut unum sint.*"

He was unconscious when, at 6:00 P.M., seven senior cardinals mustered around his bedside. As they loomed over him, Capovilla whispered their names one by one into the pope's ear—Tisserant, Dean of the Sacred College; then Benedetto Aloisi Masella, the cardinal-chamberlain, who takes over the government of the Church when the pope dies; Cicognani, the secretary of state; Ottaviani; Santiago Luis Copello; Alberto di Jorio, head of the Vatican's finances; Fernando Cento, the cardinal-major Penitentiary. In March 1962, Pope John had created several new cardinals, including three *in pectore,* that is, without disclosing their identities. They were generally thought to be Eastern European bishops, and the pope had exercised his right to keep their names to himself until a politically more appropriate moment. The cardinals now hoped to hold a bedside consistory—a meeting of the college of cardinals—so that the pope could name the three new members and thus prevent the secret from dying with him. In the darkened room the cardinals prayed for the pontiff. Presently, he stirred and beckoned to Capovilla to come closer. Was he going to reveal the names? All bent forward to hear what he had to say. With great difficulty he whispered to Capovilla; "When all this is over, don't forget to go and see your mother." Then he sank back and closed his eyes.

The same evening, Cardinal Bea went to the Vatican to see Pope John. As his Mercedes swung into Saint Peter's Square, it was engulfed in a huge crowd. Men and women stood or knelt, alone or in groups. The slow, mechanical chimes of the Vatican Radio callsign, *Christus vincit,* oozed from thousands of transistors, drowning out the murmured prayers. *Christus vincit, Christus regnat, Christus imperat*—the familiar hymn to Christ triumphant, so different from the dying pope's vision of the benign Redeemer, rang out hour after hour, interrupted only by prayers for the pope and the latest bulletin on his condition. Powerful searchlights mounted on trucks raked the brown walls of the old palace, the harsh light hammering against the shuttered windows of the room where the old man lay dying in an old oak bed.

Cardinal Bea's car nosed its way slowly through the crowd toward the Arch of the Bell; Swiss Guards waved it through the gate. Bea was borne round the huge stone mass of the rear of Saint Peter's Basilica into the quiet, deserted streets of Vatican City, past more guard posts manned by Swiss Guards and papal gendarmes, and then through the long tunnel leading to the Belvedere Courtyard, where he took the elevator to the pope's private apartment. Outside the bedroom stood a pile of bundles and cheap suitcases belonging to members of Pope John's family who had arrived earlier from Sotto Il Monte, escorted by Cardinal Montini: the pope's sister Annunziata; his three surviving brothers, Zaverio, Alfredo, and Giuseppe. The pope's niece, Sister Anna, had also been brought to Rome from her missionary convent in Asmara, Ethiopia.

When Bea entered the bedroom they were huddled together like children who were awed by their surroundings, gazing silently at their brother from a respectful distance. Bea approached the pope's bed, but the dying man seemed scarcely to recognize his close collaborator. At any rate, as Bea told his secretary during the drive home, he did not say anything the cardinal could understand. Bea would never see Pope John alive again.

Gasbarrini took Capovilla aside and told him that, although the pope was putting up a terrific fight, and his heart beat was regular, and his temperature remained around thirty-eight degrees (100.4 degrees Farenheit) thanks to a strong constitution and an iron will, his condition was slowly deteriorating. A rumor swept the Vatican that he was already dead. This was quickly denied by the press office, but not quickly enough to prevent two European newspapers from going on the stands on White Sunday with the premature news of the pontiff's death. The early edition of *De Telegraaf,* Amsterdam's highly respected morning daily paper, had sold three thousand copies, mostly in the southern Holland area which has the largest concentration of Dutch Catholics, before a corrected edition was produced. In Switzerland, the German-language tabloid *Blick* ran a seven-column headline: A GREAT POPE IS DEAD. Whereupon, angry Catholics in Lucerne retaliated by printing and distributing leaflets saying: *Blick ne parait plus* ("*Blick* has ceased publication"). *Blick* printed an apology, blaming the mistake on an inadvertent switch of front-page plates a third of the way through the paper's print run from one which said that the pope was dying to another which had been standing by for immediate use and which reported that the pope had died. In fact, the stories were identical on both plates except for an introduction reporting his death. The issue sold twenty thousand more copies than *Blick*'s usual Sunday circulation of one hundred fifty thousand.

The events of two decades—the monumental work of Pius XII, the renovation begun by John XXIII and his Vatican Council—had radically changed old attitudes and purged away ancient inhibitions with respect to the Roman Church and made it the focus of unprecedented press attention and curiosity. The Church was good "copy." Each in his own way, Pius XII and John XXIII were powerful media figures. Erudite, mystical, reclusive, Pius exercised the attraction of an enigma: the more he withdrew from public view, the more fascinating he became to the press. Toward the end of his life he even claimed to have seen visions. At the same time, he made headlines by establishing for the first time the attitude of the Church toward such important social and scientific developments as psychoanalysis, birth control, natural childbirth, and atomic energy. John closed the gap between the abstract element of the papacy and the human element. In 1962, a group of Notre Dame University alumni presented him with a new Cadillac. In such circumstances, Pope Pius was quite capable of delivering a learned discourse on the place of the automobile in modern society, with a complete section on how the internal combustion engine works. Pope John concluded his brief speech of thanks to the alumni with these words: "I bless you all, and also your cars. I presume you all have cars. Anyway, my blessings to you, with or without cars."

The spread of television, and in particular the advent of Telstar, which coincided with his pontificate, played an important part in making Pope John known to millions. On the screen, his personality radiated warmth and goodness. Here was a pope who displayed no great learning, who seemed too down-to-earth to ever have visions—and, in fact, was privately skeptical about his predecessor's—but who spoke to the good in everyone, Catholic and non-Catholic alike. As he lay dying, the full power of world television was focussed on the Vatican. Camera crews converged on Rome to film his last days. But a good or bad press is largely a matter of indifference to the Church as it moves down the ages with Christ at its head, on its supernatural mission of salvation. As a result, little importance was attached in the Vatican to keeping up with the burgeoning expectations of the press.

Even in the present situation, few concessions were made to accommodate the awesomely complex requirements of the world press. The small Vatican press department, which was considered barely adequate to handle the normal flow of business, was left to face an unprecedented invasion of reporters and communications hardware alone, with frustrating results for the invaders. Day and night, scores of journalists filled the Vatican press office, its location on the edge of the city, just inside Saint Anne's Gate doubtless reflecting official determination to keep the press as far away as possible. Indeed, journalists were not permitted to venture deeper without a special pass.

On Whitsunday morning, the press office was a maelstrom of polyglot activity. Japanese reporters compared notes with American columnists; the man from *Pravda* translated *L'Osservatore Romano* with a little help from two West German priests; wire service reporters kept telephone lines open day and night to their offices in Rome in an effort to be first with any significant new change in the Pope's condition. After nearly a week of round-the-clock occupation they worked in surroundings of utter squalor: ash trays full to capacity; tables littered with empty bottles of beer; dirty *espresso* cups; and unfinished glasses of Scotch whisky. Half-eaten food had been thrust aside to make room for typewriters, and the floor was carpeted with old newspapers and balls of discarded paper.

A Vatican Radio bulletin would quickly reduce the place to silence: "The face is placid and serene, and shows no sign of suffering . . ." A spasm of action followed when typewriters sprang to life, and a babble of words poured into telephones and tape recorders. Then came a lull until the next morsel was offered. Someone proposed a minute of prayer before reporting the death of Pope John, when it came; the proposal was ignored. Someone else kept book on the exact time of death, but he had few takers, for who knew if the Vatican would release the time of death?

But if reporters had a hard time providing grist for the information mills, the visual aspect was even harder to convey. Virtually barred from setting foot within Vatican City walls altogether, the television cameramen and photographers kept vigil in Saint Peter's Square, their lenses trained on the pope's bedroom window. From time to time, an arriving cardinal provided a brief diversion, as he drove through the Vatican gates

in his limousine on his way to see the pope. But the principal
focus of attention was the crowd which, in its prayerful concern for the dying pontiff, proved to be a moving and dignified
subject.

At the stroke of noon on Sunday, the hour when the pope
used to appear at his window, black clouds materialized over
Saint Peter's and a thundershower drove the crowd to shelter
under the colonnade. From their transistors they learned that
Pope John had "serenely entered his death agony." The reality, however, was somewhat less serene. The doctors were
having to remove his urine by a painful process of extraction
in order to prevent his system from becoming poisoned.

His deteriorating state decided them that the time had
come, as a matter of humanity, to stop using every means to
keep the pope alive. The oxygen mask was removed; the mor-
phine injections were stopped. "Clinically, the Holy Father is
already dead," Mazzoni told Capovilla. "He is in the hands
of God."

In the darkened room, kneeling figures prayed for his deliv-
erance: "O God, have pity on Thy servant, Pope John XXIII,
and gather him to your side." Old Monsignor Cavagna, who
knew death when he saw it, knelt very close to the dying man
and whispered prayers into his ear.

A mass for the pope's intentions was to be said in Saint
Peter's Square at seven in the evening, and by late afternoon
crowds had already begun to pour into the square. When Cardinal Traglia, the archpriest of Saint Peter's, mounted the
steps of the altar erected outside the basilica there were over
one hundred thousand present. The statues on the great colonnade glowed golden in the fading sun; the fountains splashed
blissfully around the central obelisk.

In a room adjoining the pope's bedroom, his family, Monsignor Capovilla, and the others had gathered around a television set to follow the mass. From his place near the door,
Gasbarrini heard the Pope's labored breathing suddenly catch
and go silent. The physician hurried into the bedroom, bent

over the pope and took hold of his wrist. There was no pulse. He looked up with tears in his eyes and shook his free hand to the others who had quickly followed him to the bedside. Pope John had died alone.

Capovilla snapped on the lights and called Archbishop Dell'Acqua. With the death of the pontiff, the secretary's official position was automatically at an end. The archbishop arrived immediately. He kissed the dead pope's hand, and then telephoned the dean of the College of Cardinals and the cardinal-chamberlain to assume control of the Church. Then he hurried to where Casimirri and Father Pappalardo were waiting and told them to announce the death of Pope John.

The press office was half empty because several journalists had gone to Saint Peter's Square to hear the mass when the priest who had been acting as official spokesman burst in, waving his arms and wailing, *"E morto! E morto!"* The room scrambled into action; reporters came running in from the square. In his haste, the Associated Press reporter, who had been cradling a telephone receiver and balancing his chair on its rear legs, fell backward.

In Saint Peter's Square, Cardinal Traglia was reading the closing Gospel of Saint John when the crowd noticed the shutters of Pope John's window swing open and the lights go on inside. Even before the announcement came, they knew. A sadness almost palpable in its intensity filled the vast square. Many wept; many others prayed; but the crowd was silent, and as the news spread the silence and the sadness seemed to roll slowly over all of Rome. The clamor of the city paused to mark a moment in its history, the passing of the two hundred sixty-sixth pontiff. Then the bells of its five hundred churches began to toll the chimes of the dead: nine strokes in groups of three, filling the air for half an hour.

At the North American College, where young American Catholics are trained for the priesthood, the seminarians were entering the dining room for their evening meal when the news came. They hurried to Saint Peter's Square, and a group of them brought out their breviaries and began to recite the office of the dead. Later that night, Richard Liddy, a young student at the College, wrote to his parents in New Jersey, "The memories of all the times I had seen him alive came into my mind, of how lively he was when he talked to people, bouncing up and down and gesticulating, and you could watch his feet tapping on the floor when he made a point. I've never read a description of that liveliness or gotten an impression of it from any newspaper accounts."

The Vacant Throne of Peter

At 8:00 P.M. ON THE EVENING OF JUNE 3, Cardinal Benedetto Aloisi Masella, cardinal-chamberlain, or *camerlengo*, of the Holy Roman Church, entered the Vatican Palace. In his hand he carried his staff of office, resembling a marshal's baton, surmounted by an eagle. Immediately the great bronze doors under Bernini's colonnade clanged shut behind him, signaling the start of the Vatican's official period of mourning. Accompanied by Cardinal Tisserant, two curia notaries, and other officials, the *camerlengo* went directly to the dead pontiff who lay in his bed, eyes closed, hands naturally at his side, as if in a deep sleep. In one corner of the now brightly lit bedroom, John's brothers stood motionless, like cart horses waiting for the command to move. The exhausted doctors were slumped in chairs in another corner. Sister Anna wept quietly. Presently, she produced a small pair of scissors from her pocket and snipped a few strands of the pope's hair. These she wrapped in a piece of paper which she buried in the folds of her habit. Then she continued to weep. Also present was the sculptor Manzù. He had been called to make a death mask of Pope John, and was waiting to start work.

Cardinal Masella tapped the pope's forehead three times with a small gold mallet, calling out distinctly to him in Italian: *Roncalli Angelo, sei vivo o morto?* ("Are you dead or alive?") When there was no reply from the bed, the cardinal hit Pope John again with the hammer, repeating the question. *Roncalli Angelo, sei vivo o morto?* After another short pause, he repeated the ritual a third time. *Roncalli Angelo, sei vivo o morto?* Then he solemnly pronounced the words *Vere Papa mortuus est* ("The pope is truly dead.") The ancient formula had neither dignity nor reason for Manzù, who turned to address the doctors in a loud angry voice. *"Porca miseria,* you're here, can't they ask you if he's dead or not?"

In fact, the next step in the procedure was for the *camerlengo* to examine the death certificate drawn up by Gasbarrini. It gave the cause of death as peritoneal complications due to gastric heteroplasia.

Meanwhile, Manzù and two assistants whom he had brought with him quickly prepared the pope's death mask. First, John's face was coated thickly with vaseline. Then a thin nylon cord was placed so that it divided the face vertically in half, running down the brow, along the ridge of the nose, and over the mouth and chin. The nostrils were blocked with cotton and the mouth propped shut with a wooden block placed under the chin. Next, the face was completely encased in plaster to produce a mold of the pope's features for casting in bronze. While the plaster was still soft, the nylon cord was gently pulled up, dividing the mask into two sections that came away easily and well when it had hardened. On impulse, the communist sculptor also made a cast of Pope John's right hand, because it was the hand that had signed *Pacem in Terris.*

But the pope was truly dead, and until the election of a new pontiff, the power was once again vested in Cardinal Aloisi Masella—once again, because he had already been *camerlengo* during the interregnum which followed the death of Pope Pius XII. Masella, seventy-six years old, was the archetypal member of the Roman ecclesiastical elite. A small, urbane aristocrat who owned huge tracts of tobacco land in the Liri Valley south of Rome, he came from a family whose record of service to the papacy went back several generations. His great uncle Gaetano had also been a distinguished cardinal. Aloisi Masella himself attended the Accademia dei Nobili and then went straight into the diplomatic service of the Holy See, eventually serving as nuncio in Portugal, Brazil, and Chile. Pius XII, who was a great admirer of his diplomatic style, called him "the nuncio of the storms," because of his consummate skill in handling difficult situations. In seventeen years as a curia cardinal he had gained a reputation as a moderate. He had been the Curia's candidate for pope in the 1958 conclave, but lost to the man he had now officially pronounced dead.

As *camerlengo*, Aloisi Masella in effect presided over a "caretaker" cabinet of all the members of the Sacred College of Cardinals, meeting in daily general congregations. Their main task during the interregnum was to organize, as soon as possible, a conclave for the election of Pope John's successor. Papal authority, which according to canon law comes directly from Christ through the apostolic succession, does not reside in the cardinals during the vacancy, but is preserved within Christ, to reappear in the person of the individual whom they elect as the next pope.

But until the next pope was elected, the government of the Church was at a virtual standstill, and only essential services could be performed. No briefs, bulls, or other important documents relating to the practice of the faith could be issued; no new arrangements entered into with foreign governments; no alterations undertaken in Saint Peter's basilica or the Apostolic Palace; no new appointments made by the *camerlengo*, or any other official. In fact, most Vatican posts relating to the government of the Church—the eight sacred congregations, the tribunals, secretariats, and other offices—were automatically suspended with the death of the pontiff.

Aside from the *camerlengo* himself, only a handful of senior prelates continued to perform their official duties during the interregnum. The cardinal-chancellor was one; others included the cardinal-vicar of Rome, the pope's immediate subordinate in his capacity as bishop of Rome; and the cardinal-major penitentiary, who has the power to absolve "reserved" sins which other confessors do not, and continues to do so during the interregnum for the good of men's souls. The cardinal-secretary of state handed over most of his functions to the dean of the Sacred College, one of whose first tasks was to send notes to the heads of all friendly governments officially informing them of the death of Pope John: "In accordance with the mysterious disposition of the Divine Will, it has come to pass that the Supreme Pontiff of the Catholic Church, His Holiness Pope John XXIII, has passed away in sanctity . . ."

The pope was truly dead. His body was now in the hands of the Servants of Mary (the Servites), the black-robed friars of the Conventual branch of the Franciscan order, who hear confessions in Saint Peter's in all the major languages. It is their traditional privilege to wash the pontiff's mortal remains and prepare them for burial. On his head was a golden miter, and red gloves and slippers were on his hands and feet. Later, the pope would lie in state in Saint Peter's, but first he was laid out in a hall of the Apostolic Palace to receive the homage of the curia.

The Vatican's security system—Swiss Guards, pontifical gendarmes, iron gates that close at night—has always attracted would-be gatecrashers. For years, the students of the North American College ran a strictly unofficial annual contest to see who could infiltrate the greatest number of papal audiences and liturgical ceremonies. As evidence of success, the gatecrasher had to produce a photograph showing him positioned close to the pontiff. Religious ceremonies in Saint Peter's Square were relatively easy targets. The standard method was to arrive at the basilica carrying a surplice (the short, white garment frequently worn by priests in religious ceremonies), squeeze up to the front of the crowds and, when the papal procession arrived, quickly don the surplice and ease into the line of churchmen. Papal functions inside the Apostolic Palace were a bigger challenge because the aspiring gatecrasher had first to elude the vigilance of the Swiss Guards at the bronze doors who scrutinized all passes with typical thoroughness, and who kept three submachine guns hidden from view inside a large umbrella stand near the door.

Two young Texan student priests were the undisputed champions of their day. A photograph in the 1962 North American College Year Book shows Pope John handing to James Plagens and James Putman a gift which had just been presented to him during a large audience. He had seen them around him so often that he apparently mistook them for members of the ceremonial staff. On the morning following the Pope's death Plagens and Putman resolved to view the pontiff in the Apostolic Palace. This necessitated penetrating deeper into unauthorized territory than they had ever ventured before, but the two young priests saw their exploit as a personal tribute to Pope John. Arriving at the bronze doors, they succeeded in convincing the Swiss Guards on duty that they belonged to the entourage of a prelate who happened at that moment to be entering the building. Once inside, they melted into the flow of churchmen moving through a succession of halls, expecting at any moment to be challenged, until suddenly they found themselves in a chamber where the pope's body lay on a low bier, hands clasped placidly over his stomach. On either side stood a member of the Pontifical Guard. A huge Murano glass chandelier hanging from the ceiling sparkled in the sunlight. Draped behind the dead pontiff was the banner of Venice, his old archdiocese: red and gold with the winged lion of Saint Mark. Along the walls were six altars at which masses for the dead were said throughout the day.

For some time, Plagens and Putman stood in a corner watching cardinals, bishops and diplomats arrive, kiss the Pope's red-slippered right foot, and kneel briefly in prayer. Two Vatican officials then guided each visitor unobtrusively toward the exit. At last, the young Americans mustered the courage to approach the pope, and this time there was no photographer to record their quiet farewell. As the two of them walked slowly back out of the Apostolic Palace and into Saint Peter's Square, they came to a solemn decision: this was to be their last gatecrash.

Messages of sympathy poured into the Vatican, including a brief tribute from Nikita Khrushchev which was subsequently published in the Soviet press. Catholics in Eastern Europe found themselves in rare agreement with their communist regimes as, taking their cue from Moscow, each one saluted the dead pope. The Hungarian party paper described him as "a wise, far-sighted, and respected political personality." In Poland, where many buildings were decked with Polish banners and black crepe streamers, the party paper *Trybuna Ludu* reported that there was "deep grief not only among believers but also all people who followed with admiration and sympathy [John's] efforts for the cause of peace and peaceful coexistence." After announcing that Pope John had died, Warsaw radio canceled its programs of light music for the remainder of the day, replacing them with sterner classical stuff.

Though it was not mentioned in the communist press, the future of Vatican relations with Eastern Europe now depended wholly on John's successor, who was in no way committed to pursue the dead pontiff's policies. A conservative pope could put the clock back at will to the cold war days of Pius XII; but until a new pope had been elected, negotiations in Hungary, Poland, and Yugoslavia, all of which were being carried out by Monsignor Casaroli, were frozen. Word went out to East European diplomats in Rome to lobby for the election of a pope who was interested in advancing the new detente between the Church and Eastern Europe's communist regimes. With no direct relations with the Holy See, and very limited access to cardinals, Eastern European diplomats could achieve little except through the cooperation of friendly diplomatic missions such as those of Cuba and Egypt. The Russians found themselves bereft of their best Vatican contact: on the night following John's death Loris Capovilla quietly left the papal apartments and found temporary shelter with Cardinal Gustavo Testa, Pope John's Curia friend, until the new pontiff, following tradition, determined his future. (With him went many of Pope John's personal papers, including his spiritual diary, later to be published under the title *Diary of a Soul,* and his private day-to-day diary.)

In the White House, John's death produced a guarded sense of relief, for Kennedy had not been altogether comfortable at the prospect of his forthcoming private audience with the pope. A short message of condolence was sent to the cardinal-dean. The text had been prepared for President Kennedy's signature by the State Department as soon as it was known that John's end was approaching. Kennedy deleted one sentence from the submitted draft, the only reference to the pope's work in the area of international affairs. The sentence read: "We recognize him as a man who dedicated himself until the last moment to the search for peace in this troubled world."

The pope's aspirations as a mediator found a brief, ironic echo at the Geneva Disarmament Talks when the United States and Soviet delegates briefly put aside their differences in order to pay tribute to his work for peace.

These sympathetic comments from the Communist bloc did nothing to improve the rapidly deteriorating relations between Moscow and Peking. To the Chinese, it was another indication of Soviet decline into decadence. Mao's China ignored the pope's death altogether, but the Hong Kong communist paper *Ching Po,* commenting on Khrushchev's tribute to the pope, suggested sneeringly that the Soviet leader's next move ought to be "to baptize the Soviet people as another step toward capitalism." *Ching Po* told Khrushchev: "Go to the Vatican, and walk behind the leaders of the Christian world and offer congratulations to the new pope."

On the evening of June 3, Pope John's body was carried in procession to Saint Peter's Basilica to lie in state. He was borne on a bier down the main staircase of the Apostolic Palace, through the bronze doors and into the square on the shoulders of the same *sediati* who had kept him aloft in the *sedia gestatoria* which he so disliked. As his body—cold, white, and lifeless—bobbed gently above the heads of the huge crowd, with the band playing Chopin's Funeral March, more than one observer noted the tight little smiles on the faces of his vehement and sometimes venomous Curia opponents. To many of those who identified him with the upheaval provoked in the Church by the Vatican Council, his death seemed an act of Providence. The council was automatically suspended when the pope died, and conservative hopes hinged on electing a successor who would not reconvene it.

At the door of the basilica, the bier was turned around so that the pope would enter feet first. John was carried between the rows of empty green council seats looking, in his own phrase, "like ploughed furrows waiting for a fresh seeding," and placed on a catafalque under the black spiral columns of Bernini's great dome, while the choir of the Sistine Chapel intoned the 129th Psalm, *De Profundis:* "Out of the depths I have cried to thee, O Lord: Lord, hear my voice . . . With the Lord there is mercy: and with him plentiful redemption."

For the next two days and nights, a river of humanity flowed gently through the main doors of Saint Peter's and down the nave thirty abreast to where Pope John XXIII lay in state, his face pasta-white against the red cushion on which his head rested, his gold vestments glowing brightly in the spotlights. Twenty tall candles burned around him—six in front of the tall catafalque, six more behind it, and four on each side of it. A quartet of pontifical guards stood one at each corner, and three feet away from them, four Swiss Guards, their halberds resting point-downwards on the ground; then four Palatine Guards in their dark blue tunics and black shakos, and finally four private chamberlains of the papal household wearing red damask surcoats and knee breeches. More than a million people interrupted their daily routine to say a last, silent goodbye to the fatherly old pope. Like the crowd that would come to receive his Sunday morning blessing, it was a human patchwork of priests, nuns, tourists, mothers with small children, soldiers, students, workers and members of the Roman nobility. Some clutched rosaries or prayer books, but many more brought their shopping baskets or their work tools, and although it was one of the biggest crowds in Rome's recent history—about half its total population, it was reported—it was also remarkably orderly. However, between 6:00 A.M. on June 5, when the basilica opened, to 10:00 P.M. on June 6, when the lying in state ended, 504 people reported having been robbed in Saint Peter's.

Meanwhile, the Sacred College had begun to hold daily meetings or general congregations to handle the affairs of the vacant See. Thirty-two cardinals took the traditional oath of secrecy at the first general congregation, mostly members of the Roman curia, and therefore residents of the Eternal City. Twenty-one were Italians, three French, three Spanish, two British, one Armenian, one Argentinian, one Portuguese, and one German. Seated around a hollow rectangular table in the Consistorial Hall of the Vatican Palace, they were an unusually sober sight, having exchanged the iridescence of their customary scarlet silk for woolen cassocks in violet, the liturgical color of mourning. Cardinal Aloisi Masella presided in his capacity of visible head of the Roman Church during the interregnum, but all decisions were taken by vote, sometimes only after considerable debate in Latin, the only permitted language of business. Drawing up and approving detailed plans for the Pope's burial and the conclave in this way—the principal task of the daily congregations—was a long and difficult undertaking. It would have been impossible without frequent recourse to the monumental dictionary used in producing the Latin versions of papal documents (*Lexicon Eorum Vocabulorum Quae Difficilius Latinae Redduntur*), highly esteemed by classical scholars. But even this demonstrates how difficult it is to express fully contemporary ideas in the language of Cicero and Erasmus. For example, *imaginum transmissio per electricas undas* seems a rather roundabout way to express "television," while *mundanus* for "international" and *Australasia* for "Australia" are among the many misleading translations.

By tradition, the congregation's first task was to destroy the seal in the heavy fisherman's ring bearing the image of Peter the Apostle casting his net and used by the pope to seal official documents. It was crushed in an old iron press and the pieces shown to each cardinal in turn. This was not, as one might suppose, a symbolic act to mark the end of the pontificate. Its origins went back to more turbulent times when the death of a pope was sometimes followed by a power struggle in the papal court, and the pope's personal seal was destroyed to prevent the forging of documents. During the vacancy, the cardinal-chamberlain uses his own seal consisting of a parasol and the crossed papal keys (the parasol being an ancient symbol of authority which originated in China).

The transitional nature of the vacancy was underlined when the cardinals, at their first congregation, picked June 19 as the start of the conclave, thus extending the interregnum almost to its limit of eighteen days after the pope's death laid down by the constitution governing papal elections; but the cardinals had to allow sufficient time for the construction of the largest and most complex conclave area in the history of papal elections. Until 1922, the conclave had had to begin within ten days. In that year the deadline was extended to between fifteen and eighteen days because the newly created North American cardinals often failed to make the Atlantic crossing in time. In 1914, all three cardinals from Canada and the United States arrived in Rome after the election of the new pope, and in 1922 Cardinal O'Connell of Boston missed his second papal conclave, after which Bostonians nicknamed him "Gangplank Billy."

At the next daily general congregation, the first four new arrivals took their places alongside the Curia cardinals. They were Ritter of St. Louis, Mayer of Chicago, Doepfner of Munich, and Lienart of Lille, all critics of the Curia during the Vatican Council debates—especially Lienart. In the days that followed, other cardinals arrived in Rome and the progressive voice in the government of the leaderless church grew stronger. But even so, the governing council of cardinals tended to be conservative by mandate as well as by composition. They were little more than custodians of the status quo, with no authority to introduce new measures or promulgate changes. Moreover, the Curia cardinals had the advantage of familiarity with the bureaucratic system, which responded less promptly to outsiders, even cardinals.

But even within these limitations, the range of decisions taken was wide and the problems discussed were many and varied. Some topics were introduced for the sole purpose of hearing the views of potential candidates for the papacy, but the general congregations also confronted some complex situations. For example, Archbishop John Heenan of Westminster approached the apostolic delegate seeking guidance because, for the first time since the Reformation, a memorial service was to be held for the dead pontiff in Westminster Abbey and the Anglican hierarchy invited the Catholic hierarchy to send representatives.

Heenan's dilemma was not whether to accept the invitation —to do otherwise would have run counter to the very spirit of Pope John's pontificate—but at what level. In other words, he wanted to know who was to represent the English Catholics. The apostolic delegate relayed Henan's question to Rome, and it was debated at length during one of the general congregations. To the cardinals, the decision was important because it would establish a precedent for other requests for similar ecumenical services which, given Pope John's universal popularity, were certain to be many. Progressive cardinals felt that since John was the ecumenical pope, English churchmen ought to go to Westminster Abbey. The conservative view was that the presence of senior Catholic clergy at the Anglican service would be dangerously premature. In the end, the more cautious approach prevailed, and the cardinals instructed Heenan that a delegation of prominent English Catholic laymen ought to be present at Westminster Abbey, but no clergy.

The cardinals also tackled the question of Cardinal Mindszenty. The cardinal had learned the news of Pope John's death from a Radio Free Europe broadcast. He looked out of the window and noted that the number of police cars outside the legation had increased to five. "Very soon," he told Owen T. Jones, the American *chargé d'affaires ad interim* in Budapest, "I shall receive a message from Rome that I must attend the conclave. The increase in the number of police outside means that the regime is still determined to arrest me."

Jones did his best to calm the cardinal's nerves. But the American diplomat also drafted a telegram to Washington urging the State Department to take advantage of the moment and offer to negotiate Mindszenty's safe conduct on Rome's behalf. The cardinal's departure, Jones argued, would remove a major obstacle in the way of improving American-Hungarian relations. It was his view that, far from wishing to recapture the cardinal, the Hungarian regime was equally anxious to have him out of Hungary as a prelude to normalizing relations with the United States. The Hungarians would readily allow him to leave, as long as he did so quietly, and for good.

Washington's reply was to take issue with Jones's assertion that the cardinal was a factor in relations between Hungary and the United States. "While the solution to the Mindszenty problem would be helpful it is in no way indispensable to . . . future progress in improvement of bilateral relations," Jones was told. "To view the matter otherwise would be tantamount to making United States actions and policies in Hungarian affairs ultimately dependent on the cardinal's wishes and decisions."

Jones, however, knew better. Over the years, Hungarian

officials had made it clear to American diplomats that there could be no question of normal relations while Cardinal Mindszenty continued to be harbored in the United States legation. As a result, the flow of business between the two governments was limited to essentials. Hungary's continuous refusal to accept the nomination of a United States ambassador to Budapest was one of the consequences of the Mindszenty question. Bilateral negotiations on trade and other questions were either frozen in their 1956 positions, when they were interrupted by the popular uprising.

What was behind the State Department's extraordinary contention that Mindszenty's presence in the legation for the past eight years had not acted as a brake on relations between the two countries? Could Washington really have believed that this state of affairs, unprecedented in postwar diplomacy, had not upset the waters? Left to make their own professional decisions, the foreign policy experts of Foggy Bottom would have reached a different conclusion, but the question of whether or not to press the Vatican for Mindszenty's departure within the context of the forthcoming conclave was discussed at a meeting of the National Security Council chaired by Kennedy. The meeting rejected Owen Jones's thesis and decreed that no initiative whatsoever should be taken in the matter.

This instruction was communicated to the embassy in Rome in a secret telegram personally approved by the secretary of state:

DEPARTMENT DOES NOT REPEAT NOT PLAN ANY INITIATIVE EITHER THROUGH ESTABLISHED CHANNEL HERE OR THROUGH EMBASSY ROME TO RAISE QUESTION OF ATTENDANCE BY CARDINAL MINDSZENTY AT CONCLAVE FOR ELECTION NEW POPE. EMBASSY SHOULD TAKE NO INITIATIVE IN SOUNDING OUT VATICAN VIEWS OR INTENTION THIS MATTER.

ON OTHER HAND IF VATICAN OFFICIALS APPROACH EMBASSY IN MATTER, YOU SHOULD ACCEPT WHATEVER MES-

SAGE IS GIVEN YOU AND INFORM BOTH DEPARTMENT
ANDLEGATION BUDAPEST. THE EMBASSY AND LEGATION
SHOULD THEN AWAIT SPECIFIC INSTRUCTIONS. IF SUCH
VATICAN APPROACH INCLUDES VATICAN INQUIRY OR RE-
QUEST RE U.S. COOPERATION AIMED AT ARRANGEMENTS,
SUCH AS THOSE SOUGHT IN OCTOBER 1958, PERMITTING
CARDINAL MINDSZENTY DEPART HUNGARY UNDER HUN-
GARIAN GUARANTEE SAFE CONDUCT AND PROCEED ROME
TAKE PART IN ELECTION NEW POPE, EMBASSY AUTHO-
RIZED ASSURE VATICAN OF U.S. READINESS COOPERATE
EVERY POSSIBLE APPROPRIATE WAY.

IN EVENT LOCAL PRESS INQUIRIES ON QUESTION
MINDSZENTY'S ATTENDANCE AT FORTHCOMING CON-
CLAVE, EMBASSY AND LEGATION BUDAPEST SHOULD SAY
THAT THIS IS STRICTLY CHURCH AFFAIR AND HENCE U.S.
COMMENT INAPPROPRIATE.

As usual, the Kennedy administration was anxious to avoid
any whiff of Catholic church involvement in American foreign
policy. The ghost of the papacy was ever present in the White
House. Sporadic alarms of suspicious Vatican activity on
American shores kept Kennedy wary of letting down his
guard. Only a month before, his opponents had fomented a
hue and cry when *Immobiliare Generale,* an Italian real estate
company in which the Vatican held the controlling interest,
broke ground for a huge apartment complex in Washington D.C. The pope, it was said, was attempting to establish a
foothold in the capital. The apartment complex was named
Watergate.

As it turned out, the White House decision suited the Vatican's purpose well, for the cardinals themselves had already
decided that, unless there was pressure to do so from Washington, it was not in the Church's best interests to try to persuade Mindszenty to leave Budapest. The Hungarian Primate
was Rome's best card in the negotiations with the regime. But
the negotiations could not be resumed until a new pontiff was

elected and, consequently, the cardinals could obtain no concessions in return for Mindszenty's departure.

On June 14, in the early morning, a message clattered on the legation telex in Budapest. It was addressed to Cardinal Mindszenty. It read:

AD NORMAM CONSTITUTIONIS VACANTIS APOSTOLICAE SEDIS HONORI MIHI CUCO TECUM COMMUNICARE PUR-PURATORUM PATRUM CONCLAVE ELIGENDO PONTIFICI SUMMUS: QUIC DESIDERATISSIMUS IOANNI XXIII SUCCE-DAT. DIE XIX HUIUS MENSIS JUNII HORA DECIMA SEPTA IN ALDIBUS APOSTOLICAS VATICANUS INITIUM ESSE SUMP-TURUM: SACRUM CARDINALIUM COLLEGIUM IN FRA-TERNA RECORDIATIONE ATQUE FUSIS PRECIPUS AD DIVINAM PARACLITUM HISCE DIEBUS TIBI ANIMO ARCTIS-SIME CONIUNCTUM MANET CARDINALIS TISSERANT DE-CANUS.*

The text was immediately relayed to Washington with a request not only for a translation—there being no Latinists in the U.S. Legislation—but also for guidance. Meanwhile, in response to the cardinal's usual inquiries, the staff lied cheer-fully that nothing had arrived for him from the Vatican. It was after eight that evening when Jones, on instructions from Washington, handed the telegram to Mindszenty. The cardi-nal read it through carefully, noting with visible relief that it contained no summons to Rome. "Very nice, very nice," he repeated several times.

Perhaps hoping for an unexpected change of heart, Jones said, "If you wish to go to Rome, my government would be

* "In accordance with the norms of the constitution of the Vacant Apostolic See, I have the honor to inform you that the conclave of cardinals for the election of the supreme pontiff to succeed the most loved John XXIII begins on the nineteenth day of this month of June at 17:00 in the Vatican Apostolic Palace. The Sacred College of Cardinals remains united with you in brotherly remembrance, and in prayer with the Holy Spirit. Cardinal Tisserant, Dean."

happy to try to arrange a safe conduct for you. But there has been no request to do so from the Holy See."

The dark clouds rushed back to Mindszenty's face. "Does your government wish me to leave?"

Not at all, the American replied. His government wished merely to accommodate the cardinal.

There was no need, Mindszenty said. No need at all. As for the message from the Vatican, he would prepare a note of thanks in a day or two; there was no hurry.

Two days later, the Hungarian primate sent thanks to the Sacred College and said he would pray to the Holy Spirit to guide them in their choice of a new pontiff.

Despite the continuous speculation, the Vatican kept quiet about the prospects of Mindszenty's appearance in Rome. On June 16, the cardinals drew lots for their cells in the conclave. Mindszenty was allotted cell 21, a room with two windows which was the office of the prelate in charge of issuing tickets for papal audiences, but observant reporters noted that the new mattress on the narrow bed had not been removed from its plastic wrapping.

CHAPTER IX

Princes of the Church

THE POPE IS AN ABSOLUTE MONARCH. There is no legislature in the Roman Catholic church. He is advised, not constitutionally imposed upon by lawmakers, and his principal advisers are the cardinals. This function is theirs by long tradition. In early Christian times a cardinal was any member of the clergy permanently appointed, or *incardinato*—the Latin word meaning hinged—to a parish church; hence, it is generally believed, the origin of the term *cardinal*. Its application was gradually narrowed down to the clergy of Rome, until, by the twelfth century, it had come to signify one of the forty-five members of the senate of the Church, in other words, the Sacred College.

The three orders or ranks into which this body is divided— cardinal-bishops, cardinal-priests, and cardinal-deacons—correspond to the three categories into which the Roman clergy was divided: the bishops of the seven sees near Rome known as the suburbicarian dioceses; the twenty-five priests of the city's parishes; and the thirteen district deacons whose business it was to care for the poor. The seven dioceses were, and still are, Ostia, Velletri, Palestrina, Albano, Sabina-Poggio

Mirteto, Frascati, Porto-Santa Rufina. Because of their situation near the city, a close relationship developed between their incumbents and the bishop of Rome, that is, the pope. Today, these dioceses are held by the cardinal-bishops, the loftiest of the three ranks. Until Pope John's pontificate they had the care, as well as the title of these ancient sees, the dean of the Sacred College always holding Ostia. But by the early 1960s many of them had grown into important suburbs, and the pope felt that they needed the attention of a resident bishop, leaving the cardinals—all of them Curia cardinals—with only the title. Cardinal Tisserant made no secret of his disappointment at being deprived of his diocese of Ostia which for over twenty years had been one of his main concerns.

The link with the ancient clergy of Rome is further maintained in the fact that cardinal-priests and cardinal-deacons on their elevation are each assigned a church in Rome and become its protector, whether they reside in the city or not. A common Vatican practice in Pope John's day was to entrust any Roman church in need of costly repairs to an American cardinal, who was automatically assumed to be wealthy and could be counted upon to contribute toward the cost of the work; or even to go the whole hog as Cardinal Spellman had done. Spellman had restored his titular church, Saint John and Paul on the Gianiculum Hill, to its former baroque splendor out of his own pocket.

The number of cardinals was raised to seventy in 1586 by Pope Sixtus, and remained fixed at that number until Pope John XXIII increased it to ninety. In the first of the three consistories of his pontificate, held two months after his election, he distributed a record number of fifty-four red hats. The new cardinals were drawn from the papal diplomatic service, the Vatican congregations, and the archbishoprics of the Church at large. The papal envoy to a country considered important to the Vatican's interests could still reasonably expect to receive a red hat at the end of his tour of duty, as Pope

John himself had done on leaving Paris. So could a prelate who had risen to the top of one of the Roman congregations, as Cardinal Ottaviani had done in the Holy Office.

But beginning with Pius XII's pontificate, the number of archbishops outside Rome "raised to the purple" had increased significantly. The purpose of this shift in emphasis was to make the Sacred College more representative of the whole Church. As a result, already under Pope Pius the Italian cardinals had lost their majority. Pope John widened the gap still further. When he died, the College was the largest and the most international it had ever been. Out of eighty-five cardinals, more than half owed their elevation to him. Thirty-five were Italians, while the remaining fifty came from seventeen other countries, including the first cardinal from the Indian sub-continent, Cardinal Valerian Gracias, the Archbishop of Bombay, and the first black cardinal in modern times (although some of the early popes could have been black).

In the long ceremony of his elevation (since modified) each cardinal used to have to kneel at the feet of the pontiff who opened and shut the prelate's mouth three times. This was meant to signify the cardinal's newly acquired right to participate in the secret deliberations of the Sacred College, presided over by the pope, but a cardinal's finest hour comes when the Throne of Saint Peter is vacant and he is called upon, along with his fellow cardinals, to choose a successor to the Apostle. This function, too, is theirs by long tradition. They were confirmed as the exclusive electors of the popes by the Third Lateran Council of 1179. Before that, popes had been chosen in turn by acclamation, by the emperors of the declining Roman Empire, the German kings, the Roman nobility, the medieval kings, the emperors of the Holy Roman Empire, and by designation of the predecessor. Acts of violence frequently accompanied the pope's accession, such as when Saint Damasus, an austere Spanish monk, was acclaimed pope by the Roman clergy in the fourth century. The enraged supporters of another of the leading contenders, Ursinicus, invaded the churches of Rome, murdering hundreds of priests and worshipers.

Modern conclaves are more orderly affairs and also much shorter, usually lasting a few days. Leo XIII, in 1876, was elected pope in thirty-six hours, and Pius XII in thirty, on the eve of World War II. The conclaves of Pope Pius XI and Pope John XXIII both took three days, but it was not always thus. The early conclaves sometimes took months to reach a decision, complicated by the cardinals' zest for intrigue, and the power plays of Europe's kings and princelings. Urban IV was elected after three months. His successor, Clement IV's conclave lasted four months. Then in the thirteenth century, impatient pilgrims hit upon the idea of locking up the cardinals in order to hasten their decision, and this became an institution in 1274 after one of the most famous conclaves in papal history.

When Pope Clement IV died in 1268, none of the eighteen cardinals meeting in the Umbrian town of Viterbo had much stomach for the task of guiding the church through the stormy years of the late Middle Ages. Thus the conclave dragged on without a decision, the months becoming a year, and then two years, while the affairs of the church were left untended. A procession of crowned heads, among them the king of France, journeyed to Viterbo to impress upon the cardinals that the times demanded a strong hand at the helm of Saint Peter's Barque, but the deadlock could not be broken.

With no supreme authority to impose the law, the atmosphere became bitter and explosive. Old feuds began to surface. One morning, while the cardinals were at mass, Cardinal Guy de Montfort sidled up to Prince Henry of Cornwall, an enemy of his family, and stabbed him in the heart. The alarmed people of Viterbo consulted the Franciscan Saint Bonaventure who advised them to follow the example of the pilgrims at some recent conclaves and lock the electors in the papal palace. When even this failed to accelerate the decision, all the doors and windows were walled in, and food was passed to the cardinals through a rotating hatch. A special guard was formed to ensure their isolation. At least one other cardinal died inside—apparently from natural causes—but still there was no election.

Meals were reduced to one a day, sometimes consisting of only bread and water. As a last resort, in the fall of 1271, the Viterbesi climbed on the roof and dismantled it tile by tile, exposing the interior to the oncoming rains. The cardinals attempted to resolve the situation by offering the papacy to Saint Philip Benizi, a figure of great piety in a troubled age, but he got wind of their intentions and went into hiding. At the end of three and a half years, they agreed on a compromise candidate who was neither a cardinal, nor even a priest, but Tebaldo Visconti, the Papal legate in Syria. He accepted and took the name of Gregory X. The new pope immediately enshrined the measures taken by the people of Viterbo in an historic decree governing future papal elections entitled *Ubi Periculum Maius*. In it, the term conclave—from the Latin *clavis* (key) meaning a locked place—was used for the first time in connection with the choice of a pontiff.

Pope Gregory's fifteen rules were simple, detailed, and severe. The cardinals were required to convene "in the very building where the pope had lived," and to occupy a hall or space sufficiently large to accommodate them "in common, without dividing walls, curtains, or other fabric between them, with only one private room, and completely locked in so that no one can get either in or out." Outside contact was forbidden, and food was passed to the electors through a window kept open for the purpose. Each cardinal was allowed to take into the conclave two assistants, or "conclavists." Voting was to begin immediately to elect a new pontiff, who had to receive two thirds of the ballot. "Three days after the cardinals have entered the conclave," the decree stipulated, "if no new pontiff has been elected, the priests and others responsible for the supervision of the conclave must prevent more than one dish being prepared for the cardinals' meals, either at lunch or dinner for the next five days. When these five days have elapsed they will allow them nothing but bread and water until the election has been concluded." The rules went into force for the first time following Gregory X's death, and his successor, Pope Innocent V, was elected in a matter of hours.

After that, practice often ignored precept as the cardinals once more fell into their dilatory ways. The election of Nicholas III in 1277 took six months, as did that of the next pontiff, Martin IV. After the death of Honorius IV in 1287, the papacy remained vacant for eleven months until at last the cardinals settled on Pope Nicholas IV. When *he* died, there was another long interregnum, this time lasting twenty-seven months, before his successor, Saint Celestine V, was chosen. The next pope, Boniface VIII, reaffirmed the rules of the conclave. Their gradual acceptance thereafter (with occasional lapses) owed much to the growing realization among the princes of the church that the system reinforced their position as an electoral elite with full control of the papal succession.

Various pontiffs have taken much of the rigor out of Gregory X's fifteen rules. The cardinals are no longer required to live in one room, for example, and the bread-and-water diet has also been abolished, but the emphasis on complete isolation to ensure a secret ballot free from outside pressure still forms the basis of modern day papal elections. It is this isolation which perpetuates the principle of physical discomfort as an incentive to reaching a quick decision.

In the eighteenth and nineteenth centuries, popes were elected in the Quirinal Palace, then the papal summer palace, now the official residence of the president of Italy, but following the unification of Italy and the consequent dissolution of the Papal States, the pontiff withdrew in protest inside the walls of Vatican City. As a result, all conclaves beginning with that of Pius IX in 1876 have taken place in roughly the same area of the Apostolic Palace that is closest to the Sistine Chapel, where the cardinals vote.

As preparation of that same conclave area proceeded apace,

speculation over who would be the next pope reached its peak. It seemed that everyone in Rome had a theory—including the Central Intelligence Agency. The following was included in Kennedy's weekend reading folder for June 15–16:

Information Report
CENTRAL INTELLIGENCE AGENCY

Country: Italy   Report No TDCS DB–3/654,973
Subject: Successor to John XXIII
         Situation appraisal
Source: Staff officer of this organization. Commentary.

Following is a [CIA] appraisal of the present situation. It is not an official judgment by this Agency or any component. It represents the observations and interpretations of a staff officer based on information available to him at the time of its preparation. Prepared for internal use, this commentary is disseminated in the belief that it may be useful to the Department of State in assessing the situation for its purposes.

Based on background knowledge, exhaustive scanning of the press, and discussions with personalities in various fields, the following speculations concerning the successor of Pope John XXIII are offered.

A complicating factor in predicting who the next pope will be is the increased size of the College of Cardinals, which is now 82, compared to 55 in 1958. The average time that the 1958 group had been cardinals was much longer than the average for the present group. Moreover, in 1958, it was easier to identify each of the cardinals with one of three major categories: Liberal, Conservative, or Moderate. The present College contains 44 cardinals created by Pope John XXIII, but some are far from being in the Liberal group . . .

The possibility of a non-Italian pope might be examined first. As in 1958, this is a subject of great speculation in the press and among "experts." In our opinion, such an eventuality is unlikely. Pope John's reign has shown that renovation which has been sought for years and which had often been identified with the possible accession of a non-Italian, can take place with an Italian. The problem is now seen to be the internationalization of the Curia, which can be undertaken by anyone following in Pope John's footsteps. It therefore seems less likely than in 1958 that a non-Italian will be elected. We believe that the desire for a non-Italian pope is not really strong among cardinals, who are not interested in resurrecting national problems, problems that have been buried for centuries.

The Italian popes of this century have not given cause to regret that they have been nationalistic and continuation of the Italian tradition now would save the Church from new difficulties. Even the Curia problem is not one of Italian nationality, but rather its narrow tradition in connection with the Roman bureaucracy. It is difficult to see how non-Italians could agree among themselves who should have the honor of being the first to break the Italian tradition, and such an attempt would almost certainly cause Italians to close ranks and block it . . .

A prime consideration is certain to be the next pope's attitude toward Vatican Council II and Pope John's policies in general. We think that the prevailing mood will be to continue them, but perhaps to check certain aspects which many cardinals, including some Italian, think have gone too far. This is especially true with respect to Church relations with the Communist world, which seems to have created some chinks in the non-Italian Liberal front. Even if Pope John's successor is committed to his general policies, the tendency is usually to go more slowly and to take stock.

It might also be said that what is needed now is not further innovation, but implementation. It is difficult to see how the conclave can ignore the fact that Pope John's reign has created a definite worldwide image of the papacy and of great expectations and that they now must in some manner be carried forward. It might be argued that cardinals have never shown themselves to be overly concerned with public opinion, but public opinion regarding the Church has never been brought to bear nor stirred up to the extent it has in recent years . . .

A number of cardinals probably would be ruled out at once because of age or infirmities. It does not seem likely that an interim candidate will be sought, barring an unbreakable deadlock, since what Pope John's policies need now is continuity. It is felt that the average age of serious contenders will be at least lower than John's was and that it will tend more to return to what has been the age of popes over the last 150 years. While this might appear arbitrary, it would eliminate 15 of 28 Italians, some of whom are not likely candidates for other considerations of health and policies also: Morano, Fossati, Pizzardo, Micara, Masella, Bracci, Chiarlo, Cicognani, Valeri, Cento, Di Jorio, Ciriaci, Bacci, Testa, and Ruffini. All of the foregoing are over 75.

Of the 13 remaining Italians, Castaldi, Ottaviani, and Traglia might be eliminated because they are known as definite opponents of Pope John's policies. The one remaining well known conservative, Siri of Genoa, might also be eliminated because of his relative youth, as well as his opposition to Pope John. However, the Conservative group among Italians is strong and Siri has many friends abroad. This, together with his undoubted personal qualifications and his proven ability to lean toward the more moderate wing of the conservatives, gives him some chance.

Among the strongly committed Liberals, Montini of Milan stands out and almost everyone queried comes up with his name sooner rather than later. Montini is certainly going into the conclave as the favorite of the masses. Against Montini there might be the consideration that he is too committed and has overextended himself on the Italian scene. Also, the Council must have given all the cardinals opportunities to get to know each other and, unlike past conclaves, it will not be necessary to form opinions at the last minute. Perhaps some of the alleged pettiness that his fellow Italian cardinals have reportedly frequently observed in Montini has also been apparent to non-Italians. Montini's record at Milan has also not appeared brilliant when compared with records of other heads of large dioceses, particularly foreign ones. In addition, Montini is certainly going to be opposed to the end by the majority of Italians, who can probably force a compromise candidate through if they insist. In this effort they are almost certain of the support of the Spaniards, many Latin Americans, and perhaps two North Americans. Urbani of Venice, a Liberal, is almost too young and suffers from coming from the same city as Pope John. The stock of the other Liberal diocesan cardinal, Lercaro (of Bologna), has gone down consistently in recent years.

In the Curia there are a number of unknowns, in the sense that the public at least has not had an opportunity in the relatively short time they have been cardinals to form firm judgments on where the cardinals stand on the issues at stake . . . Confalonieri of the (Sacred Congregation of) the Consistory, Marella, Archpriest of Saint

Peter's, and Antoniutti, who serves on a number of Congregations, are three definite possibilities. All three are acceptable to the Conservatives, but are open minded and inclined to follow Pope John's ideas with certain modifications which would not prejudice the Liberals against them. Marella and Antoniutti particularly have wide experience abroad in papal diplomatic service, but Antoniutti may suffer for his service in Spain. Marella, on the other hand, seems to have been popular in Paris, his last post, and is reportedly acceptable to French.

In brief, the following seem to be the most probable candidates: Siri, likeliest of the Conservatives; Montini, favorite of the Liberals; Confalonieri, Marella, Antoniutti, three logical compromise candidates from the Curia; Giobbe, Forni, and Ferretto, three unknowns who are at least in the running, based on age. To this group must be added Agagianian and Alfrink as the most likely non-Italians.

The report ended with the results of a straw poll of the CIA's best Italian sources and paid informers—its network of "friendly" politicians; members of SID, the Italian counter-intelligence service; churchmen; and others. Though the majority said they preferred Cardinal Siri, most predicted with regret that Cardinal Montini would be the next pope.

Thorough and painstaking, the agency's assessment offered no new insights into the pre-conclave negotiations. It was an outsider's view—a distant account of the fray that brought no whiff of the gunpowder from the big guns. If the CIA numbered any cardinals among its contacts they were evidently on the fringes of the action. A strong bias ran through its seven pages, either its own or that of the station's Italian informers, who tended to be right of center. This was especially true of the agency's SID contacts. (The cynical view of the Italian counterintelligence was that it was split into three factions: the right wing worked for the CIA; the center for the French secret service; the left for Soviet intelligence; and none of it for the Italian government).

This explains the agency's belief that Cardinal Siri was the conservative candidate, for the brilliant, lantern jawed Archbishop of Genoa and chairman of the Italian Bishops' Conference filled the right-wing political bill to perfection. Siri led the opposition among many Italian bishops to Pope John's policy of *disimpegno*, detachment from Italy's national political affairs. Churchmen who wanted to continue the offensive against communism looked to Siri for leadership, and he was not inhibited about giving it. With this political crusade went a rigid and unbending attitude toward change in the Church and a distaste for the innovations promulgated by the Vatican Council. In 1963, evening mass had still to be introduced in the archdiocese of Genoa because the archbishop disapproved of it.

It was true, as the report stated, that Siri's political and pastoral conservatism won him many friends in the Spanish and Latin American hierarchies, but in asserting that he had shown himself capable of leaning toward the more moderate wing of the conservatives, the CIA was being taken in by the wishful thinking of its right-wing Italian sources, for Siri had a reputation for unrelenting inflexibility.

On June 16, it was reported that a group of prominent Italian, Spanish, and South American conservatives or—as they were often called, *integralists*—had held a pre-conclave conclave of their own, presided over by Cardinal Ottaviani. Their purpose was to pick a politically realistic candidate, one capable of attracting the support of moderate or *centrist* cardinals and hopefully creating a bandwagon situation that would win over the less committed progressives. It was a strategy that virtually ruled out the most prominent conservatives, among them Cardinal Siri.

The conservative choice fell on Cardinal Ildebrando Antoniutti, a pale, subtle diplomat who owed his emergence to the support of the Spanish and South American cardinals. Antoniutti had spent nine years as nuncio in Madrid, until Pope John made him a cardinal in 1962 and he received his red *biretta* from his personal friend, General Franco. Earlier in his career, Antoniutti had been apostolic delegate in Canada and spoke good English and Eskimo; he had translated the Bible into Eskimo. His conservative backers evidently hoped that his Canadian experience would be a point in his favor with the North American cardinals.

Antoniutti was never publicly identified as the *integralist* candidate. The technique was for conservative cardinals to mention his name as the choice of the moderate group, but liberal lobbyists and supporters began to point out that Antoniutti's name was on the reactionary letter to Pope John. Xerox copies of an address full of ringing triumphalism delivered on October 28, 1962, at the Lateran University surfaced all over the Vatican, and virtually every cardinal received one. This was an age, Antoniutti had said, in which "errors are so many ... while the one and indivisible truth of the Church conserves the freshness of its originality, the glow of its most pure light, the perfume of its imperishable substance."

As for Christian unity, Antoniutti had declared at the Lateran, "it is not possible unless those who are outside the Church accept the unity of the faith with a measure of humility." Hardly an echo of Pope John's open door ecumenical policy. Rome bookmakers gave odds of fifteen to one on Antoniutti.

In the forthcoming conclave, Antoniutti could count on the awesome solidity of the Italian Curia group, buttressed by all but one of the Spanish cardinals, the majority of the South American cardinals, four Italian pastoral cardinals, and one each from Ireland, the Philippines, and the United States to total thirty-four. The liberal group, often called *Roncalliani*, was strongly pastoral in flavor and included the dominant liberal voices in the Vatican Council: the two German cardinals; the eight French cardinals, who formed a compact, disciplined voting block; four North Americans; six Italians; three South Americans; and one each from Spain, India, Africa, Formosa, Japan, and Australia respectively. But with an expected electorate totaling about eighty cardinals, no one group could muster the necessary two-thirds plus one majority of fifty-five votes to elect its candidate without significant defections from the other two groups, and Rome was a hive of negotiations and lobbying. The electors themselves knew each other better than at any previous conclave in modern times. In past elections, the pastoral cardinals had had to rely heavily on the Curia cardinals for information about each other—to the obvious advantage of the Curia cardinals. But the Vatican Council had given every cardinal the opportunity to meet even his farthest-flung colleagues, and to form definite impressions of where each one stood on the important issues facing the Church.

Moreover, the general congregations provided further opportunities for observation and consultation. Each day around 1:30 P.M. when their meeting on the third floor of the Apostolic Palace was over, there was an evocative scene out of the Renaissance as the emerging cardinals separated into twos and threes and paused for a while to talk as they strolled slowly together back and forth. Sunlight streamed in through the glass enclosure of the loggia, illuminating the mythological scenes of Raphael's frescoes on the ceiling above their heads. Then they descended by elevator to the Courtyard of Saint Damasus, or farther still to the Belvedere, and said goodbye until the following day.

That was only part of a busy crisscross of informal contacts and exchanges that formed the texture of the suspenseful preconclave period. Continental and national groups, for instance, spent time together as a matter of course because most of them lodged in their country's religious houses or seminaries. The Spanish cardinals were together at the Spanish Pontifical College. The cardinals from the United States stayed at the North American College (except for Cardinal Spellman, who, as usual, was at the Grand Hotel). Most of the South American block lived at the Latin American College, and the Brazilians at their country's college where Cardinal Bea was a permanent resident. It was natural to refer back to the others after visiting with cardinals of the Curia, or other countries, and the process multiplied.

Yet it was the order of the day, especially among non-Italian cardinals, to describe the conclave as a religious rather than a political event and to refuse to discuss any specific names directly with the press, at least not seriously. When an American reporter managed to waylay Cardinal Agagianian as he left the general congregation one afternoon and attempted to discuss with him the forthcoming election, Agagianian laughed nervously and replied in heavily accented English, "Oh, that is in the hands of God. Yes, the hands of God." And Cardinal Jaime de Barros Camara of Rio de Janeiro declared, "The choice of the pope is the work of the Holy Ghost who directs the Church. Anyone who is elected will be the pope that should be. God will choose him according to the needs of the time. We have lost a great pope, but we can be sure that his successor will give the Church the direction that God wants."

To be sure, the election is held in a church. The help of the Holy Ghost is invoked before the voting starts. And as each cardinal casts his ballot he declares that in making his choice he is an instrument of the Divine Will. But while the pope is a religious leader, he is elected by a political process, and the making of the pope has remarkable similarities with all other political processes. Not only are there issues; and not only are some cardinals considered candidates. There are also campaigns, smoke-filled rooms (more cardinals in 1963 were smokers than not), block voting, and maneuvering of a kind that would be immediately recognizable to any Chicago ward captain. Only the most innocent would believe that a papal election is so different from any other human election as to be devoid of politics.

In theory, blatant campaigning is strictly forbidden, and any cardinal rash enough to attempt to advance his cause in an obvious way is destined to fail. The rules also forbid the cardinals to commit their vote to a particular *papabile* in advance of the conclave. Frank, wide-ranging discussions about the relative merits of different candidates are allowed, and even before Pope John was buried the cardinals had begun to form alliances and to reach "understandings."

The liberal faction was not as homogenous a group as the integralists. Each cardinal responded to the spirit of Pope John's *aggiornamento*, but individuals disagreed with various aspects of it in application. The widest area of dissent was political rather than religious and concerned Pope John's East European policy. Cardinal Wyszynski, the only East European cardinal, was ambivalent about the Vatican's negotiations, apparently feeling that Rome's approach often lacked toughness and led to too many concessions. The German cardinals were equally concerned because any Vatican-Polish agreement would imply recognition of Poland's claims to the Oder-Neisse border, to Germany's disadvantage. In fact, the Germans had come to Rome inclined toward choosing a pontiff who was committed to consolidating John's reforms, but was less adventurous in his East European policy. Initially, they had hoped to elect Cardinal Cicognani. At close quarters, however, Cicognani's problems of age and infirmity came to full light, and the Germans abandoned the idea. The more progressive South Americans worried that the sight of the Vatican openly dealing with the regimes of Eastern Europe would strengthen the Communist parties in their own countries, and so did Cardinal Giacomo Lercaro of Bologna. Others understood the importance of John's process of reconstruction and wanted to see it continued. Given his close association with Pope John, as well as his extraordinary talent for friendly persuasion, Cardinal Bea was the obvious man to rally the *Roncalliani* behind the candidate whom the dead pontiff considered his natural heir—Giovanni Battista Montini of Milan.

The "experts" (including the CIA, if they qualified as such) maintained that Giacomo Lercaro of Bologna and Giovanni Urbani, the Patriarch of Venice, were also on the progressive short-list together with Montini. But while both Lercaro and

Urbani may have had their supporters who would have liked
to see their candidacy gain momentum, the *Roncalliani*'s first
choice by a very long chalk was Montini.

In the press and in private conversations, his conservative
opponents made much of the streak of indecision which had
clearly bedeviled the archbishop during his eight years in
Milan. This was, in fact, a more significant criticism than the
allegation of "pettiness" in the CIA report. Unlike Pope John
XXIII, his critics argued, he would find it difficult to act
directly and spontaneously on any major issue. On the contrary, his doubts and hesitations made him prone to contradic-
tory decisions, as had happened all too often in the past.

One week he was the champion of the labor unions, the
next week he was on the side of the industrialists. One week
he stood between a left-wing Catholic weekly and the Holy
Office's anger over the publication of a controversial article,
the next week he was asking the Holy Office to rap the Milan
Jesuits on the knuckles for publishing a favorable review of
Federico Fellini's new movie *La Dolce Vita*. One week he
eagerly sought advice, the next, one of his collaborators was
brusquely rebuffed for expressing an opinion. As if to hammer
the point home, a story began to circulate that Pope John
himself had once been heard to describe the archbishop of
Milan as *amletico* ("Hamlet-like"). Surely a firmer hand was
needed at the helm of Peter's bark?

John was a man of instinctive decisions who would under-
standably have been amused if not troubled by the more
painful, more intricate mental processes of the archbishop of
Milan, but it was well known among the cardinals that the
dead pope had regarded Montini as his most obvious successor. In his last hours the pope had told his secretary, Monsignor Capovilla, "As for the conclave, my successor will be
Cardinal Montini. I fully expect the Sacred College to vote for
him." In his spiritual diary Pope John had expressed the hope
that Cardinal Montini would inherit the papal tiara, thus en-

suring that the work of *Aggiornamento* would continue. The relevant passage was omitted from *L'Osservatore Romano*'s published extracts of the pope's diary, doubtless on instructions from the Curia, but the *Roncalliani* made sure that it was leaked to the press.

Pope John made Montini a cardinal in his first consistory, naming him first on the list, which was a mark of honor. Thereafter, the Pope seemed to go out of his way to show the cardinal special consideration. On November 5, 1961, the third anniversary of his pontificate, and also his eightieth birthday, he picked Archbishop Montini from among all the cardinals to celebrate mass in Saint Peter's Basilica, referring to him in his address as "worthy successor to Saint Charles," another signal honor considering John's admiration for Saint Charles Borromeo of Milan, about whom he had written a five-volume historical study.

During the first session of the Vatican Council a year later, Montini was the only cardinal invited to live in the Apostolic Palace as the pope's personal guest. More important than the public attention which John lavished on Montini was the frequent use that he made of the latter's immense experience and acknowledged ability. Montini supporters detected the archbishop's hand in Pope John's landmark speech to the bishops at the opening of the Vatican Ecumenical Council. And, prior to its publication, the social encyclical *Mater et Magistra* went back and forth several times between Rome and Milan for additions and comments by Cardinal Montini. In 1961 the pope sent him to the United States, and in 1962 on fact-finding trips to Latin America and West Africa (the first visit by a European cardinal to the African continent), where he witnessed at first hand the rapidly growing Catholic presence in the Third World.

Montini himself quickly made it clear where he stood on the question of continuing Pope John's work. The night following John's death, Montini had celebrated a memorial mass in Milan's vast Vigorelli Bicycle Stadium, and there, before an estimated crowd of one hundred thousand, he delivered what was inevitably interpreted as his electoral speech. Pope John, he said, had "outlined certain paths which it would not only be wise to remember, but to follow . . . Fixing our gaze on his tomb, which is now sealed, we should consider his legacy, which the tomb could not contain, and his spirit, which has suffused our age, and which death cannot extinguish. Could we ever turn aside from the path to the future, so boldly opened by Pope John? Surely not."

Any other cardinal would surely have damaged his chances with such a blatant breach of the traditional reticence expected of *papabile* cardinals, but Montini's candidacy had all the logic of beads clicking along an abacus. He simply filled the progressive bill better than anyone else. The hopes of those working for closer Christian unity were pinned on him because of his long-standing interest in furthering the ecumenical movement. In 1956, for example, he had invited as his guests at the archbishop's palace a group of Anglican clergymen and their families in order to learn about the Church of England. His commitment to liturgical reform, and especially to the replacement of Latin with the vernacular in the Mass and other church services, was well known. His long period in the Secretariat of State gave him the capacity to tackle the immense and detailed problem of reforming the Vatican curia—a problem which Pope John, by temperament a pastor and not a central administrator, had ignored in order to give priority to the fundamental problems affecting the Church itself.

Politically, Montini supported Pope John's approach: less direct involvement at home, and greatly increased readiness to deal with the communist world. In 1961, he clashed with Cardinal Siri during a meeting of Italian cardinals in Pope John's study called by the pontiff to discuss the hierarchy's approach to Italy's political situation. Siri pressed for an all-out anticommunist campaign from the pulpits, while Montini strongly advocated Pope John's hands-off policy. When the Balzan Peace Foundation voted to award the Peace Prize to Pope John, the pontiff at first hesitated to accept it. The unanimous decision had been made possible by Premier Khrushchev, and John was chary of putting himself in the Soviet leader's debt. But he was persuaded by Cardinal Montini. The cardinal argued that the Balzan Prize would dramatize the Church's work for peace, and pave the way for the publication of *Pacem in Terris.*

On paper, Montini's record in the council was not outstanding, although he had been very influential behind the scenes in the commissions. He had spoken on only two occasions in the council debates, resisting attempts by progressive bishops (especially German bishops) to draft him as one of their leading spokesmen. This prudence, too, worked in his favor with his supporters among the cardinals because by carefully balancing his opinions and trimming his sails in the winds of controversy he had not alienated the Curia conservatives. As Archbishop Vagnozzi, who belonged to the Ottaviani faction, confided to State Department officials in Washington, before the election, the Curia cardinals considered Cardinal Montini a moderate and would in the last resort support him in preference to a candidate of more extreme views, particularly a foreign one.

One morning, a prelate approached Cardinal Gustavo Testa in the Apostolic Palace with a message from Archbishop Dell'Acqua. Would the cardinal be willing to campaign for Archbishop Montini among the Curia cardinals in an attempt to shake loose some votes from the conservative block? Testa was a curialist, the prefect for the Congregation for Oriental Churches. But he owed both his position and his red hat to a close personal friendship with the dead pope. In arguing his case, the prelate did not fail to stress that Montini had been Pope John's choice. Testa was at first dubious about Montini because of the latter's reputation for indecisiveness. He was after all also aware that Pope John had called Montini *amle-*

tico. "Do you really know him?" he asked. "These could be crucial years for the Church." But the prelate persisted, and the cardinal finally agreed to cooperate—"out of respect for Dell'Acqua, not out of conviction," he added.

CHAPTER X

Conclave

O<small>N THE EVE OF HIS DEPARTURE</small> for Rome following Pope John's death, Cardinal Spellman received a visit in his Madison Avenue residence behind Saint Patrick's Cathedral from a senior CIA officer. He had come, he told Spellman, not only as a concerned American official, but also as a concerned Catholic, to make certain political observations about the papal succession.

Under Pope John, he went on, the Church swung sharply to the left. This was proving particularly dangerous in South America where social-minded bishops, taking their cue from such papal documents as *Pacem in Terris*, were embarking on activities, forming alliances, and preaching sermons that undermined the authority of their governments. "Of course, these bishops often have a genuine social grievance," the CIA man conceded, "and they mean well. But their open opposition is creating great instability in more than one country, and strengthening the communists." What were the chances of the cardinals in Rome electing a successor who would restrain this corrosive process which, in any case, would end up harming the Church as well?

The CIA man must have known, in making his approach, that Spellman, or "Spelly" as he was universally known in American ecclesiastical circles, had not been an admirer of Pope John. Shortly before the pope's fatal illness, a member of Spellman's staff wrote a speech for him in which he included a passage praising Pope John's work. Spellman deleted the passage. "I guess you don't think Pope John is the greatest man in the world, huh?" the speech writer inquired. "Just between you and me, doctor, I do not," was Spellman's frank reply.

No wonder: John's reforms often ran counter both to Spelly's deep-rooted Irish traditionalism and to his political convictions. The cardinal who spent every Christmas night with United States troops, first in Korea and later in Vietnam, preaching a midnight sermon on the justness of their cause was not easily reconciled with Pope John's policy of *rapprochement* with the communist regimes of Eastern Europe. Besides, he saw it as a repudiation of his mentor and friend, Pope Pius XII, to whom anticommunism was a holy crusade. It was during Pope John's pontificate that Spelly's personal influence in the Vatican began to wane, and he no longer exercised a special and privileged power in the Church. Other, more liberal voices in the American Church, such as those of Mayer and Ritter, had been heard in the Council debates. Some of Spelly's nominations for bishops began to be passed over. He was no longer, as he used sometimes to be called, "the American pope."

Much as he admired the CIA and approved of its work, Spellman was not about to divulge his voting plans and he dismissed the subject with the standard answer about the vote being a secret to everyone except the cardinals themselves. But the CIA officer had made his point.

At the time, the CIA was preaching to the converted. Spelly journeyed to Rome intending to vote for a conservative candidate. That meant that Joseph McIntyre of Los Angeles would do the same. McIntyre owed his appointment to Spelly, whose chancellor he once was in the New York archdiocese, and wherever Spelly went the cardinal archbishop of Los Angeles never failed to follow. The three remaining United States cardinals—Cushing, Ritter, and Mayer—shared the outlook of the European progressives and accepted Montini as soon as Bea proposed him to them.

But Spellman was not impressed with the conservative choice. He had never cared for the senior Curia prelates, especially Ottaviani: they were arrogant and devious. For their part, the curialists had not forgotten how Spellman used to go over their heads to Pius himself to get what he wanted, and they resented him. But old antagonisms aside, Spellman simply considered Antoniutti a poor choice who did not possess the caliber of a modern-day pope. His personal preference was Cardinal Siri. He admired Siri's strength, and shared his views. Besides, they had both been proteges of Pius XII, and had received their red hats from the pope's hands during the same consistory. Siri also had long pastoral experience which, in Spellman's eyes was more useful to a pontiff than diplomatic experience.

In the days leading up to the conclave, however, it became clear that the northern European cardinals were immovable in their opposition to Siri. The archbishop of Genoa was too diehard for the likes of Alfrink, Suenens, and Doepfner to stomach. So, on the evening before the conclave, Spelly went to see Montini at the Lombard College where the latter was staying. The conversation centered on political questions. Later, one of Spellman's close friends in Rome confided to an American diplomat that the archbishop of Milan had gained another vote—or rather, two more votes. "Spelly is simply too much of a politician not to recognize the difference between a bandwagon and a hearse," Spellman's friend explained.

What kind of a man was Montini, the man to beat in the election? After a lifetime in the top echelons of the Church, the biographical details of his life and career were better known than those of any other cardinal, and it was a life of

industry and devotion to duty frequently rewarded by setbacks and disappointments. He was born on September 30,
1897 in Concesio, a small town near Brescia, about thirty
miles west of Bergamo, birthplace of Angelo Roncalli. But
Montini's background differed greatly from his predecessor's
peasant origins. Montini's family belonged to the upper middle class. Four generations had occupied the same prosperous
seventeenth-century townhouse surrounded by a high yellow
wall. From an early age Montini was marinated in Catholic
politics. His father, Giorgio, had been a parliamentary deputy,
and then editor of the Brescia Catholic paper, *Il Cittadino.*
Thus Montini was used to meeting his father's political
friends who included Don Luigi Sturzo, founder of the *Partito
Popolare,* forerunner of the Christian Democrat Party. An
elder brother also went into active politics and became a
Christian Democrat senator.

Ill health plagued Montini's childhood and early youth,
forcing him to drop out of regular school and isolating him
from the company of other children. He was tutored privately
and acquired an early reputation for studiousness and intro-
spection. As happened with Roncalli, his devout mother encouraged him to join the priesthood, and he was ordained in
Brescia at the age of twenty-three, on May 29, 1920. The cha-
suble that he wore was made from the material of his mother's
wedding dress. In the fall of that year, the bishop of Brescia
picked him to go to Rome for further study and the selective
process by which promising young priests float to the top was
set in motion.

Initially, young Don Giovanni Battista Montini enrolled in
the Gregorian University as a theological student, but with his
family's political connections he had no difficulty gaining direct entry into the Secretariat of State. The following year,
1921, he got his first and only foreign posting: he was appointed secretary in the apostolic nunciature in Warsaw.
He left for Poland in May, but within five months his frail
health had forced him back to Rome where his efficiency and

industry saw him rise practically to the top in the Vatican administration.

At twenty-six he became a *minutante* (equivalent to second secretary of embassy) in the Secretariat and was at the same time appointed chaplain assistant to the FUCI (*Federazione Universitaria Cattolici Italiani*), the Catholic university students federation. The appointment brought under Montini's influence prominent FUCI members such as Aldo Moro, Emilio Colombo, and Giulio Andreotti, the future leaders of the postwar Christian Democrat party. When fascist hecklers began to break up FUCI meetings, Montini advised the federation to disband itself in order to avoid violence.

In 1937, Montini—by now a monsignor—was appointed substitute secretary of state along with Monsignor Domenico Tardini, who was to become his nemesis. Both worked directly under Cardinal Pacelli, the Secretary of State and were destined to remain his close collaborators for twenty years, building their careers in his shadow. From Pacelli young Monsignor Montini received vigorous training in the former's style of detailed application, punctuality, formality—Montini was once rebuked for bringing him an urgent telegram when incorrectly dressed. On becoming Pius XII, Pacelli reconfirmed them in their posts.

For most of his pontificate, Pius was his own secretary of state with their constant assistance. It was an arrangement that suited Pius right down to the ground. It meant there was no official spokesman of the Holy See other than the pope himself. There was no one to insist upon the adoption of a line of policy or action that the pope might not like. There was no voice other than his own, and no one to deflect the limelight from the occupant of the throne of Saint Peter, as he himself had sometimes done when he was cardinal secretary of state.

The British Minister to the Holy See, Sir D'Arcy Osborne, who was one of the few envoys who had a good relationship with Pope Pius, once boldly complained to the pontiff of the inconvenience of there being no secretary of state, and suggested that it was in the best interests of the Holy See to appoint a new one.

Osborne reported to London that the pope's reply was that "he found the present arrangement quite satisfactory, explaining that he saw one or both of the undersecretaries (Montini and Tardini) daily and that this provided for the effective conduct of the affairs of the Secretariat of State." Osborne went on to report that he had recounted this conversation to Monsignor Montini, but the hard-pressed prelate, "Could not agree with His Holiness that the present arrangement was satisfactory." Pope Pius was indifferent to the views of his overworked collaborators, whom he expected to be on call virtually round the clock, and continued to resist all attempts to persuade him to fill the vacant post. The pope's obliviousness to the physical demands he made on his staff was legendary. He once left a functionary of the Secretariat of State on his knees for an hour discussing a complicated political situation.

Meanwhile, a deep-seated enmity developed between Tardini and Montini. Given their opposite temperaments, personal conflicts were inevitable. The former was irascible and outspoken, with a native Roman's earthiness, a brilliant Catherine wheel of speech and motion. The latter, equally brilliant behind his wall of North Italian reserve, had a personality like a tightly furled umbrella. But the important clash was political rather than temperamental. Tardini was a conservative, with a conservative's solution to the Christian Democrats' chronic inability to gain an absolute parliamentary majority so as to be able to govern without outside support. He wanted the Church to put the full weight of its authority behind a proposed coalition consisting of the Christian Democrats and right-wing parties, a formula strongly supported by the American embassy of the time.

Montini owed his reputation as a progressive in political and social matters at least partly to his opposition to this notion of a center-right accord. He belonged to a small group of

Italian prelates who favored gradual social reform as the most effective antidote to communism, and he felt that this would in time work to the advantage of the more liberal wing of the Christian Democrat Party, his former associates in the FUCI.

In 1953, Pope Pius held what was to be his last consistory. During the ceremony two things happened, completely unrelated at the time, which invested it with a special historical significance. One was that Angelo Roncalli, the new patriarch of Venice, was made a cardinal, the other that Giovanni Battista Montini was not. In the course of it, the pope announced that both Tardini and Montini had declined to be made cardinals. One explanation given (not by the pope, who gave none at all) was that Tardini had refused, thus virtually forcing Montini to follow suit. Tardini, it was said, feared that, once his counterpart had been made a cardinal, Pius would appoint him secretary of state, and the way would be clear for him to become pope. What would have happened had Montini succeeded his mentor, instead of Cardinal Roncalli, is a matter of speculation. The course of the church would have been radically different. It is virtually certain that he would not have called the Vatican Council.

In 1954, Montini and Tardini quarreled sharply on the political issue. This time, a coalition of Montini's adversaries, headed by Tardini and Sister Pasqualina Lenhert, the formidable German nun who commanded the approaches to Pius XII in his later years, prevailed upon Pius to fire Montini. It was announced that Montini had been appointed archbishop of Milan. The fact that it was the largest and most important diocese in Italy softened the blow, but Pius did not make Montini a cardinal, even though Milan is a see which by custom has a cardinal-archbishop. A man of Pius's familiarity with, and taste for, formality would have realized that in denying Montini his red hat not only was he cutting off his chances of ascending the throne of Peter, but he was also diminishing his stature.

A friend went to visit him in his Vatican office a few days

after the appointment was announced, and Montini burst into tears. Still, he was determined to make the most of it. When he drove into Milan, in January 1955, preceded by ninety cases of books, he stopped the car, and knelt to kiss the ground. "I pray," he said, still on his knees in a rare moment of lyricism, "that the roar of your machines becomes music and the smoke of your chimneys, incense."

His main thrust was a campaign of spiritual renewal among the huge, largely immigrant working population, uprooted from its southern traditions and greatly susceptible to communist influence. He called himself the workers' archbishop. He celebrated mass in working-class districts of the city. He went down into the mines. He toured factories, approaching the workers with his sad, strained little smile and outstretched hand, ignoring their boos and jeers, In the end, they usually shook his hand. He set up new parishes in communist strongholds, and built churches near the factories. But in the pre-conclave maneuvering, his conservative opponents were quick to point out that his record as archbishop was, at best, a mixed one. Communism had maintained its strength in Milan, and many of the new churches had remained empty.

Many cardinals were going into the conclave itself with two or three names on their mind. One of them was almost certain to be Montini: the other candidates would be measured against him. The conviction that Montini was either the man to elect or to beat, depending on the individual point of view, spread beyond the small circle of cardinal-electors—for example, to Bonaventura Gammarelli, the ecclesiastical tailor situated behind the Pantheon in Rome who traditionally supplied the vestments worn by the new pontiff as soon as he was elected. (After that, it was up to the pope himself to decide whether or not to retain the firm as his official tailor.)

As his family's firm had done before every conclave for more than two hundred years, Gammarelli prepared three white wool cassocks in three different sizes, each with an attached capelet, silk-lined, plus one high, white silk waist sash ending in gold tassels, a *rochetta* made from a bolt of exquisite antique Flemish lace bought earlier and saved for just such an eventuality, and a red watered silk *mozzetta* to go over the other two garments. The cassock was made in three sizes so that the newly elected pope could exchange his cardinal's robes for the one closest to his size. It was Gammarelli's practice to tailor the cassocks to the measurements of the three cardinals whom the firm felt had the best chance of success, and it prided itself on always guessing right. One of the cassocks was made to Montini's size (he had been one of their clients for years).

To the Central Intelligence Agency, Montini was very much the man to beat in the 1963 conclave. Since his days at Pius XII's elbow in the Vatican, the agency had thought him too progressive in his social and political outlook to be considered a reliable ally. When he was removed to Milan, American intelligence circles received the news with considerable satisfaction. Yet he remained an important figure in the Church, even in Milan, with wide ecclesiastical and political contacts, and every Rome chief of station made it his business to get to know him. At least one orphanage and one charity whose principal benefactor was the archbishop of Milan appeared from time to time among the Rome station's "project money" disbursements.

But Montini also had another political enemy in General Franco of Spain. Aside from a general antipathy to Montini's politics, Franco was still fuming over a clumsily handled appeal for clemency by the archbishop in the fall of 1962. Montini had sent a highly publicized telegram to the *Caudillo* urging him to commute the death sentence of a young Spanish anarchist. Franco immediately fired off an equally widely publicized reply. He had, he said, learned the contents of Montini's telegram from the press before receiving it himself. Besides, he pointed out, the archbishop had got it wrong: the anarchist had not been condemned to death at all, but had been sentenced to life imprisonment. This was true: Montini

had apparently let himself be persuaded to send the appeal to
Franco by Milanese left-wing students, without first checking
their information. Angered by Montini's impetuous action,
Franco had passed on to the Spanish cardinals his expectation
that they not vote for him in the conclave. The senior members of the Spanish hierarchy were in the forefront of the
stop-Montini movement. They were convinced that the obvious breach of ecclesiastical etiquette which he had committed by intervening uninvited in the affairs of an important
Catholic foreign country reflected a gradual, and to their
minds dangerous, drift by the Italian hierarchy as a whole
toward a more accommodating policy toward the left, and this
was a state of affairs Montini as pope would not correct.

The conclave began on Wednesday, June 19. In the morning, the eighty cardinals who were in Rome gathered in St.
Peter's for the Mass of the Holy Ghost, a solemn invocation of
divine intervention, at the altar of the throne in the basilica
apse. The celebrant was Cardinal Tisserant, intoning his dis-
tinctive French-accented Latin. High above the altar, sunlight
from a fine June morning suffused the golden glass window
with, in the center, a white dove in flight, symbol of the Holy
Spirit.

After mass and the prescribed prayers for God's guidance in
the coming task of choosing a pope came the traditional Latin
sermon *De Eligendo Pontifice* ("On Electing a Pontiff"), delivered by Monsignor Amleto Tondini, the Curia's leading
Latinist who was in charge of translating official documents
into the official language of the Church. Because he was also
Ottaviani's creature, every impeccably constructed sentence
enumerating the qualities desirable in the new pope contained an implied criticism of the old one. John XXIII's
Church, charged with the energy and filled with the promise
of the Council, was scarcely recognizable in the doom-laden
elegance of Tondini's Curia-inspired picture of it.

Threatened by dissent, beset by dangerously ambiguous
teaching and ideas, exploited by atheistic governments for

their own ends, "the barque of Peter needs a helmsman who is firm, prudent, and good." Firm in order to restate without hesitation the sacred dogmas of the faith; to fight the spread of erroneous theories, such as scientism, relativism, and materialism; to defend openly those who suffered persecution in the cause of justice—the inference here being that as a result of Pope John's East European policy, persecuted Catholics in communist countries had been left in the lurch.

The new pope needed to be prudent in his conduct of international affairs which, according to Tondini "contained many thorns and few roses." Violence and hate, he said, dominated relations between people—a far cry from the dead pope's fundamental conviction that there was good in all men. Was it, therefore, pessimistic to have reservations regarding the motives and sincerity of "not a few of those who applauded so enthusiastically the Pope of Peace," but who at the same time opposed the religious and moral principles for which he stood?

"Prudent also in continuing the work of the Vatican Council." The council was a grand enterprise. Catholics throughout the world wished to see it brought to a satisfactory conclusion. But, Tondini added, "It will be the task of the pope whom you, Most Eminent Fathers, are on the point of choosing from among yourselves, to decide the appropriate time for the resumption of this great assembly. It will be his task to decide, above all, if the issues, and the documents, have received sufficient reflection . . ."

At the end of the mass, the cardinals flowed down the apse in two slow moving lines inside two wooden barriers erected along the central length of the basilica. Dressed in violet robes, they drew a buzz of admiring whispers from the worshipers pressed along the railings. Tourists' cameras clicked to record rare closeups, children's hands reached out to touch their robes. At the Altar of the Confession, reserved for the pontiff's exclusive use, under Bernini's baldachin on its four spiraling columns of black marble, the two files of cardinals split laterally and converged again in the transept to turn toward a side chapel and thence into the sacristy. Some of them looked impassively ahead. Others smiled back gladly at the public thrusting toward them against the barriers. Cardinal Rugambwa drew special attention as the only black face in the procession. Cardinal Montini passed by, his head bowed, lost in his own thoughts. A group of nuns pointed to him and began whispering excitedly among themselves: *"Ecco il Papa! Ecco il Papa!"* Montini looked around at them, shocked, and put his finger quickly to his lips, signaling them to be silent.

In the afternoon the cardinals arrived with their suitcases to be locked in the conclave area where they would live in almost total isolation from the outside world until the moment of election. Most prelates had packed for a short conclave: "You can telephone me on Friday afternoon or evening at the Brazilian College," Cardinal Bea told a member of the Christian Unity Secretariat staff who accompanied him to the Vatican. Bea evidently expected the conclave to last less than forty-eight hours. "I only hope they (the Curia group) don't take it too hard . . ." Among the last to arrive was Montini. He had spent the afternoon visiting Archbishop Slipyi, a spot of last minute homework on the Church under communism which was bound to be a dominant issue in conclave discussion.

Voting would not begin until the following morning when there would be four daily ballots, two in the morning and two in the afternoon, but as a first step the cardinals gathered in the Sistine Chapel to take the conclave oath. Cardinal Tisserant read from the constitution governing the Vacant See the rules of the papal election, including the clause binding the electors to secrecy, and the clause which in effect repudiated the ancient "Right of Exception," which gave Catholic sovereigns the power to veto a candidate, and which was last exercised in 1914 by the Emperor Franz Josef against Cardinal Merry del Val, whom the Austrians suspected of being pro-

French. Each cardinal in turn then swore to uphold the conclave rules.

One final—and largely formal—step remained before the
conclave area could be sealed off. Accompanied by the Vatican architect responsible for converting the Apostolic Palace
into the conclave site, Prince Sigismondo Chigi delle Rovere,
hereditary Marshal of the Conclave, in doublet and cape, em-
barked on a meticulous search of the premises for stowaways
and (more realistically) forbidden cameras and radios. With
the Marshal went the Colonel Commandant of the Swiss
Guard, Colonel Nuenlist, who shared the task of ensuring the
security of the conclave. The colonel was a stern disciplinar-
ian on secondment from the Swiss army. He walked with a
slight limp, the result of a gunshot wound inflicted by a muti-
nous Swiss Guardsman. In his plumed helmet, breastplate,
and breeches, he looked as if he had stepped out of the fresco
of the battle of Lepanto on the South wall of the *Sala Regia*,
adjoining the Sistine Chapel.

With a Roman Catholic director at Langley, the agency's
headquarters in Virginia, and a Catholic president in the
White House who was, moreover, more impressed with the
mystique of intelligence gathering than he ought to have
been, the Rome station was expected almost as a matter of
prestige to beat the news media at their game and be first with
the result of the conclave. This entailed learning the identity
of the new pontiff in advance of the official announcement
from the balcony of Saint Peter's Basilica immediately following the election itself—usually a matter of minutes.

The CIA's motives went beyond pleasing its director and
impressing the President. Not for the first time in Church history, the international political situation was a central factor in
the selection of a new pope: political issues were certain to
loom large in the cardinals' secret discussions, and the agency
was deeply interested in what was said. In any event, the
agency flashed the news of the election to Langley several
minutes ahead of the wire service bulletins. How did the CIA

do it? Some Italian intelligence sources have always maintained that the agency bugged the papal conclave. It is also possible that the CIA had succeeded in planting an informer inside the conclave. With the conclave area of the Apostolic Palace totally sealed, the "mole" would have had to use a transmitter. All windows overlooking Saint Peter's Square had been papered over to prevent signaling, and all telephones in the area disconnected. The sole means of communication with those inside was through two closely guarded hatches fitted with revolving horizontal drums for delivery of food, messages, personal mail, and other articles.

The larger of the drums, made of a light metal and painted yellow, had a large aperture cut in the side through which to fill the inside. It had been erected in the space between the wooden doors of the arched entrance of the *Cortile del Pappagallo* the ("Courtyard of the Parrot")—and it was used in a way that eliminated any possibility of human contact with the conclave inmates. The outer doors were opened and supplies placed inside the drum. Then the drum was spun round so that the aperture faced the inner door, and the outer door was locked again. At a given signal, officials inside the conclave opened the inner door, unloaded the contents of the drum, and returned it to its original position ready for the next delivery. In the *Cortile San Damaso*, in the heart of the Apostolic Palace itself, was a second, smaller drum (about two feet in diameter) for messages and letters which had first to be "censored" by the conclave staff either inside or outside the conclave area.

CHAPTER XI

Pope and President

No GREATER SUSPENSE could compete with the atmosphere of expectancy created around the enclosed prelates. Not only among the Roman Catholic faithful, waiting for their head, or the betting enthusiasts in the shadow of Saint Peter's itself. Formality and history, uncertainty, controversy and real power, combined with frequent invocations of the supernatural, provided the elements of a unique, comprehensive human experience. Scores of television cameras were beamed on the tiny chimney erected on the roof of the Sistine Chapel to transmit live throughout the world, via the new communications satellites, the puffs of white or black smoke that followed every voting session of two ballots each and were supposed to signal the outcome (in most cases, wisps of noncommittal grey smoke trailed across the sky, leaving the faithful baffled). Newspapers prepared special editions. Romans altered their schedule to be able to be at Saint Peter's at the historic moment of election.

The first vote on the morning of June 20 took place in an atmosphere of high excitement. Hardly a word was spoken as each successive cardinal in order of precedence, approached

the altar with the folded ballot in his hand (having disguised
his writing to keep his identity a secret), knelt down and declared: "I call to witness Christ the Lord who will be my
judge, that my vote is given to one who before God I consider
should be elected." Then he dropped his vote in a chalice that
stood on the altar to serve as a ballot urn and returned to his
seat.

With the last ballot cast, the three cardinals who had been
appointed as scrutators mixed and totaled the votes to ensure
against duplicate votes, and then proceeded to the scrutiny of
the ballots. The first cardinal scrutator took a ballot paper out
of the chalice, unfolded it, silently noted the name on his tally
sheet which listed the names of all the cardinals, and passed
it to the second cardinal. The latter did the same as the first
and then passed the ballot to the third, who read out the name
aloud so that the cardinals could fill in their own tally sheets.

Predictably, the first ballot was widely dispersed among a
scattering of realistic as well as throwaway votes. Several cardinals had observed the tradition of casting so-called courtesy
ballots to honor friends and respected colleagues who were
not *papabili.* Ottaviani received several votes from loyal conservatives: Bea from equally admiring *Roncalliani.* The Germans voted for Cicognani. But the first round of voting also
put forward the serious contestants. Already the predicted
main lines of the tussle between Montini and Antoniutti made
a significant appearance, each one receiving about a score of
votes apiece.

The second ballot confirmed the trend, though no one
emerged with what could be discerned as a decisive lead.
When the voting papers of the inconclusive first ballot had
been skewered together with needle and string and put aside,
fresh ballots were distributed and the cardinals moved
quickly to another vote, following the same procedure. This
time, Montini forged ahead with slightly less than thirty votes,
while Antoniutti drew about twenty. But Cardinal Lercaro,
the kindly, forward-thinking Archbishop of Bologna, surfaced

as a challenging third contender with about twenty votes, clearly at the expense of Montini's further progress. Some cardinals, it seemed, were hesitating between the complex, wordly former Curia diplomat, and the good, less complicated pastor.

At 11:54, the black smoke of no election appeared above the waiting crowd outside as the long garland of one hundred sixty ballots, the second vote having been threaded with the first, burned in the stove together with the cardinals' notes and tally sheets.

Intense discussion was already under way when the cardinals broke for lunch, walking the eighty yards out of the Sistine Chapel, under Bernini's sculpted marble drapes at the entrance to the *Sala Ducale* ("Ducal Hall"), and along the glass enclosed loggia (its windows painted over to shut out the view of Saint Peter's Square below) to their dining room in the *Sala Pontificia* of the famous Borgia apartments on the second floor of the Apostolic Palace. In the ornate, high-ceilinged room, the cardinals took their assigned places at the long tables. Over a lunch of *pasta* followed by veal and washed down by Chianti wine, they consulted. The siesta hour was forgotten as cardinals and conclavists (each cardinal was accompanied by one prelate to act as conclavist or assistant) floated from room to room, or paced the loggias deep in conversation.

In his efforts to rally support for Montini, Cardinal Gustavo Testa, Pope John's friend, had won over a valuable ally. This was Cardinal Clemente Micara, the vicar of Rome, and an influential figure among the Curia faction. The best sources on the conclave credit the diminutive prelate with winning over at least a half dozen cardinals to Montini in the conclave.

A diplomat of long experience who knew Montini well, Micara argued that (1) in terms of training and qualifications to develop the Church's new political approach not only toward Eastern Europe but also in such vitally important areas as the emerging Third World, Montini had no equal among the cardinals; (2) in terms of reforming the church as a whole, Montini would, despite his reputation as a "liberal," by nature and instinct lean toward a moderate approach; (3) in terms of the "foreign" threat, meaning the possibility of a non-Italian pope, Montini was the only cardinal from Italy who could count on the broad foreign support needed by an Italian to get himself elected. If his candidacy were to be blocked, Micara warned his colleagues, the non-Italians might regroup behind one of their own and perhaps succeed in getting a non-Italian elected.

Montini had yet another influential supporter in Cardinal Cicognani, another senior prelate with Curia influence. When Cardinal König first sought his backing for the archbishop of Milan, before the start of the conclave, he soon found himself preaching to the converted. "I believe that we (i.e. the cardinals) have the only man who can do it," Cicognani told König. In the conclave, Cicognani sought actively to advance Montini's cause as the man most qualified to lead the Church through the years of evolution, and the white haired, benign prelate bustled about the conclave among his colleagues with very good effect.

Montini did not have to proclaim his intention to continue his predecessor's policy of rapprochement toward the communist world. His record as a strong supporter of what Pope John was doing in this area spoke for him, and concern over this course of action remained one of the principal causes of opposition among the Italian conservatives. Cardinal Wyszynski emerged as a strong advocate of the need to continue Pope John's line in Eastern Europe, and he won many converts.

At least some of the effects of the previous hours of bargaining were already felt in the afternoon voting session. On the first ballot, the Bea-Testa-Micara faction closed ranks, and the "pastoral alternative" of Cardinal Lercaro gave way to a solid block of around fifty votes for Montini—by far the largest vote, but still at least four short of the required two-thirds plus one majority. Antoniutti retained his twenty votes, but a new name emerged, that of Francesco Roberti, who received about a dozen votes. Roberti was a Vatican jurist who had been made a cardinal at the end of a long and distinguished career in the ecclesiastical courts. He was virtually unknown outside curialist circles but, as far as anyone was able to judge, qualified as a moderate.

The signal was clear: the conservatives were firm in their opposition to Montini, who had presumably reached the ceiling of his committed support, but not in their adherence to Antoniutti. A compromise candidate would be acceptable, and Roberti seemed to be their nominee. Thus the movement to get their best man elected seemed to have fallen back on the less edifying strategy of stopping Montini.

When the result of the first ballot was known. Cardinal Testa was reported to have marched over to where Di Jorio and other curialists happened to be seated close together and given vent to his exasperation. In a voice loud enough to be heard through most of the chapel, he appealed to them to use their influence to stop what he termed the deliberate obstruction of the election. Siri heard him, and rose to protest to Cardinal Tisserant. The bearded dean of the Sacred College, known in the Vatican as *Il Francese* ("the Frenchman"), had been an intelligence officer in the French Army's *Deuxième Bureau* in Syria during World War I. Traces of a military manner had persisted throughout his subsequent career as an Orientalist of wide repute in the Vatican library of which he rose to become the prefect, introducing from the United States the Dewey System of cataloging books. In the 1958 conclave, he was overheard rebuking Cardinal Roncalli in the Sistine Chapel, *"Eminenza,* you are wearing the wrong kind of shoes."

To which the soon-to-be pontiff replied, *"Eminenza,* surely we have more important things to worry about than shoes."

Such a stickler for regulations was even less likely to tolerate Testa's outburst, and he sharply instructed the cardinal to return to his seat. The tension was high when the cardinals voted again. The result of the ballot showed no movement. The impasse was complete.

A day of balloting was nothing in the context of past conclaves lasting years and months, but the presence of the television cameras positioned in Saint Peter's Square, their powerful lights seeping into the conclave area through shuttered windows, brought home to the cardinals as never before that the world was watching and waiting. There was a growing consensus in the conclave to avoid a long election that implied deep divisions among the cardinals.

The conservatives were in fact divided over what to do next. Cardinal Siri headed a group favoring a firm stand until a compromise candidate acceptable to both sides could be found, but with Antoniutti hopelessly stalled, Ottaviani was inclined to "take the train to Geneva." The conservative jibe at the cardinals who supported Montini had a double edge. The train from Rome to Geneva stopped en route in Montini's archdiocese. Besides that, however, Geneva was the headquarters of the World Council of Churches, and the diehards feared that a committed ecumenist like Montini would allow the Church of Rome to slip under Protestant influence.

Ottaviani, however, was concerned that if the two conclave blocks were fragmented as a result of a long deadlock, things could get out of hand, and there was always the danger that someone less acceptable than Montini might emerge out of nowhere to win the election by default. Ottaviani let it be known that, with certain guarantees, Montini himself could become the compromise candidate the conservatives sought —he was at least a known quantity.

In that strange atmosphere of improvisation and inspiration, the necessity of a solution seemed to have taken hold. On the evening of June 20, Montini was seen entering Cardinal Cicognani's cell. When the archbishop of Milan emerged, about an hour later, he walked straight to his own cell without saying a word to anyone. Yet within half an hour the word had spread that Montini had agreed that, in the event of his election, he would confirm the aged secretary of state in his post. More than a human gesture toward an old man, the commitment was seen as an attempt to reassure the curialists, who had good reason to believe that Montini's original intention had been to appoint an energetic young cardinal to the post to counter his own hesitant nature and push him to take action. What was worse from their point of view, the likeliest candidate was rumored to be the Curia's old adversary, Cardinal Suenens.

Later that evening, as he strolled in the *Galleria del Lapidario* close to his room, Montini seemed more somber than ever.

Cardinal König tried to cheer him up. "You have not far to go now," he told Montini.

The remark brought an anguished reply that the inheritance of John was a frightening burden. Montini was among those who believed that his predecessor had had a special grace, a supernatural reinforcement of his personality.

"I continue to hope not to be elected," he told König. "So far, in fact, the votes rise to a certain level and then stop. I hope it will stay that way, but at the moment, I am in the dark and see nothing."

Montini went on to speak of the importance of continuing John's work, and of his conviction that the pope's Eastern European policy was the right road to follow. He must have known that there was now little chance of avoiding the papal chalice. With Ottaviani's veto apparently lifted, some of his erstwhile opponents would probably vote for him the following morning, thus ensuring his election.

He had been dismayed to find himself the center of a maelstrom of political wheeling and dealing, with the conclavists playing an overly active part—at least to his way of thinking. (In revising the Rules of the Conclave some years later, he was to remember their intrigues and bar them from attending the election.)

Next day, even before the morning's ballot, Montini was

treated with a marked deference, as if he were already pope.
After he had said mass in the *Sala dei Paramenti,* he spotted a
conclavist at another altar about to begin his own mass, and
went to act as his server—as many cardinals had already done
and were doing for other conclavists. But a prelate quickly
came forward to take his place, enabling him to go and have
his breakfast.

Voting began in an atmosphere of great anticipation. In their
eagerness, the cardinals even appeared to speed up the balloting process. Then, during the count there were some early
moments of anxiety when the previous day's three-name
spread began once more to take shape. Soon, however, the
scrutator's even chant of "Montini . . . Antoniutti . . . Roberti"
began to break up into a more irregular pattern dominated by
one name—Montini. Toward the end of the count the conclavists stationed outside heard a burst of applause from inside
the locked chapel. Montini had passed the fifty-four mark, but
the tally went on until all eighty ballots had been accounted
for. Montini's final total was fifty seven votes, just three more
than the required majority. Although seven conservatives had
presumably swung over, twenty-two had held out till the bitter end.

Even without the triumph of a large majority, Montini had
still been elected two hundred sixty-second pontiff of the
Roman Catholic Church. When he was approached and asked
if he accepted the election, eyewitnesses spoke of a momen-
tary pause during which the cardinal's emotions showed
plainly in his expression, and he seemed to shrink from the
enormous task. Then he replied, *Accepto in nomine Domini.*

"Having given his consent," the conclave regulations
stated, "the elected man is immediately the true Pope, and at
that moment acquires and can exercise full and absolute jurisdiction over the whole world."

Montini was led behind the altar, where he took off his
cardinal's robes, standing for an instant in thick black wool
trousers which he wore summer and winter because of his

fear of draughts and colds. Then he donned the white cassock tailored to his exact measurements by the prophetic Gammarelli. Archbishop Carpino, the secretary of the conclave, knelt to offer him the white silk *zucchetto*, lined with lambskin so as not to slip off the pontiff's head. Traditionally, the newly elected pontiff places his discarded red *zucchetto* on the head of the kneeling secretary, thereby making him a cardinal on the spot. But enough modern popes have ignored the practice to create a human moment of tension around the figure of the kneeling prelate.

All eyes were on the new pope to see what he would do. To Carpino's visible disappointment, the new pope absently thrust the red *zucchetto* into his pocket. It was all over in an instant, and the ceremonial machinery trundled on. The pope was led back to his throne in front of the Sistine Chapel altar and the cardinals approached one by one to kiss his right foot in act of homage to the newly elected supreme head of the Roman Catholic Church. As each old prelate in turn prostrated himself creakily on the ground, the pope solicitously raised his red slipper slightly to make the obeisance a little easier.

While the obeisance was in progress, a blank tally form was circulating among the cardinals for their signatures. It belonged to Cardinal Spellman, who was a keen autograph collector. But a member of the prefect of ceremonies's staff intercepted it and added it to the pile of ballots and papers relating to the final round of voting which, according to instruments left by Pope John XXIII, were to be put in a sealed envelope and conserved in the Vatican Archives. Old newspapers would be burned in the stove in their place.

"*Eminenza*," the prelate chided Spellman, "it's against the rules to take any documents out of the conclave." But Spellman was not about to be robbed of a prize collector's item. Armed with another tally form, he went purposefully from one cardinal to the next until there was an autograph of every cardinal present in the conclave with the exception of the newly elected pope. En route, however, Spellman had acquired another trophy: the name card from Montini's place in the Sistine Chapel, and when the American cardinal's turn came to do homage, he produced it and asked the pope to sign it. The pope wrote: "Paulus PP VI" in a small, precise hand. It was the first time he signed his papal name.

It was 11:22 on the first day of summer when a sudden spurt of unmistakable white smoke against a brilliant blue sky announced the election of a new successor to the throne of Saint Peter. Soon a long white column drifted lazily upwards from the narrow makeshift chimney. Almost instantaneously, the square began to fill with thousands of Romans. They seemed to spring up from between the cobbles. Schoolchildren and nuns catapulted out of classrooms into the streets. Busses and cars west of the Tiber came to a halt, disgorging passengers and drivers who ran to the square as the word spread, "*È bianco!*" A detachment of Palatine Guards led by their band and followed by Italian troops marched onto the square, taking up their positions in review order in front of the porch of the great basilica. When the double glass doors of the central loggia were thrown open the crowd, which by now exceeded one hundred thousand, seethed with excitement. The cameras under colored umbrellas to shield them from the sun seemed to strain forward on their tripods.

It was 12:20 when Cardinal Ottaviani stepped out onto the loggia (the cardinals having in the meantime sung a *Te Deum* of thanksgiving for the successful conclusion of the conclave, and witnessed the signing of the election document). As senior cardinal-deacon it was Ottaviani's task to make the formal announcement. Clearly relishing the suspense, he waited for the hubbub to die down before launching into the Latin formula.

Annuntio vobis gaudium magnum. Habemus papam.
Eminentissimum ac Reverendissimum Dominum. . . .
Dominum . . . Johannem Baptistam Sancti Apostoli
Ecclesiae Cardinalem Montini.

Only the first two names were needed to identify the new pope, for there was no other Giovanni Battista among the cardinals. The remainder of Ottaviani's announcement was lost in an eruption of cheering. Ottaviani waited, smiling blankly out at the sunlight. Then he went on:

Qui sibi nomen imposuit . . . Paulus Sextus.

While the crowd continued to cheer, Ottaviani withdrew surrounded by purple-clad prelates.

Montini was pope. Paul VI. There was no real surprise about it, but the result of a papal election is never certain until the small figure appears on the loggia of the basilica to give the pontiff's name. Canon Bernard Pawley, the archbishop of Canterbury's representative at the Vatican Council, had watched the announcement in the office of the Secretariat for Christian Unity. Pawley had been a member of the group of Anglican clergymen who had stayed with Montini in Milan. He immediately left the building, returning shortly with a bottle of champagne to drink a toast with Cardinal Bea's staff.

The crowd in Saint Peter's Square began to cheer again when the windows of the side loggias were thrown open, and the cardinals began to cram themselves onto the balconies. The cheers swelled into a roar when Pope Paul himself appeared, smiling a tense smile, arms outstretched, waving his hands from the wrist at the sea of fluttering white handkerchiefs below him. He was flanked by Archbishop Dante and Monsignor Capoferri, and at a sign from the former, he began the formula of the papal blessing *Urbi et Orbi,* to the city of Rome and to the world.

"Blessed be the name of the Lord." His voice was clear, though not particularly musical.

"Now and forever," responded the crowd.

"Our help is from the Lord," chanted Pope Paul.

"Who made heaven and earth."

Then, with the grace of a born ceremonialist, he raised his arm high above his head and began making the sign of the

cross in a slow, sweeping semicircle to cover the whole earth
before him: "May the blessing of Almighty God, Father, Son,
and Holy Ghost descend upon you and remain forever."

The news of Montini's election was flashed to Langley and
thence to President Kennedy who was in Dublin on the first
stop of his European tour which also was to take him to Berlin
and Rome. The agency quickly prepared a profile of the new
pontiff in anticipation of Kennedy's papal audience, already
scheduled for July 2 before Pope John's death, but long
thought unlikely to take place because of the pope's illness.
The two-page profile contained no startling revelation, but the
speed with which it was compiled and sent to Kennedy indicated the existence of personal files, or at the very least access
to accurate information about Church personalities. It gave
details of his family background and political connections and
outlined his Vatican career. It also pointed out that he was
generally considered a liberal on social questions and had
been an early supporter of the opening to the left in Italian
politics.

The news also flashed to Moscow and Premier Nikita
Khrushchev's message of congratulations to the new pope was
among the first to arrive. Montini was the archbishop who
had carried a cross through the streets of Milan mourning the
dead of the Hungarian Revolution. At the time, the press in
Eastern Europe had said he was "praying for men who had
killed their brothers"—meaning that the regime's troops had
only fired in self-defense. But the governments of Poland,
Czechoslovakia, and Hungary dutifully followed the Soviet
lead in sending congratulations to Pope Paul on his election, and soon afterward another message arrived from East
Germany.

Clearly, the Communist bloc did not intend to break off
contacts with the Vatican now that their instigator, Pope John,
was dead. The new pope, for his part, was equally determined
to build an East European policy on the foundations laid
down by his predecessor. Here was an issue tailor-made to his

long experience in diplomacy. He was still in the conclave when he had his first talks with Cardinal König to review the status of Vatican relations with each communist country.

Then at 5:00 P.M. that afternoon, the conclave doors in the *Cortile del Pappagallo* were unlocked, and the cardinals began streaming out with the alacrity of schoolboys quitting school. Cardinal Cushing, who recognized a political process when he saw one, grumbled to waiting members of his staff, "That's the last conclave I go to. We could have settled the whole thing in twenty minutes. Instead of which we sat around in there for three days."

In the conclave, Cushing had been the protagonist of a minor crisis stemming from the way he felt about the Curia and the Curia about him. When he was made a cardinal in 1959, a planeload of American prelates had flown to Rome for his consistory. Cicognani, then apostolic delegate to Washington, had accompanied them. During the flight, Cico (as he was known in American ecclesiastical circles) had taken Spelly aside. *"Eminenza,"* he said. "Monsignor Cushing is a man of outstanding qualities. He could do great things for the Church, but the Curia does not understand him. You and I are going to have to look after him."

Time had done little to further that understanding. Part of the problem was that Cushing did not speak Italian. This put him at an immediate disadvantage in Rome where Curia bureaucrats would not condescend to speak anything else. But aside from a language problem there was the fact that alone among the United States cardinals, Cushing was not a product of the North American College in Rome, the traditional breeding ground for senior American prelates, which made him an unknown quantity in the Vatican. A young student priest at the large American establishment on the hill overlooking the Vatican inevitably came into contact with the central government of the Church, and this tended to help him to cope with its parochiality in the future. The more ambitious among them could get themselves plugged into the Vatican's old boy network, perhaps by befriending a rising Curia figure, as Spellman had done with Pius XII.

There was no doubt in the mind of Archbishop Joseph O'Connor, who had been Rector of the North American College for so long he seemed eternally destined to hold the post, that his charges were the cream of young American priesthood. He was fond of pointing out to them that, as graduates of the college, a glorious career in Vatican diplomacy was theirs for the asking. Most young priests, however, were more interested in returning to parish work at home.

But Cushing had followed a less privileged route to prominence. He had trained for the priesthood at a Boston seminary, and no one had asked him to join the papal diplomatic service. What he was asked to do was to raise money for the Church, and it was as a fund raiser of outstanding skill and effectiveness that he made his mark first nationally and then on Rome. Cushing was personally responsible for channeling more money to Rome, especially for missionary work, than any other individual before or since. A more secure personality would have learned to cope with the fact that he was a "ranker" among West Pointers, but Cushing never did. He always felt and behaved like an outsider when he visited the Vatican. He fell back on self-parody as a defense mechanism, and became "The Cush"—the gruff, back-slapping giant of popular legend.

The Cush never ventured to Rome without his secretary, a Boston priest named John Sennott who not only spoke fluent Italian and was an alumnus of the North American College, but had also been its chief administrator for eight years. Besides acting as the cardinal's interpreter, Sennott ran interference for him in his dealing with Curia prelates. Of course, Sennott had arrived with Cushing to act as his conclavist in the papal election. In Rome, the cardinal discovered that the Curia had assigned to him another conclavist in the person of Monsignor Daniel Cronin, an American ecclesiastical diplomat working in the Secretariat of State. But Cushing was as immovable as Saint Peter's Basilica itself: he refused to give up Sennott as his conclavist, and actually threatened not to enter the conclave if his secretary was refused admission. The Curia was equally insistent on its own appointee in case the unpredictable American cardinal needed to be restrained. When the Cush stuck to his guns, both sides appealed to Cardinal Tisserant, and the dean of the sacred college decreed that Cushing could keep both conclavists. When Cardinal Spellman learned of this unique dispensation, he immediately demanded the same privilege. If the archbishop of Boston rated two conclavists, the archbishop of New York deserved the same treatment at the very least. But by then the conclave doors were closed, and it was too late.

The evening following the election, Pope Paul summoned the archbishop of Boston to the Vatican Palace to ask him what topics President Kennedy would want to discuss at his papal audience. Cushing arrived with Sennott trailing inevitably behind him, but he was told that no interpreter would be necessary as the pontiff would speak English. So the cardinal lumbered into the pope's study alone. He found Pope Paul standing at his white desk behind a barricade of documents. He looked so at home in his new surroundings that Cushing blurted, "Holy Father, you look as if you've been here all your life." He was rewarded with a watery smile.

The pope was full of praise for Kennedy and expressed great pleasure that his first official visit should be with the president of the beloved United States. He said he wanted to discuss world peace with the president, and to make a statement on racial discrimination. He also wanted to transmit words of encouragement to Church schools in the United States which were then in the throes of a congressional battle to win federal funding. But Cushing was well versed in Kennedy's thinking. "Great care should be taken to prevent the discussions from becoming part of political propaganda in the United States," he replied cautiously.

Paul looked puzzled. Propaganda?

Well, Cushing replied, such subjects as racial problems and
schools carried strong political implications. "I strongly rec-
ommend that any problem of national significance be
avoided," Cushing went on boldly. "I believe that the audience should be confined to questions of world peace." No
other cardinal could have warned the newly elected pontiff to
stay out of American domestic affairs and gotten away with it.
When Pope Paul agreed, Cushing pressed his advantage. If
any communiqué was necessary, he insisted, it should state
simply that the audience had taken place without revealing
the substance of the discussion.

Pope Paul's hopes of starting off his pontificate with a meeting of political significance had been torpedoed, but the Vatican did not give up. Later the same day, Monsignor Cardinale
approached the United States Embassy to suggest that, as
Kennedy would already be in Rome on his state visit to Italy,
would he consider attending Pope Paul's coronation ceremony on June 30? This request presented the traveling White
House with a difficult decision. The president could hardly
refuse without appearing to snub the new pope, but at the
same time the notion of attending the coronation was totally
inconsistent with the policy Kennedy had so far followed with
respect to the Vatican. So the White House quickly altered
Kennedy's schedule so as to postpone his arrival in Rome by
twenty-four hours to July 1. It was announced that he would
spend Pope Paul's coronation day getting some much needed
rest at a villa on Lake Como. Kennedy clearly felt that any
criticism resulting from being in Italy and not in Rome at the
ceremony—which was, in any case, likely to die out after the
papal audience—was preferable to what he would have to
face at home if he was seen there, sitting among the Catholic
leaders of such countries as Italy, Belgium, and Ireland.

When Pope Paul VI was crowned on the evening of the feast
of Saint Peter and Paul in the basilica square, the United
States delegation was led by Chief Justice Earl Warren. Over
four hundred thousand crammed the square to watch the an-

cient ceremony which, as a consequence of subsequent developments, could well have been the last papal coronation in history. At 6:00 P.M. the pope was borne out of the Apostolic Palace on the *sedia gestatoria* under a large golden canopy, surrounded by the full panoply of a papal court enjoying its last moment of glory before the new pope's Vatican reforms reduced much of it to obsolescence: Swiss Guards, Noble Guards, Gentlemen of the Sword and Cape, Mace Bearers, Standard Bearers, Sword Bearers, Cup Bearers surrounded the throne as it bobbed above the heads of the crowd on the shoulders of a dozen *sediari.* On either side of the pontiff was carried a large ceremonial fan made from ostrich feathers, another soon-to-disappear vestige of the imperial papacy.

The pope himself was wrapped in a voluminous, gold-embroidered cape known as the *falda,* exclusively for papal use. His thin face behind his glasses was nervous, almost furtive, and his smile strained, betraying the awkwardness in crowds that was to become the bane of his pontificate. As the crowd cheered, and the television cameras feasted their lenses on the splendor of the scene, the pope clung to the arm of his throne with his left hand, while with his right he traced little crosses in the air. Three times the procession was halted so that a silver container of burning flax could be held up to the pope, and the loud voice of a master of ceremonies reminded him, *"Beatissime Pater, sic transit gloria mundi."* Each time, Pope Paul placed his right hand over his heart and stared gravely at the smoking material, but each time the procession moved on, and the pope continued to bless his faithful, with the exalting hymn *Tu Es Petrus,* sung by the Sistine Chapel choir ringing in his ears.

After mass celebrated by the pope against a magnificent Roman sunset, Ottaviani, as senior cardinal-deacon, took the triple tiara in both hands and, raising it about a foot above the pope's head, began to bring it blindly down in the solemn moment of coronation. The cardinal's aim was off, but one of the ever-watchful masters of ceremonies corrected the tiara's

line of descent by pulling Ottaviani backwards by his vestments at just the right moment, and Giovanni Battista Montini
was crowned the two hundred sixty-second successor to Saint
Peter without mishap.

No pontiff in recent history ascended the throne with such
an inheritance of worldwide anticipation and goodwill. No
one doubted that Pope Paul was John's logical successor. No
one doubted that he would remain true to the legacy of his
predecessor. With his great knowledge and experience of Vatican administration, he would be able to extend the Johannine
program of renewal and reform of the Church and strengthen
the spiritual values and the sense of unity that Pope John
aroused among men of goodwill everywhere. At the same
time, no one was more aware than the pope himself of the
implications of his succession. Not by nature or training an
innovator, he was on the threshold of a pontificate committed
to innovation. He was a man who consented to try the unprecedented only after wrestling with deep mental reservations,
yet much of what he would feel he had to do, especially in the
early years was unprecedented.

Montini's decision that Pope John's policies were to be followed was to lead him down paths which were against everything which by character and experience he could be
expected to represent, and perhaps because he had no real
instinct for change, even his most adventurous ideas did not
match up to the root and branch reform which progressive
bishops were expecting from him. But if there were difficulties in following one of the most loved men in recent history
there were also advantages, for the new pontiff's performance
would be watched with sympathy. This was the real transformation of the papacy in the twentieth century. It looked out
on the world and captured the world's surprised interest.

Two days after the coronation, on the third day of his visit
to Rome, President Kennedy was speeding along the streets
of the city heading for his private audience with the pope. By
his side in the presidential Lincoln sat Secretary of State Dean

Rusk. Though it was shortly before 10:00 A.M., both men were wearing white tie and tails. There had been a last-minute flap when the presidential entourage realized that they did not know what actually took place during a papal audience, and what was the correct dress. It is a measure of Kennedy's reliance on the agency that he turned for guidance not to the protocol office of the State Department, but to the CIA, and a telegram was flashed from Langley telling him what to expect and what to wear.

At the president's feet lay a folder marked "Papal Audience with Pope Paul VI," a compilation of background information (including the CIA profile of Paul), and suggested topics for discussion. Ralph Dungan recommended raising the question of recalling Archbishop Vagnozzi, the apostolic delegate in Washington, who was unpopular with all but the more conservative American Catholics, and who consequently presented a distorted view of the United States Church to the Vatican, and to replace him with a man who was more in tune with the reforms taking place in the Church.

Dungan even ventured a proposal on the touchy subject of Vatican–United States diplomatic relations: bring back President Roosevelt's compromise formula of appointing a personal representative to the pope with limited diplomatic status. The CIA wanted Kennedy to induce Pope Paul to bring the influence of the Vietnamese hierarchy to bear on the Bhuddist monks in Vietnam to soften their anti-war stance.

During the ride, Kennedy was more interested in discussing Italian politics than his forthcoming audience. The previous evening, he had attended an official reception in his honor at the Quirinal Palace, official residence of the Italian head of state. Several leading politicians had been presented to him, including Palmiro Togliatti. The brief encounter had piqued Kennedy's interest in the Communist party secretary, and he bombarded Rusk with questions. He regretted not having had the opportunity for a longer conversation with Togliatti, he said.

Eventually, however, Rusk managed to steer the conversation to the question of United States relations with the Vatican.

"You know, Mr. President, I think the time has come when we should certainly think about establishing diplomatic relations with the Holy See," Rusk began. "It would be beneficial." If one concedes the reality of Church influence in the world, he argued, it would seem wise for the United States to be able to talk frankly and continuously with the pope on the most vital and delicate issues of policy. This could be done only through regular diplomatic contact and conversely, the failure to have such contact could hamper the conduct of American foreign policy in certain areas . . .

But Kennedy abruptly cut off Rusk's argument in midsentence. "Maybe the time has come for someone else, but it isn't right for me, the first Catholic president. If Harry Truman, a Baptist, didn't feel he could do it, I certainly don't." There was an awkward silence, and the secretary changed the subject.

As the presidential motorcade drove into the *Cortile San Damaso*, a company of Swiss Guards presented arms with their halberds. Kennedy acknowledged the salute. Then a squadron of prelates of the papal household led the president and his party—so large, in fact, that the prelates refused to admit the whole group to the papal audience—to the pontiff's third floor library. On the way, Kennedy quietly made it clear that he did not intend to follow the practice of Catholic heads of state and genuflect before the pope, nor was he going to kiss the papal ring. He was assured by Monsignor Cardinale, in his capacity as chief of protocol, that Pope Paul was expecting nothing more than a cordial handshake. Very well, Kennedy went on, but he would not bow as they shook hands either. "In the first place, I have a bad back, and if I bow I might not be able to get up again," he said, but he gave no other reasons, nor did he have to; the president's position was by now well known in the Vatican.

The audience itself was in two parts: first, a private conversation between Kennedy and Pope Paul in the latter's inner sanctum, the papal library, with only an interpreter present. Then the two of them would emerge into an adjoining antechamber where Kennedy would introduce the senior members of his staff—including McGeorge Bundy, Pierre Salinger (the White House spokesman), Rusk, and Theodore Sorensen; and Kennedy and the pope would each make a brief statement.

Clearly then, any discussions of substance would have to take place in the first part of the visit. As it turned out, however, Kennedy's determination to prevent any tinge of political significance from creeping into his discussions with the pope and Paul's own desire not to embarrass his first official guest by taking the initiative combined to reduce the encounter to the level of an obligatory event in any leader's official visit to Rome. When Pope Paul said he rejoiced at the good relations between the United States and the Holy See, he may have been offering Kennedy an opening to bring up the subject of diplomatic ties; but Kennedy failed to react on cue. There was no mention of a resumption of the prewar Roosevelt formula; Archbishop Vagnozzi's name was never brought up. Instead the talk drifted on to the New York World's Fair. Kennedy thanked Paul for permitting Michelangelo's magnificent *Pietà* in Saint Peter's Basilica to be shipped to the United States and exhibited in the Vatican pavilion.

The pope then apologized for Cardinal Mindszenty's presence in the American legation in Budapest, and the difficulties in United States–Hungarian relations arising from it. "No, no, not at all, please don't apologize," Kennedy replied with surprising force. "We regard this as a human rights issue, not a political question, and we are prepared to go right down to the wire. As far as we are concerned, the cardinal can go on staying right where he is." The pope was somewhat startled by Kennedy's reaction. It was the only animated moment of the thirty-minute audience. No mention was made of racial problems, schools, Vietnam, or world peace.

When the time came for the presentations, shouts and scuffling could be heard in the background. By prior agreement, Pope Paul was introduced to eleven top administration officials, but the Kennedy party contained nearly twenty people whose names were not on the original guest list, including a group of American White House correspondents who were traveling on the presidential plane, Air Force One. Vatican prelates had herded the surplus into a large room and literally placed them under guard, but when word got out that the pope was greeting the president's men, they staged a breakout, hoping to meet him too. Nervous clerics and Swiss Guards held them back, rough-handling some of them in the process. The pope appeared not to notice the commotion.

While Kennedy departed the Vatican, William Sherman, Igino Cardinale's contact in the embassy, remained behind to pick up the original text of Pope Paul's speech for inclusion in the presidential official files, the Vatican having already been advised that a copy would not do. Sherman had to wait while the pontiff erased his penciled annotations to help his English pronunciation. For example, over the name of Pope John XXIII, he had written "Pope John the twenty-third."

Meanwhile, Kennedy was heading for his next engagement, a visit to the North American College. His aides waited expectantly for some comment on the audience from the president. With Kennedy, they could often judge the impact of a meeting by how he talked about it immediately afterwards. Instead, he picked up the trend of his earlier conversation about Togliatti. It was as if his half hour with the pope had left no imprint on his mind. At the American College, Cardinal Cushing presented to him the gifts Pope John XXIII had intended to give him had the pope lived long enough: a beautifully illustrated book on the Vatican's art treasures, an ikon, and several of Manzù's medals. John's former associates had asked Cushing to make the presentation after approaching several senior

Curia cardinals and being turned down by each of them. None wished to be associated with the dead pontiff. *Morto un papa, se ne fa un altro.* ("A pope dies, another comes in his place.")

It is arguable that Kennedy's rigidity with regard to the Vatican resulted in missed political and diplomatic opportunities. Who can say where Pope John's determined efforts to initiate a three-way dialogue would have led had both sides been willing to accept his historic concept of a politically active pontiff? Who can say how papal intervention in the Vietnam war would have affected events had it come sooner than Pope Paul's briefly hopeful negotiated Christmas truce? On the other hand, it can safely be said that by adhering to his Houston commitment with such firmness, Kennedy contributed greatly to the disappearance of the religious issue from American presidential politics. The pope did not dictate United States foreign policy. Mass was not said in the White House (actually, mass had been celebrated in the White House on one occasion long before—by Cardinal Spellman during the first Eisenhower Administration—but hardly anyone knew it.) The sacrosanctity of the separation of church and state was safe.

The Vatican prelates did not press for diplomatic relations with Kennedy, but someone else did. The morning after his papal audience, Kennedy was on his way to place a wreath at the tomb of Italy's Unknown Soldier. Beside him in the car was Giulio Andreotti, the minister of defense, who asked why the U.S. continued to hesitate about diplomatic ties with the Holy See. Several non-Catholic countries, including Arab countries, had missions accredited to the papacy, Andreotti argued, and it seemed strange that the U.S. should hold out.

Andreotti was not likely to have raised the point had he not received a high-level request from Church circles. Since Pope Paul VI had been his political mentor, it was safe to assume that the level could not have been higher. When Kennedy explained the political hazards to a Catholic president of establishing diplomatic relations with Rome, Andreotti said, "You feel you cannot take the step because you are a Catholic, a Protestant president would have little interest in doing so because he is not Catholic, so who will?" Kennedy was silent. Then he said, "If I'm reelected in 1964, I'll do it in my second term."

CHAPTER XII

The "Visitor" Departs

Hᴉsᴛᴏʀʏ ᴍᴜsᴛ ʙᴇ ʟᴇFᴛ ᴛᴏ ᴊᴜᴅɢᴇ the fifteen-year papacy of Pope Paul VI, a reign of crises, controversy, and new precedents. Many of his difficulties, as well as his advantages, originated in his inheritance. John was, of course, a hard man to follow because of the strength of his personality. Moreover, though the council had been the result of John's inspiration, it was Paul who faced the long and challenging task of implementing the reforms which the council sanctioned, and of controlling the remarkable energies which it released. Besides his determination to remain faithful to John's example, he was also himself convinced of the necessity for the Church to change its posture, especially in relation to other Christian churches and to secular bodies, but he also recognized the dangers the process held for the embodied truths and essential traditions of the Roman Catholic church. The resulting conflict between change and preservation brought out his "Hamlet" streak. His doubts and hesitations were visible, and they bore heavily upon him. A firmer hand would probably have been preferable.

From the start, however, Pope Paul showed a surer touch at

directing the international affairs of the Holy See. There was
even a feeling that diplomacy took up too much of his thinking
at the expense of the pressing problems of the Church. The
fact was that, due to his long training, he felt more at home
with diplomatic telegrams and reports from nuncios than with
theological problems ("Better news from Santo Domingo
today," he once told a crowd gathered in Saint Peter's Square
for his blessing.)

His talks with Cardinal König while still in the conclave
reflected the high place reserved on his list of priorities for
improving the situation of the Church and the faithful in Eastern Europe. Thus there was hardly a pause in the development of Pope John's initiatives in this direction. From the
communist bloc, meanwhile, came further indications of a desire to continue the contacts. The messages of congratulation
to the new pontiff had been the first signal. Three months
later, Norman Cousins's request to Khrushchev in December
1962 for the release of Archbishop Josef Beran of Prague bore
fruit. The Czechoslovak primate arrived to a Roman exile.

The Vatican immediately began attempts to build on this
advantage. The gains were small and slow in coming, for the
entrenched regime of President Antonin Novotny made
concessions grudgingly in any field. The most significant gain
for Vatican diplomacy was the appointment of an apostolic
administrator to Beran's see of Prague, which had been without a bishop for over fifteen years. There were still many
impeded bishops, and all but two seminaries remained forc-
ibly closed. Czechoslovakia was, and continued to be, the Vatican's toughest challenge in Eastern Europe after Albania.

But the release of Archbishop Beran was really the outcome
of earlier contacts under Pope John. Paul VI scored his first
solid achievement in Hungary where Monsignor Agostino
Casaroli had established tentative contact with the regime in
the spring of 1963. Though Casaroli remained undersecretary
of state for extraordinary affairs and nominal deputy to Archbishop Samoré, he rapidly emerged as the Vatican prelate re-

sponsible for Church contacts in Eastern Europe, reporting directly to the pontiff who personally supervised the conduct of the negotiations. Casaroli's first objective in Hungary was to secure the regime's agreement to the appointment of bishops to as many vacant sees as possible, but if the Church's expectations were modest, Cardinal Mindszenty's were not. The Hungarian primate would settle for little less than the regime's total capitulation in religious matters.

In a letter to the pope, written while Casaroli was holding talks in Budapest, the Hungarian primate outlined his minimum conditions for normalization of church-state relations in his country: (1) abolition of birth control and legalized abortion; (2) abolition of "socialist" ceremonies, secular weddings, funerals, and baptisms introduced by the communist regime to replace the church ceremonies; (3) reconstruction of the destroyed Regnum Maximus church which formerly occupied the site where the giant statue to Stalin was erected; (4) release of political prisoners. The primate's argument was that the regime's present policy of accommodation for the sake of appearances, plus Soviet pressure, gave the Church a strong bargaining advantage.

But Mindszenty's views were not sought by Casaroli, nor did Casaroli allow the primate's situation as a refugee in the United States legation to come up in the negotiations, which dragged on intermittently for eleven months. The Hungarian regime tried to pretend that Mindszenty's archdiocese of Esztergom was one of the vacant sees to which the Church hoped to appoint bishops. The Hungarians evidently expected Casaroli to challenge this contention and thus be drawn into a discussion on the cardinal, but as the talks inched along, the prelate made it clear that Mindszenty was not going to be part of the present bargain. The Holy See was still a long way from introducing their only negotiable asset into the talks. So Mindszenty was to remain official head of the Hungarian Church —at least for the moment.

In the primate's view, the Church's partial accord with the

Hungarian regime, signed in the spring of 1964, still gave
away too much in exchange for too little. When Casaroli revealed the details to him, the cardinal listened with mounting
anger. His first reaction was to issue a public statement disso-
ciating himself from the agreement, but the Vatican prelate
quietly pointed out that the terms of his asylum forbade him
from making such statements.

The problem was not a disagreement over tactics. Mindszenty and the Vatican were fighting different wars. Mindszenty burned with a crusader's fervor to destroy the enemy.
The Vatican hoped for modest practical gains. Seen from
Rome's perspective, the accord was a landmark in the drive to
regain lost ground in Eastern Europe. It demonstrated that
patient negotiation could produce results without sacrificing
fundamental principles. The Church had made a start in re-
building its fragmented hierarchy. Six titular bishops were
appointed to vacant sees as "apostolic administrators" with
regime approval, and with the understanding that they would
be advanced to full residential status by mutual agreement in
the future. The bishops, in short, were on probation.

In addition, the Church registered an important psycholog-
ical gain in having government commissars removed from the
episcopal curias. These party watchdogs lived in the bishop's
house, censored the bishop's mail and generally dominated
diocesan life. Under the new agreement, the commissar continued to exercise his surveillance—but from a house across
the street.

Also enshrined in the accord was a guarantee of religious
instruction in schools. This clause was largely a farce, for it
required an act of courage for a parent to insist on religious
instruction for his child, and such a request would sooner or
later tell against either child or parent. (Before World War II,
there were over three thousand Catholic schools in Hungary.
In 1964, there were less than ten.) The Church realized this
as well as anybody, but the existence of a formal commitment
made it possible to protest abuse.

Washington was disappointed that no progress had been made in securing Mindszenty's departure from its legation, and State Department officials said as much to the apostolic delegate in the United States, Archbishop Vagnozzi. Lyndon Johnson was less sympathetic than his predecessor had been to the cardinal's situation. The complicating presence of Mindszenty in the legation made it difficult to extend to Hungary the prevailing American policy of improving relations with East European regimes, especially through increased trade. Washington felt that "The Guest" (as the cardinal was usually referred to in State Department telegrams) had in some respects overstayed his welcome. At the same time, the American government was determined to continue to play a secondary role in negotiating his departure in order to prevent the issue from looming even larger in United States–Hungarian relations. So Washington began to apply gentle pressure whenever possible on both Budapest and the Vatican to come up with a solution.

The Hungarians needed little convincing. They saw the cardinal as an obstacle blocking access to the much-needed American technological know-how which would become available once ties between the two countries returned to normal as a result of his negotiated departure. "We do not want (the Mindszenty problem) to keep our relations abnormal for another thirty years," Premier Janos Kadar assured an American visitor in 1963. The Vatican, however, was in less of a hurry to prevail upon the cardinal to leave his country, and in trying to prod the Church into action Washington felt the lack of diplomatic relations.

Without direct instructions from Rome, the primate was unlikely to seek asylum in the West. He felt that he had a political responsibility as well as a religious one. Although the regime had long ago abolished his constitutional role as regent, Mindszenty still saw himself as the highest-ranking legitimate civil authority, and as long as even the remotest possibility of another uprising existed, he should stand ready to assert that authority and appoint a government. So the cardinal remained entrenched in the legation, celebrating mass every Sunday for the staff, and requiring close personal attention. Every Saturday, the *chargé d'affaires* would visit him and be lectured by him for over an hour on the terrible error of judgment which the Church was making in negotiating with the Kadar regime, which could not be trusted.

Then, in August 1965, Mindszenty became suddenly and seriously ill and began to spit blood. Three United States Army doctors were rushed to Budapest from West Germany; they arrived with an elaborate X-ray apparatus. The medical officer at the American embassy in Belgrade, who regularly examined the cardinal, was also summoned.

Mindszenty was found to be suffering from tuberculosis. When his condition improved he explained to his American hosts that he had contracted the disease while in prison, but believed that he had fully recovered before seeking refuge in the legation nine years earlier. For that reason, he said, he had never considered it necessary to mention his illness. Mindszenty's relapse caused an infection scare in the legation. Staffers began to give the cardinal a wide berth, but medical tests showed that the danger had passed, and the cardinal's small congregation gradually drifted back to Sunday mass. All the same, the episode raised serious questions about the legation's ability to cope with a serious recurrence of the cardinal's condition, and his departure seemed more desirable than before.

In the fall of that year, Mindszenty was once again a subject of discussion in a papal audience with the president of the United States. On this occasion, the president in question was Lyndon Johnson, and what he had to say about the cardinal eloquently reflected the change in Washington's approach to the problem. Johnson gave Pope Paul the usual American assurances that Mindszenty was welcome at the legation for as long as his personal safety and freedom required such an arrangement, but at the same time the United States government was "anxious to see the matter settled as soon as it seemed possible."

In December, "the visitor" himself made one of his periodic appeals to Washington for reassurance that he could remain in the legation. For the first time, the reply that he received contained a note of truculence. The State Department's letter, delivered by the *chargé*, Elim O'Shaughnessy, said,

> The refuge of your eminence in the Legation constitutes an extremely difficult and delicate situation. The prolongation of this situation for the indefinite future would not, in the considered view of the United States Government, serve the interests of the Hungarian people or those of your eminence. My government hopes, therefore, that an acceptable solution of the problem of refuge can be found . . .
>
> We are troubled by our inability to meet effectively the medical responsibilities on the Legation premises . . . We do not have at hand the medical facilities to undertake a thorough investigation of other body areas which may be affected by your illness nor to provide emergency treatment for the various medical episodes which may arise. For this reason, as well as for reasons stated above, we feel it most important that a reasonable solution consistent with the purpose for which refuge was granted be sought as soon as possible.

The letter plunged Mindszenty into a deep gloom. The Americans had turned against him. Soon, "those men from the Vatican," as he called Monsignor Casaroli and his aide Monsignor Bongianino, would arrive with a papal summons to Rome. But though State Department officials conveyed the American government's sentiments to Vagnozzi, the Vatican took no action. At this point, contacts between Rome and Budapest had soured and lost their momentum.

In 1965, Nikita Khrushchev, last of the trio of leading players in the dramatic story of Pope John's peace drive, fell from power in the Kremlin. With Khrushchev gone, Moscow became less openly favorable to improving relations with the Church, and its satellites found themselves with greater autonomy to determine their individual policy toward religious freedom. The Hungarian authorities toughened their position in the negotiations with the Church, insisting on a resolution of the Mindszenty problem. The cardinal was to go to Rome (or at any rate, to the West), renounce his title as primate, and refrain from making anti-regime statements. Perhaps to demonstrate that it meant business, the regime suddenly rounded up a number of priests and charged them with sedition. In the fall of 1965, Casaroli visited Hungary but when foreign ministry officials learned he had no new proposals, they refused to receive him.

No reason for the rebuff was communicated to Casaroli directly. On his arrival in Budapest, he was welcomed by a low-level government official who was polite but noncommittal. Then he was left to cool his heels at the Italian Embassy, where he was staying, for several days. When he finally gave up and left for Rome, the same official, polite as ever, saw him off at the airport.

Then a senior Hungarian diplomat in Washington telephoned his State Department contact to say, "Tell Casaroli that if the Vatican has something to say which could lead to a solution of the (Mindszenty) problem he would be received at the cabinet level."

To "test the language," the State Department man replied, "The Hungarian government would be happy to receive Casaroli—"

"Not happy," the Hungarian interrupted. "That would give the impression that the Hungarian government is under pressure to negotiate and weaken its position. Our aim is to solve the problem in such a way that it cannot be exploited as a cold war issue."

The use of the United States as a channel of communication underlined the extent to which Mindszenty's continued presence in the American Mission had set back budding relations between Rome and the Hungarian regime and at the same time how much things had improved between Hungary and

Washington, in spite of the cardinal. Nineteen sixty-seven was a poor year in the Vatican–Budapest talks. By contrast, the Hungarian regime and the United States reached an agreement to raise the level of their diplomatic missions to embassies, and to exchange ambassadors for the first time since 1956.

Neither the Americans nor the Vatican saw fit to inform the cardinal of this development. The Americans felt it was properly Rome's responsibility. But Rome never lost an opportunity to demonstrate to the Americans that things would go much more smoothly if formal relations existed and took its time communicating with Mindszenty. The wheels of Church diplomacy tended to grind at an even slower pace than usual when the United States was involved. When an American diplomat complained about ecclesiastical foot-dragging to Archbishop Vagnozzi in Washington, the apostolic delegate shrugged elaborately and replied that "unorthodox" channels tended to cause delays. This gentle pressure had the new pontiff's full backing, for he had long been an advocate of trying to persuade the American government to agree to formal relations. As substitute secretary of state he had been at the center of the Mark Clark initiative. When it failed, he was deeply disappointed. To make matters worse, Pius XII had somehow held him responsible for its failure.

In June 1967, seven months after the signing of the United States–Hungarian accord, the pope dispatched Cardinal König to confirm to Mindszenty what he had long ago read in the newspapers: the newly appointed American ambassador would shortly be arriving in Budapest. The Hungarian primate requested König to ask the Vatican to arrange for his immediate departure to the West. Mindszenty appeared determined to leave before the arrival of the official whose quarters he now occupied.

Speaking quietly but with great determination, Mindszenty went on to say that his continued presence in the embassy after the new ambassador's arrival would be out of the question, since it would give the impression that he approved of

Washington's willingness to improve relations with the regime. In the absence of an arrangement for him to go to the
West he would walk out of the embassy and give himself up
to the Hungarian police. He was the ranking personage in the
Hungarian nation constitutionally as well as ecclesiastically,
he said, and he must share the suffering that his people were
going through.

Somewhat taken aback by this unexpected switch in the
Hungarian primate's longstanding position of refusing to
budge, Cardinal König said that he would immediately report
to the pontiff. When he left for Rome, the United States *chargé*
cabled a detailed report to Washington. Cardinal Mindszenty,
he wrote, "repeatedly indicated that appointment of an ambassador has made him decide to leave Hungary.

"His decision appears unconditional: he has made no reference to the conditions he had raised in past for giving up his
refuge. He seems prepared to go to the West on whatever
terms can be arranged. He hopes that he can settle down in
Vienna, where he can be near Hungary, and also, he probably
feels, be freer than in Rome. He evidently hopes that all of
this can be arranged by Cardinal König, whom he likes and
trusts, rather than papal envoys such as Archbishop Casaroli
and Monsignor Bongianino who visited him in the past."

The *chargé* added that Mindszenty "gave no indication as
to how he thinks the consent of the Hungarian regime for his
departure will be obtained: this is undoubtedly a humiliating
point which he prefers not to think about . . .

"If the cardinal's hopes for departure to West fail to mater-
ialize, believe we must prepare seriously for possibility he
has raised that he will walk out of embassy. Department's
thinking on best way of handling such contingency is requested soonest. In view of cardinal's frankness regarding his
intention of walking out and his statement that before doing
so he would express gratitude to President and to U.S. for
refuge, am inclined to think that he would give us final notice
before attempting such a step and that he would choose to do

it in day time, in public view. It would be difficult for him to get to front door of embassy unseen by staff even if he wished to do so, but we are taking additional precautions just in case.

"If he remains determined to take this step it might be possible for us to influence the way in which it is taken, e.g., obtaining suitable statement from him on purpose in leaving, and give him assistance and protection in leaving such as escort and car to any address he may choose up to point when Hungarian authorities intervene which may, of course, be at our very doorstep."

Meanwhile, a CIA operative on post at the American mission reported to Langley that the Hungarian regime had considered the possibility that the cardinal might one day walk out and vacillated between two options—exiling him to the West, and confining him to a village. The Hungarians felt that Mindszenty was a forgotten man in his own country and that his reappearance was not likely to create problems internally. All the same, if he were jailed, it would arouse sympathy for him.

Expulsion seemed the most desirable option, but it raised the likelihood that, once in the West, he would become a vocal critic of the regime and a focal point of emigré opposition. On balance, therefore, the Hungarians would probably opt for confinement in a village, probably Mindszenty's native village.

While the cardinal was taking his afternoon constitutional, the agent conducted a thorough search of his documents and belongings but reported finding nothing that could shed further light on the threatened walkout.

Was Mindszenty bluffing? Possibly, but Washington was taking no chances. Contingency press guidance was prepared so that everyone would know what to say in such an eventuality. Then a State Department desk officer called at the apostolic delegation of Massachusetts Avenue, the capital's "Embassy Row," to impress upon Archbishop Giovanni Raimondi (who had succeeded Vagnozzi as apostolic delegate) the need for the Vatican to deflect Mindszenty from such a course.

The officer went on to say that the Johnson Administration was concerned that it might run into criticism from American Catholics for allowing Mindszenty to fall into the hands of the communists. (He did not add that, with the Presidential elections less than twelve months away, Catholic reaction at home was an important factor.) The State Department had considered briefing a few prominent Catholic laymen, he said, but this would hardly take care of the situation, for it still left the possibility of uninformed prelates anywhere in the country making critical comments. Perhaps the delegate would consider making a press statement if the walkout should occur which in effect would serve as a guideline for the entire hierarchy and which would indicate that everything possible had been done by the United States government.

Raimondi countered by asking the Americans to delay the arrival of the new ambassador to Budapest to give the Vatican more time to find a way out of the situation. The United States agreed and, on October 4, Ambassador Martin Hillenbrand, en route to Budapest, was stopped in his tracks in Vienna and instructed to stay put for fourteen days.

The delay was little more than a gesture for the cardinal's benefit. Both sides knew that no satisfactory arrangement could be made in that short a time. The Vatican had no intention of taking Mindszenty's departure out of the framework of the bilateral negotiations on church–state relations in Hungary. To do so would considerably weaken its position.

The Mindszenty "dossier" had suffered from papal neglect. Pope Paul was acting as his own Secretary of State, the aged Cicognani being no more than an experienced but occasional adviser, and when a problem was not high on the pontiff's list of priorities, it tended to slip down on everyone else's. From 1965, Pope Paul, alarmed at the growing dimensions of the Vietnam conflict, made peace in Asia the number one concern of the Holy See's diplomatic effort. This made closer ties with the United States doubly important and deliberate Vatican procrastination on matters involving Washington became more pronounced. The question of Mindszenty's future fitted nicely into this context. By threatening to walk out, however, the Hungarian primate had forced himself on the pontiff's attention.

On October 5, the pope sent word to Mindszenty through Cardinal König that the Holy See was negotiating the terms of the primate's departure to the West. But meanwhile, the pope's message continued, Mindszenty was to consider the harm that he would be doing to the Holy See, to the Church in general, and to the United States, if he gave himself up to the Hungarian authorities. Mindszenty's brooding face seemed to become more disconsolate than ever, but he replied (in Latin, as usual) that he felt he could not go against the pope's wishes.

The talks were held in Rome. The Hungarian delegation was headed by a member of the politburo who was ostensibly in Italy on vacation. But on the eve of Ambassador Hillenbrand's scheduled arrival Mindszenty had another visitor from the Vatican, Monsignor Giuseppe Cheli, a member of Casaroli's staff. It was not König, but Mindszenty noted with satisfaction that it was not Casaroli or Bogianino. The cardinal took this as a concession to his feeling about the two prelates. Cheli conveyed the pope's assurances that negotiations with the Hungarians were continuing with all possible speed, and that in spite of obstacles hope remained of a satisfactory agreement. But the negotiations involved a number of wider questions affecting the Hungarian church, and not Mindszenty's situation alone. They were very complex. In short, no solution was possible before the American ambassador arrived.

The Holy Father, the prelate continued, had the deepest sympathy for Mindszenty's position, but wished him to wait patiently until the talks were successfully concluded. The cardinal responded with a gesture of acquiescence and the words: "What else can we do?"

At the further request of the Holy See, Hillenbrand was kept at bay in Vienna for two more days. It was clear to the Americans, however, that Rome and Budapest were nowhere close to an agreement. Indeed, Mindszenty had so far hardly been mentioned in the discussions. So, on October 20, Hillenbrand finally flew to Budapest to take up his post.

"On the day of the ambassador's expected arrival, Cardinal is resigned to a situation which he hoped to avoid," the embassy cabled Washington. "During conversation this afternoon he spoke sadly of his principles, which he regards as violated by necessity of waiting on in embassy, even though he is doing so in obedience to higher wishes of the head of his Church. He agreed, nevertheless, to meet the new ambassador should latter so desire, though he again expressed hope that he might thereafter stay out of ambassador's way . . .

"Period of deep inner struggle and uncertainty which Cardinal has been through has inevitably left him with let-down feeling, now that critical moment is past. Discouragement shows in his appearance and manner. However, his strength of conviction remains. He discussed dispassionately the tactics he believes Hungarian regime will use during further negotiations with Vatican concerning him. . . . He is unwilling to predict how long negotiations will continue, and he appears fatalistic about outcome."

Mindszenty's pessimism was well founded. The negotiations dragged on, with many setbacks, for several months, during which time the cardinal received more than one message from Rome urging him to have patience. On January 23, 1969, the Vatican and the Kadar regime came to an agreement of sorts. To the ten remaining vacant sees (including four whose bishops wished to resign because of ill health), the Vatican was allowed to appoint five bishops. The other five were filled with apostolic administrators—clearly probationary appointments, indicating that prelates who were fully acceptable to both sides remained in short supply.

The even balance of the accord was reflected in the new

arrangement regarding Mindszenty's see of Esztergom. The cardinal retained the title of primate, but a young bishop was named apostolic administrator reporting directly to Rome. At the same time, a priest with known pro-regime sympathies was named as his auxiliary. Saint Stephen, the patron saint of Hungary, was "rehabilitated," and Sunday High Mass began to be regularly celebrated in the cathedral which bears his name in Budapest. Cardinal Mindszenty's future was not included in the deal. In the negotiations, the Vatican had failed to break through the regime's opposition to teaching religious instruction in schools, or to publishing religious material for distribution, so the regime got nowhere in securing Mindszenty's departure.

Mindszenty fumed over the agreement. He became more withdrawn than ever, worked on his diaries and spoke little. A mild form of phlebitis began to afflict him and he took fewer walks in the embassy's small garden. Vatican messages thinned out—and so did the negotiations. But the latter were resumed in continuing form in June 1970, when Monsignor Cheli flew to the Hungarian capital.

After that, the venue shifted regularly between Rome and Budapest. In the following April, Hungary's Foreign Minister Janos Peter, had a private audience with Pope Paul, and in the five months that followed Cheli made four trips to Hungary. On his fifth trip, a further agreement was initialed, considerably enlarging the Vatican's right to nominate bishops and the episcopate's power to move priests between parishes.

Then, in the summer, Cardinal König visited Mindszenty and told him that the pope wanted him to come to Rome. The way the Vatican put it, Pope Paul had been watching the Hungarian primate with "growing anguish and worry" and was concerned that in his present situation he might not get the right medical care. Therefore, the pope had sought an "honorable solution" and Cardinal Mindszenty had agreed to leave.

The "honorable solution" was worked out in conjunction

with the Hungarian authorities. It included none of the old
cardinal's demands. He was not allowed to say a final Mass in
his cathedral. He did not receive permission to visit his
mother's grave. He was allowed to take his papers, and he did
remain—as he demanded—the Primate of Hungary, at least
nominally, and for a while. The cardinal had also demanded
full rehabilitation which involved abolishing the charges of
treason, espionage, and currency speculation brought against
him by the regime. Instead, on the day after he left Budapest,
the Hungarian government announced that it had granted
him amnesty, an act of communist grace which the old man
rejected.

Cardinal König and Monsignor Cheli called for him on the
morning of September 24. Mindszenty said goodbye to the
assembled embassy staff and then walked quickly out to
König's waiting Mercedes. Five black suitcases had previ-
ously been loaded into a second car. Passersby in the busy
square failed to recognize the primate. The secret police had
disappeared from in front of the embassy building for the first
time in fifteen years, but two cars followed at a discreet
distance as the prelate rode in silence toward the Austrian
frontier.

From Vienna, the cardinal flew directly to Rome where the
pope, deeply moved, received him in the open air in the Vatican Gardens, an exceptional honor, embracing him warmly
before a mass of photographers. Then Paul personally accompanied him to a special apartment prepared for him close to
the Vatican Palace in Saint John's Tower. Here, the pontiff
made the ultimate gesture of humility, placing his own pec-
toral cross round the cardinal's neck, and slipping his bishop's
ring on Mindszenty's finger.

Cardinal Mindszenty was a man of conscience caught in a
time of compromise. The Holy See had guaranteed his silence
—as was the case with Cardinal Beran and Archbishop Slipyi
before that—and the pope, in their brief first meeting, asked
the cardinal to honor the commitment that had been made on

his behalf. Soon Mindszenty was complaining to visitors that, in its way, the Vatican was proving as much a prison as the embassy in Budapest had been.

But relations between Rome and Budapest were only one factor that led to what Mindszenty regarded as the ultimate humiliation, in other words, his departure. Another was the new diplomatic understanding, reached the previous year, between the United States and the Holy See.

CHAPTER XIII

Agreement—of Sorts

L IKE HIS PREDECESSOR, Pope Paul VI strove to restore to the Church some of its historic influence in temporal affairs. His diplomacy was active, especially in his anxiety to bring an end to the Vietnam conflict. His absorption with Vietnam was natural enough. It was a menacing war. He almost desperately wished to avoid any accusation that the Holy See was morally absent at the moment of crisis, the accusation frequently levelled at Pius XII because of his refusal to pronounce strongly against Nazi atrocities.

Like Pope John's intervention in the Cuban crisis, Paul's appeals for an end to the Vietnam conflict cut right across United States interests. The Johnson administration's first preoccupation was to ensure that papal concern did not lead to open criticism of the United States. A papal condemnation of the American role in Southeast Asia would have had great impact on world opinion. It was to prevent such an eventuality, and to try to influence the pontiff to maintain at least a neutral perspective, if not a favorable one, that President Lyndon Johnson (who did not have Kennedy's reasons for being

inhibited about dealing direclty with the pope) sought an audience with Paul.

On the way home from his famous Vietnam tour in the
spring of 1965, Johnson made a special stop in Rome and had
a fifty-minute meeting with Pope Paul. He went directly from
Rome airport to the Vatican in a helicopter to avoid setting
foot on Italian soil and thus having to meet members of the
Italian government. His schedule would not allow it, the
White House explained. Such insensitive behavior deeply
hurt the Italians and drew a strong protest from Ambassador
Reinhardt, who shortly afterward quit the Foreign Service.

Johnson was never one to worry unduly about diplomatic
gaffes, however. What mattered to him was that he had had an
opportunity to satisfy himself that the pope would not constitute a large problem to his Vietnam policy and could, on the
contrary, turn out to be a benign and useful element.

In December 1965, with the full backing of the United
States, Pope Paul appealed for a Christmas truce as the minimum relaxation of conflict that both sides should agree to. He
made his plea from his "window on the world" overlooking
Saint Peter's Square, as Pope John had done during the Cuban
missile crisis: "The war in Vietnam is becoming more serious
and more bloody; the numbers of combatants grow, as do the
numbers of victims, the piteous mass of refugees, and the danger of wider conflagrations.

"Where is peace? Where is the human and Christian Christmas? We have heard mention of negotiations to resolve the
conflict. We know of certain proposals for a truce at least for
the blessed day of Christmas. And we know of many statesmen of goodwill who are seeking to resolve the difficult situation. . . . We applaud therefore those who are working loyally
to end the menacing conflict."

There was a truce. Before it was assured, the Vatican made
it quite clear that its diplomacy was working at full stretch.
Under Paul's personal guidance, prelates in the critical out-
posts of Vatican diplomacy—Washington, London, the United

Nations, and Cambodia, where the Holy See had recently set up an apostolic delegation almost exclusively for that very purpose—campaigned unceasingly to bring about a cease fire.

Pope Paul claimed, justifiably, a share of the credit for the Vietnamese Christmas truce and for the American peace initiative which followed it, and he strove to resolve the problem on an international level while the bombers were grounded.

What was surprising for some people—and perhaps the most important factor of all—was the lack of public hostility in the United States to the papal hand in international affairs. That Johnson—anxious to demonstrate that he had tried everything before moving on to the next escalation—should not be loath to hear what the pope had to say is understandable; that no one of note attacked him for doing so is more surprising. There were many possible reasons for this, including the growing criticism of the Vietnam involvement in America itself. But another was Pope John's inheritance of neutrality and peace.

Despite such signs of public acceptance, the White House remained cautious in its dealings with the Holy See. When Pope Paul VI visited New York in the summer of 1966, the Administration took great care to emphasize that the pontiff was not a guest of the United States, but of the United Nations Organization. The President went to the Waldorf Astoria to pay a call on the visitor from Rome. There is no record of LBJ's asking the pope to the ranch for barbecue, one of the few celebrities not to receive the ritual invitation.

But Johnson knew that old prejudices died hard. They had, in fact, flared up again briefly some months earlier when the first of his school bills seeking government aid for parochial schools was awaiting congressional approval. Bill Moyers, Johnson's press spokesman, one day took a call in the president's absence from a protesting senior Southern Baptist. The caller wanted to talk to the president himself about how he could have got so tangled with the Catholics.

"He's in the swimming pool with Dr. Graham," said Moyers.

"Who?" asked the diminished voice.

"The President is in the swimming pool with Dr. Billy Graham," Moyers repeated. There was a long and heavy pause.

"Our Billy?" asked the defeated caller.

But the pope pressed on with his Vietnam peace initiative. On December 29, President Johnson sent his permanent representative to the United Nations, Arthur Goldberg, to see the pontiff. On January 1, 1966, the Vatican released the text of personal letters to the heads of states of North and South Vietnam, the Soviet Union, and to Mao Tse-tung. To the latter, the pope said, "An intervention on your part would resound to your honor in the eyes of the world and permit a people sorely tried to resume in peace the work of reconstruction which is rendered impossible by the continuation of the war." In September, he sent Monsignor Sergio Pignedoli, officially the apostolic delegate, to preside over a special meeting of the Vietnamese Catholic hierarchy in Saigon.

As the prospects of a breakthrough dimmed, the pope began to blame his lack of success on the absence of a regular channel of communications between Washington and the Holy See. This point was strongly made to President Richard Nixon when he visited Rome three months after starting his first term in order to pave the way for a further escalation of the American offensive in Vietnam. But Nixon resisted the idea of diplomatic relations, promising instead to send a succession of officials to listen and explain.

It was not a satisfactory solution and the Vatican continued to press for permanent contacts. Early in 1970, Paul dispatched Archbishop Giovanni Benelli, the under-secretary of state who was especially close to him, to Washington, where he saw not only Henry Kissinger, then head of the National Security Council, and Secretary of State William Rodgers, but Nixon as well, and the question of something better than a disconnected succession of visitors was thoroughly discussed.

The pope definitely did not want another Myron Taylor, Benelli told the Americans. It had declared as much seventeen years ago in *L'Osservatore Romano* when the nomination of General Clark was withdrawn. Nixon, on the other hand, was not prepared to risk the political implications of full diplomatic relations.

There was an element of take-it-or-leave-it in the American proposal to resolve what Nixon referred to as "The Vatican business." The Holy See took it. On June 28, 1970, Ron Ziegler, the Presidential spokesman, announced that "President Nixon has appointed Henry Cabot Lodge as his personal representative to the Holy See." The choice of a former ambassador to Vietnam was appropriate enough in the light of the pope's continued concern about the Asian conflict. *L'Osservatore Romano* called the arrangement "a new and therefore experimental form of official relations," and the Vatican described Lodge as ambassador-at-large to the Holy See. If there was anything new about the formula, it was unintentional. The White House had simply resurrected the Roosevelt appointment, and it was going to have to do. They agreed that the procedure was for Lodge to visit Rome at least three times a year for a few weeks each time to see the pope, "on the basis of continuity," as Ron Ziegler put it. On his first visit Lodge raised the question of Cardinal Mindszenty. He did the same on the second trip. By his third, Mindszenty was in Rome.

Then the pontiff secured Washington's assurance that the CIA would no longer continue to use ecclesiastics as informers. Thus, the arrangement continued to function, pleasing no one but at the same time offending no one. From time to time Holy See diplomats grumbled to their American counterparts that attitudes in the United States had surely changed sufficiently to make it possible to move on to better relations. Things would surely work much better. Then, in October 1979, Pope John Paul II toured the United States and visited the White House. Considering what had gone before, the sight of the pontiff on the South Lawn shaking hands with President Jimmy Carter was nothing short of a miracle—or rather, the combination of several miracles: the changes in American attitudes toward the Roman Catholic Church and the papacy; the extraordinary personal impact of John Paul II; and the courage of President Carter in deciding to receive him. And miracles are not the product of diplomatic relations.

Index

Ackersley, Garrett, 102
Adjubei, Alexei, 78–84, 95, 96
Agagianian, Gregory Peter, 67, 150, 154
Alfrink, Cardinal, 89, 150, 163
Allende, Salvador, 24
Andreotti, Giulio, 165, 197
Angleton, James Jesus, 22
Antoniutti, Ildebrando, 150–152, 163, 176, 178, 179

Bacci, Cardinal, 149
Balzan Peace Prize, 78, 80, 159
Bea, Augustin, 20–21, 37, 38, 41, 58, 64, 65, 67, 76, 78, 79, 84, 92, 97, 118, 153, 155, 163, 172, 176, 178, 185
Benedict XV, 44
Benelli, Giovanni, 219, 220
Benizi, Saint Philip, 145
Beran, Josef, 92, 200, 214
Bernabei, Ettore, 59–61
Bidault, Georges, 52
Blum, Leon, 52
Boetto, Pietro, 22

Bogianino, Monsignor, 205, 208, 211
Boniface VIII, 146
Bracci, Cardinal, 149
Brezhnev, Leonid, 4
Browne, Michael, 90
Bundy, McGeorge, 27, 195

Cacault, François, 77
Camara, Helder, 24
Camara, James de Barros, 154
Capovilla, Loris, 10, 14, 15, 19–20, 53, 58, 69, 79, 85, 94, 96, 100, 113–117, 119, 122, 123, 131, 156
Cardinale, Igino, 21, 27, 28, 34, 58, 67, 71, 85, 100, 190, 194, 196
Carlyle, Thomas, 41
Carpino, Archbishop, 183
Carter, Jimmy, 221
Casaroli, Agostino, 96, 97, 99–100, 102–104, 108, 130, 200–202, 205, 206, 208, 211
Casimirri, Luciano, 114, 115, 123
Castaldi, Cardinal, 149
Cavagna, Alfredo, 116, 122
Celestine V, 146

Cento, Fernando, 116, 117, 149
Cheli, Giuseppe, 211, 213, 214
Chiarlo, Cardinal, 149
Christian Democrat Party, 13, 18, 22,
    23, 28, 91, 94, 95, 164–166
Churchill, Winston, 78
CIA, 21–27, 74, 76, 93, 96–99, 110–
    111, 113–114, 161–162, 147–151,
    155, 169, 173–174, 186, 193, 209,
    220
Ciappi, Lorenzo, 90, 91
Cicognani, Amleto, 14, 20, 21, 65,
    79, 116, 117, 149, 155, 178, 180–
    181, 187, 210
Ciriaci, Cardinal, 149
Clark, Mark, 30–32, 207, 220
Clement IV, 144
Colby, William E., 23
College of Cardinals, 141–146
Colombo, Emilio, 165
Colonna, Aspreno, 90
Communistic Cattolici, 12
Confalonieri, Cardinal, 149, 150
Connally, Tom, 30
Cooper, Duff, 50
Copello, Santiago Luis, 117
Corneliano, Baron, 91
Cousins, Norman, 56, 57, 64–67, 70–
    74, 76, 92, 93, 200
Cronin, Daniel, 188
Cuban missile crisis, 56–59, 71, 83
Cushing, Cardinal, 44, 61–62, 163,
    187–190, 196–197

Damasus, Saint, 143
Dartmouth Conference, 56–57
De Boynes, Norbert, 22
De Ecclesia, 88
De Gaulle, Charles, 51–52
De Luca, Don Giuseppe, 12, 14, 18,
    25, 96
De Montfort, Guy, 144
Del Val, Merry, 172–173
Dell' Acqua, Angelo, 10, 17, 20, 56,
    58, 59, 64, 79, 83–85, 92, 114–117,
    123, 159, 160

Delle Rovere, Sigismondo Chigi,
    173
Di Jorio, Alberto, 117, 149, 179
Diary of a Soul, 131
Doepfner, Cardinal, 135, 163
Dungan, Ralph, 71, 72, 193

Fanfani, Amintore, 59, 79, 82–83
Ferretto, Cardinal, 150
Forni, Cardinal, 150
Fossati, Cardinal, 149
Franco, General, 151, 169, 170
Franklin, Benjamin, 29
FUCI (Federazione Universitaria
    Cattolici Italiani), 165, 167

Gammarelli, Bonaventura, 168–169,
    183
Gasbarrini, Antonio, 62, 112, 119,
    122–123, 126
Gasparri, Enrico, 22
Giobbe, Cardinal, 150
Goldberg, Arthur, 219
Gumulka, Wladislaw, 96, 105–109
Gracias, Valerian, 143
Graham, Billy, 219
Graham, Robert A., 41
Gregory X, 145–146
Gromyko, Andrei, 6
Gronchi, Giovanni, 7, 8

Heenan, John, 135-136
Herriot, Michel, 52
Hillenbrand, Martin, 210–212
Hitler, Adolf, 47–49
Honorius IV, 146

Innocent V, 146
Italian Bishop's Conference, 13, 95,
    151
Italian Communist Party (PCI), 93,
    94

Jesuits, 5, 19, 22
John XXIII, 3, 5–21, 23–25, 27, 28,
    34–133, 142–144, 147, 148, 152,

155–159, 161, 162, 164, 167, 170,
171, 179, 181, 183, 196, 197
John Paul I, 2–4
John Paul II, 1–6
Johnson, Lyndon B., 203, 204, 210,
216–219
Jones, Owen T., 136–137, 139–140
Josef, Franz, 172

Kadar, Janos, 100, 203, 204, 212
Kalamasinas, Thomas Hercules, 23–
24
Kennedy, John, 25–29, 34–36, 57–
62, 64, 70–74, 85, 97–99, 131, 137,
138, 147, 173, 186, 189, 190, 192–
197
Kennedy, Robert, 62
Khrushchev, Nikita, 9, 11, 12, 14, 23,
57–59, 61, 64–67, 71, 74–76, 78,
80–83, 85, 92, 93, 98, 105, 130,
159, 186, 200, 205
Kissinger, Henry, 219
Kliszko, Zenon, 106, 107
König, Franziskus, 69, 102–104, 178,
181, 187, 200, 207–209, 211, 213,
214
Koulic, Alexander, 80–82

Lardone, Francesco, 38
Laval, Pierre, 78
Lenhert, Pasqualina, 167
Leo XIII, 8, 144
Lercaro, Giacomo, 149, 155, 176–
178
Liberation theology, 5
Liddy, Richard, 124
Lienart, Cardinal, 135
Lodge, Henry Cabot, 220
Luce, Clare Boothe, 56
Luciani, Albino, 2–4

McCone, John, 14, 24, 97–99
McIntire, Carl, 31
McIntyre, Joseph, 162–163

Maglione, Cardinal, 48
Manzù, Giacomo, 8, 91, 92, 125, 126,
197
Marella, Giacomo, 52, 149–150
Martin IV, 146
Masella, Benedetto Aloisi, 117, 125–
127, 133, 149
Mater et Magistra, 8, 157
Mayer, Cardinal, 135, 162, 163
Mazzoni, Dr., 115, 122
Micara, Clemente, 149, 177–178
Mindszenty, Joszef, 6, 15, 100–104,
136–140, 195, 201–215
Montini, Giovanni Battista. *See* Paul
VI
Morano, Cardinal, 149
Morlion, Felix, 56, 57, 70, 92
Moro, Aldo, 165
*Movimento Politico Cattòlico
Italiano*, 91
Moyers, Bill, 218–219
Murray, John Courtney, 61

Nagy, Imre, 102
Nazis, 47–48, 216
Nicholas III, 146
Nicholas IV, 146
Nixon, Richard, 219, 220
Non Expedit, 95
Novotny, Antonin, 200
Nuenlist, Colonel, 173

O'Connell, Cardinal, 134
O'Connor, Joseph, 188
Office of Strategic Services (OSS),
22
Orsini, Raimondo, 90
Osborne, D'Arcy, 165–166
O'Shaughnessy, Elim, 205
Ostpolitik, 24
Ottaviani, Alfredo, 7–8, 17, 21, 27,
36, 41, 79, 87–91, 117, 143, 149,
151, 159, 163, 170, 176, 180, 181,
184–185, 191–192

Pacelli, Cardinal. *See* Pius XII
Pacem in Terris, 84–87, 90–93, 95, 97, 99, 159, 161
Pappalardo, Paolo, 114, 123
Parente, Pietro, 36
Paul VI, 19, 22, 33, 77, 118, 149, 150, 155–157, 160, 163–170, 172, 176–187, 189–201, 204, 207, 210, 211, 213, 214, 216–221
Pavan, Pietro, 85
Pawley, Bernard, 185
Peter, Janos, 212
Pignedoli, Sergio, 219
Pius IX, 146
Pius X, 113
Pius XI, 7, 45, 78
Pius XII, 9, 12, 15, 22, 31–34, 40, 47–52, 55, 86, 95, 97, 101, 106, 119–120, 126, 127, 130, 143, 144, 162, 163, 165–167, 188, 207, 216
Pizzardo, Cardinal, 149
Plagens, James, 129–130
Pontifical Ecclesiastical Academy, 45
Putman, James, 129–130

Quadragesimo Anno, 7

Radini-Tedeschi, Giacomo, 42–44, 113
Raimondi, Giovanni, 209, 210
Reinhardt, Frederick, 28, 35, 83, 84, 217
Rerum Novarum, 8
Ritter, Cardinal, 135, 162, 163
Roberti, Francesco, 179
Rocca, Mario Nasalli, 91, 110
Rodano, Franco, 12, 14
Rodgers, William, 219
Roncalli, Angelo. *See* John XXIII
Roncalli, Giambattista, 116
Roncalliani, 152, 155–157, 176
Roosevelt, Franklin, 30
Ruffini, Cardinal, 149
Rugambwa, Laurean, 8, 172
Rusk, Dean, 29, 192–195

Sacred College, 141–146
Salinger, Pierre, 195
Samoré, Antonio, 17, 18, 20, 82, 100, 116, 200
Schlesinger, Arthur, Jr., 59–61
Schumann, Georges, 52
Second Vatican Council. *See* Vatican Ecumenical Council
Sennott, John, 188, 189
Sherman, William, 27, 28, 34, 35, 196
SID, 150
Siri, Cardinal, 41–42, 149–151, 158, 163, 179, 180
Sixtus, Pope, 142
Skinner, Robert P., 46
Slipyi, Josef, 65–70, 75, 83, 172, 214
Society for the Propagation of the Faith, 44
Sorensen, Theodore, 26, 57–58, 195
Spain, James W., 21, 74–76, 95
Spellman, Cardinal, 30–32, 41, 59, 142, 153, 161–163, 183–184, 187–189, 197
Stalin, Joseph, 78
Stevenson, Adlai, 33
Sturzo, Don Luigi, 164
Suenens, Cardinal, 163, 181
Suhard, Cardinal, 51

Tardini, Domenico, 9–10, 47, 49, 50, 165–167
Taylor, Myron C., 30, 33
Testa, Gustavo, 64, 131, 149, 159, 160, 177–179
Theological Commission of the Ecumenical Council, 88
Third Lateran Council of 1179, 143
Tisserant, Cardinal, 117, 125, 139, 142, 170, 172, 179, 189
Tito, Josip Broz, 4
Tittman, Harold, 30, 47
Togliatti, Palmiro, 12–14, 18, 93–94, 96, 193, 196
Tondini, Amleto, 170, 171

Traglia, Cardinal, 122, 123, 149
Truman, Harry, 30–33

Ubi Periculum Maius, 145
Urban IV, 144
Urbani, Giovanni, 149, 155, 156

Vagnozzi, Egidio, 27, 35, 159, 193,
    195, 203, 205, 207, 209
Valeri, Valerio, 51, 149
Van Lierde, Canisius, 116
Vatican City State, 39
Vatican Ecumenical Council, 5, 9–
    11, 34–40, 62, 63, 78, 88–90, 117,

119, 135, 149, 151, 153, 157, 162,
    167, 171
Vietnam, 216–219
Visconti, Tebaldo, 145
Von Papen, Franz, 48–50

Warren, Earl, 190
Willebrands, Jan, 37, 67–69, 76
Wojtyla, Karol, 1–6
Wright, John, 25
Wyszynski, Stefan, 6, 21, 38, 96

Zawieyski, Jerzy, 107–109
Ziegler, Ron, 220